GLOBALIZATION AND MARGINALITY IN GEOGRAPHICAL SPACE

Globalization and Marginality in Geographical Space

Political, Economic and Social Issues of Development in the New Millennium

Edited by

HEIKKI JUSSILA
University of Oulu, Finland

ROSER MAJORAL
University of Barcelona, Spain

FERNANDA DELGADO-CRAVIDÃO
University of Coimbra, Portugal

ASHGATE

Published by
Ashgate Publishing Limited
Gower House
Croft Road
Aldershot
Hampshire GU11 3HR
England

Ashgate Publishing Company
Suite 420
101 Cherry Street
Burlington, VT 05401-4405
USA

Reprinted 2003

Ashgate website: http://www.ashgate.com

British Library Cataloguing in Publication Data
Globalization and marginality in geographical space :
    political, economic and social issues of development in the
    new millennium. - (Dynamics of marginal and
    critical regions)
    1. Globalization - Congresses 2. Economical development -
    Social aspects 3. Regional disparities - Congresses
    4. Marginal productivity - Congresses 5. Marginality, Social
    - Congresses
    I. Jussila, Heikki II. Majoral i Moline, Roser
    330.9

Library of Congress Control Number: 00-133535

ISBN 0 7546 1476 X

Printed in Great Britain by Biddles Limited, King's Lynn.

Contents

PART 2 – POLICIES AND POLITICS OF CHANGE

PART 3 – FROM ECONOMIC TO SOCIAL ISSUES

List of Figures

List of Tables

List of Contributors

MARIA ANDREOLI	Università degli Studi di Pisa, Pisa, Italy
J. CLARK ARCHER	University of Nebraska, Lincoln, NE, USA
PAUL OLAV BERG	Bodø University College, Bodø, Norway
LUCÍLIA CAETANO	University of Coimbra, Coimbra, Portugal
MARÍA EUGENIA CEPPARO DE GROSSO	Universidad Nacional de Cuyo, Mendoza, Argentina
VINCENZINA COLOSIMO	Università degli Studi di Pisa, Pisa, Italy
ALFRED COLPAERT	University of Oulu, Oulu, Finland
FERNANDA DELGADO-CRAVIDÃO	University of Coimbra, Coimbra, Portugal
FRANCESCO DI IACOVO	Università degli Studi di Pisa, Pisa, Italy
HENRI GOVERDE	University of Nijmegen, Nijmegen, Netherlands
MATTI HÄKKILÄ	University of Oulu, Oulu, Finland
HEIKKI JUSSILA	IGU, Commission on Dynamics of Marginal and Critical Regions, Pisa, Italy
STEVEN KALE	Oregon Department of Transportation, Salem, OR, USA
WALTER LEIMGRUBER	University of Fribourg, Fribourg, Switzerland
RICHARD E. LONSDALE	University of Nebraska, Lincoln, NE, USA
FRANCISCO LÓPEZ-PALOMEQUE	Universitat de Barcelona, Barcelona, Spain
ROSER MAJORAL	Universitat de Barcelona, Barcelona, Spain
SANDRA MARQUES	University of Coimbra, Coimbra, Portugal
ASSEFA MEHRETU	Michigan State University, East Lansing, MI, USA
LUÍS MORENO	University of Lisbon, Lisbon, Portugal
TOIVO MUILU	University of Oulu, Oulu, Finland
CHRIS MUTAMBIRWA	University of Zimbabwe, Harare, Zimbabwe
JANE MUTAMBIRWA	University of Zimbabwe, Harare, Zimbabwe
ARVO NAUKKARINEN	University of Oulu, Oulu, Finland
BRUCE WM. PIGOZZI	University of Michigan, East Lansing, MI, USA
JARMO RUSANEN	University of Oulu, Oulu, Finland

DOLORES SÁNCHEZ-AGUILERA   University of Barcelona, Barcelona, Spain

PETER SCOTT   University of Tasmania, Hobart, Tasmania, Australia

LAWRENCE M. SOMMERS   University of Michigan, East Lansing, Michigan, USA

WILLIAM R. STANLEY   University of South Carolina, Columbia, South Carolina, USA

VITTORIO TELLARINI   University of Pisa, Pisa, Italy

Preface

In connection with the IGU Regional Conference, in Lisbon August 1998, the Commission on Dynamics of Marginal and Critical Regions met at the University of Coimbra, August 24-29. Following the Commission's four year programme established in The Hague during the International Congress (1996) the theme announced for this meeting was 'Consequences of Globalization and Deregulation on Marginal and Critical Region Economic Systems' and of the large number of contributions 20 are presented in this book 'Globalization and Marginality in Geographical Space' book of the Spatial Aspects of Marginality-series being published by Ashgate in association with the IGU Commission on Dynamics of Marginal and Critical Regions. The three previous books of this series are: 'Perception of Marginality' (1998), 'Marginality in Space – Past, Present and Future' (1999) and 'Environment and Marginality in Geographical Space' (2000).

This 'Globalization and Marginality in Geographical Space' book analyses and discusses the issue of marginalization and the effects that economic globalization have on marginal and critical regions from the point of view of politics and policies and the shift from economic to social issues of development. This book aims to give the reader an overview of the globalization issues, and yet keeping a close connection to practical examples of what, where and how globalization and deregulation effect marginal areas.

The editors would like to thank all the contributing authors for their work, and thanks are also due to the organisers of the Coimbra meeting that made this book possible. Although, there are many people we would like to mention, special thanks are due to professor Maria Andreoli (University of Pisa) and Hugo Cappella (University of Barcelona) and João Fernandes (University of Coimbra) who have helped us in putting things in order and also pointed out mistakes that otherwise could still have existed in this final version.

Finally the editors would like to thank Ashgate for the book series that has enabled the Commission to publish much more of its work than initially was thought.

Pisa, Barcelona and Coimbra

Heikki Jussila, Roser Majoral and Fernanda Delgado Cravidao

1 Introduction

HEIKKI JUSSILA AND ROSER MAJORAL

This book on issues of globalization and marginalization is based on the papers of the Coimbra 1998 conference of the IGU Commission on Dynamics of Marginal and critical regions. The aim of the conference was to look at the various aspects and faces of globalization and to see what kinds of effects they have on the 'weaker' regions of the world. The topic produced more than 40 papers and out of them 20 are presented in this book of *Globalization and Marginality in Geographical Space: political, economic and social issues of development in the new millennium.*

This book is the fourth in the *Spatial Aspects of Marginality*-series of books produced from the research work done under the programme of the IGU Commission on Dynamics of Marginal and Critical Regions. The aim of this book is the same with the previous books, to develop and give new visions for the readers about the marginal regions of the world. The articles in this volume look into an issue that is becoming an increasingly important: 'Globalization of World Economies'. The issues touched, discussed and analysed in this book do not cover all the aspects of the issue, but they do, however, show that geographical research can contribute significantly onto the understanding of the effect policies and politics of globalization have on the more marginal areas of the world.

This book on *Globalization and Marginality in Geographical Space* recalls the importance of the processes of globalization that have changed the way marginal and critical regions are seen in the world of today. The book consists of articles that deal the issue of globalization from different perspectives.

The first main part of the book deals with the general issue of globalization as seen from the general perspective and then approaching a closer, i.e., more micro-perspective. The articles grouped under the title *Effects of Globalization* look at the question of globalization from a 'general', although each article in the section uses a slightly different point of view. The first opening article of Leimgruber is the most theoretical, although it has concrete empirical cases that manifest the various effects that globalization process has on a given region.

The discussion of the articles in this book starts with general theoretical issues. It then moves to the issues of the economic importance and the role of transnationals (see articles by Archer and Lonsdale, by Cepparo de Grosso and by Sommers *et al.*) and nation blocs (article of Goverde) in the current globalization process of the world economy.

According to these articles this globalization process will probably lead to a situation where commodity markets are increasingly controlled by a small number of large transnational corporations with little loyalty to any particular nation or region. Consequently this may lead to an isolation of producers and other residents of 'marginal lands', since the producers operate on 'global' and the other residents on 'local' scale and yet they both would be isolated from the centres of power and authority.

The second main part of the book *Policies and Politics of Change* contains six articles that discuss the policy aspects of globalization. The articles in this section stress that in many cases the direct impacts are taken into account, but the hidden 'indirect' effects are those that in the long run may have the most important effect on development. These can bring in new resources for development or they can even create new development enclaves, the so-called *pocket development*, which e.g., Tykkyläinen (1998; 1999) and Tykkyläinen and Jussila (1998) have discussed in the case resource utilisation areas. These development enclaves can be of importance for marginal regions, since they might be the forerunners of a new era in marginal regions, an era that despite of globalization and its negative effects brings a hopeful tone for the development of these regions in the next millennium.

The second section is based on case studies of different policy options. The articles look also at the implementation of these policies in specific regions (see articles by Moreno and by Berg). The articles focus on various policy agents that have emerged due to the process of globalization and deregulation (see articles by Andreoli *et al.*, by Muilu, and by Häkkilä). The specific cases of individual articles address the issues of policies and politics from different points of view, but the common undertone is that there is a need to implement a more 'fine tuned' policy action when regarding marginal areas of the world. The politics and policies have in many cases both direct and indirect impacts on regional development (see articles by Kale and by López-Palomeque).

The third part of this book *From Economic to Social Issues* is the part that has attracted a larger number of articles than the previous parts, eight articles. The articles in this part look at issues of globalization and marginalization from the point of view of a change within the contents of measuring the effects of globalization within a region. The emphasis is on the change from economic issues toward social issues and even to individual aspects of understanding the processes of globalization and marginalization. Articles in this section produce images on the effects of marginalization and globalization in different parts of the world.

Articles in the third section *From Economic to Social Issues* are sequenced in the book by their generality in respect to the topic and the region they examine. Consequently the articles discussing more specifically issues on 'nation state' level are grouped as one block. These include the articles by Marques and Delgado, by Sánchez-Aguilera and Majoral, and by Rusanen *et al.*. These articles approach the issue from different points of view, but the main question taken up is that of population, migration or economic development. The second grouping of articles in this section has a more 'local' or 'individual' connotation. These articles include the articles by Andreoli *et al.*, by Caetano, by Scott, and by Mehretu *et al.*. The questions analysed by these writers range from the quality of life and labour issues to the question of minorities and the role of women in a society.

The basic tone of this part is the concern about the weaker in society, may it be an individual or regional images. This concern can be crystallised by the words of Scott who, when speaking about Aboriginals, says that 'without the same respect as human beings, and the same socio-economic conditions' it is difficult to obtain balanced development pattern. In this respect one needs to look for policies and politics that do go into the roots.

The three sections of this book of *Globalization and Marginality in Geographical Space* discuss the phenomenon of marginalization and how it has changed or is going to change in the next millennium. This book does not give definite answers. However, the individual articles of the book all point out the need to look for more accurate information in order to understand the various direct and especially the hidden indirect effects of globalization to the development horizons of marginal regions.

References

Tykkyläinen, M. (1998), A multicausal theory of local economic development, in C. Neil and M. Tykkyläinen, M. (eds.), *Local Economic Development, A geographical comparison of rural community restructuring*, United Nations University Press, Tokyo, pp. 347-355.

4

Tykkyläinen, M. (1999), The emergence of capitalism and struggling against marginalization in the Russian North, in H. Jussila, R. Majoral and C. Mutambirwa (eds.), *Marginality in Space*, Ashgate, Aldershot.

Tykkyläinen, M. and Jussila, H. (1998), Potentials for innovative restructuring of industry in Northwestern Russia, *Fennia* 176:1, pp. 223-245.

Part 1 – Effects of globalization

2 Globalization, deregulation, marginalization: Where are we at the end of the millennium?

WALTER LEIMGRUBER

The problem

Looking at the 20th century, one is inclined to assert that there have been few epochs in the history of mankind, which have lived through more dramatic changes in such a short time. Within a few generations, man has freed himself from many physical and biological constraints through the application of technology: not only do we cover almost unlimited distances in less and less time, we also communicate in real time around the world, we can buy almost everything – whether we need it or not – and eternal life at good health with a youthful look seems to be at the doorstep. Our scale of action both in space and time has become global; the term for this phenomenon is globalization.

In this same period, however, the gap between rich and poor, privileged and underprivileged has widened, and the image of an 80-20 or even 90-10 society is becoming reality. While neo-classical theory suggests that free market forces will even out disparities, events in fact point to the opposite direction, and polarisation theory seems to provide a more appropriate model: the rich are becoming richer, the poor poorer. As a result, a growing number of people all over the world are becoming marginalized, and conflicts at different scales around the globe have become part of the daily news similarly to the weather forecast.

As a result of globalization, pressure on the political forces towards liberalization has been increasing. The traditional role of the state as protector of a territory and its people is giving way to new public management: the state is being transformed to an enterprise, but it remains non-profit-oriented. Its chief task is to occupy itself with those segments of policy, which cannot be furnished by the private sector, i.e., which yield no monetary profit. Parallel to this, however, the state is deprived of a considerable part of its income through the reduction of tariffs and the privatization of profitable segments of its infrastructure such as telecommunication services. This process is termed deregulation.

It would be easy but also fruitless to blame our current problems simply on globalization and the weakness of the political system. In order to find their roots, we have to dig deeper. We shall try to explore both globalization and deregulation into some depth and look at their significance for the process of marginalization at different scales and from different thematic perspectives. The use of these two terms has become commonplace, and simultaneously, they are considered both the hope for the future of mankind and the root of all evil. What do they really stand for?

The global scene

Globalization first of all evokes a scale, meaning world-wide or global, but the word also means 'all-embracing' or 'general'. An enterprise can therefore be global when its activity space covers the whole world, or when its activity covers the totality of a production process or of a service.

The term globalization originates in the economy, and in this context it is still widely used. It stands for the world-wide activity-space of enterprises, whose decision centres and research and development departments are located in the Triad, whereas the production units are shifted around the globe according to the *credo* of profit-maximization/cost-reduction.

This economic definition of globalization is only part of the story. The German sociologist Ulrich Beck (1997) looks at it from a much wider perspective. In fact, every individual on the globe, without exception, is in some way or another a global actor or player. This is so obvious that we tend to overlook it. As consumers of goods and information, we are linked to the whole world every day, and as scientists we would be at a loss without our global networks.

Globalization in its economic definition is therefore an inadequate term for the description of the global phenomenon. As a consequence, Beck (1997) widens the field of notions. Thus, *globalism* is 'the idea that the world market ousts or replaces political actions, i.e. it is the ideology of the domination of the world market or of neoliberalism' (p. 26) whereas *globality* is 'the global society in the sense that the idea of closed spaces becomes fictitious. No country, no group can shut itself off from others' (p. 27). *Globalization,* then, is defined as 'the *processes,* as a consequence of which nation states and their sovereignty are suffused and linked by transnational actors, their chances of power, their orientations and their networks' (p. 28; emphasis in the original). Applied to humans, this means that we all take part in globality (we live in the global village) and are victims to the process of globalization which leads to globalism.

Many people suggest that the world's problems can be solved by acting globally, and in a way this may be true. However, this discourse is coloured by a variety of ideological backgrounds (Bertrand, 1994, p. 1), ideologies which lead to numerous and often contradictory moral and political prescriptions (liberal, developmental, ecological, federalist or Marxist political views). In addition, by privileging the global scale, the importance of all other scales is ignored and the arguments become extremely simplistic. There are many local and regional problems, which have little impact on the global system, and a global problem may not be felt at the local level. This holds good even if we agree that there is a global unity, that everything is tied to everything, that the transformation of one tiny element in the system influences all other elements. After all, as geographers we have always been thinking in different scales, and we are used to comparing them – global problems are not new to us:

> The heritage of the various geopolitics and the continuing study of the world political map will make any political geographer wary of the recent 'discovery' of the global scale in both the popular perception and modern social science (Taylor, 1996, p. 3).

The political scene

The term *deregulation* takes us into the domain of politics and stands for the current tendency of the State to back out of certain tasks or services, which it used to provide. This process can be seen as the result of a battle between contradicting theories, those favouring private economic initiative and regulation versus those standing for a substantial public engagement. Central to the current debate on deregulation is the definition of the State's primary tasks. Should it simply provide security for the individual citizens, or ought it to provide general welfare? And what would be the substance of 'security' or of 'welfare'?

At present, the prevailing neoliberal world-view considers excessive public regulation as an obstacle to the free economy and the law of the market. According to this doctrine, only an unregulated economy will be able to shed all its positive effects on mankind, therefore, the State has to concentrate on its 'primary tasks'. This sounds well in theory, but in reality, the free economy meets with a lot of obstacles, e.g. to factor mobility. If this theory promises equality among humans as its ultimate goal, we have still a long way to go.

The fallacy of this perspective is obvious: a totally free economy is as unrealistic as a totally state controlled one because in either case *power* is the driving force behind all policy. If the socialist economy was characterized by the omnipotence of the Party, the free market economy is driven by the desire for market expansion and control and by the permanent demand for growing profits. The chief actors serve this goal, and power over others is their common denominator.

The State, as a sort of social contract, is a necessity. In the absence of general agreement over its 'primary tasks', one might as well see the political system as the lesser evil. The society requires some form of supreme institution organising life for the benefit of all and respecting people's free will. The public sector is supposed to function as a regulatory force, harnessing the rich and assisting the poor. To do so, it has to operate a balance (Figure 2.1) between the economic and the normative systems, trying to satisfy one side without irritating the other.

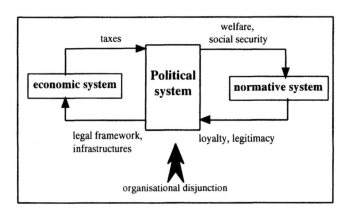

Figure 2.1   Political, economic and normative system

Source: C. Offe, 1973, quoted in Grauhan and Linder, 1974.

Reality, however, looks somewhat different, and it is here that the problem of marginalization and marginality appears.

Marginality is the situation of an area that is located 'at the margin' of a system as regards its socio-economic features. Thus, even when most of the economic and cultural power is concentrated in the centre, there are still some linkages, although sometimes very weak ones, between the margin and the other components of the systems (Andreoli, 1992, p. 24).

A marginal region is therefore not isolated from the rest of the world; it simply receives fewer benefits from it than other regions. The political system should prevent situations of inequality from arising. In order to achieve this, it ought to induce the economic system to bring some sacrifice and renounce maximum profit in order to promote social equality. In this way, the economic system could contribute to guarantee the loyalty of the normative system to the political system. Power relations, however, run differently: the political system depends on the economic system for its material survival (fiscal policy) and tends to favour asymmetrical relations (Figure 2.2). Legitimacy and loyalty approach a situation of *panem et circenses* (if people have food and pleasure, they are satisfied, and politics and economy can play their own games).

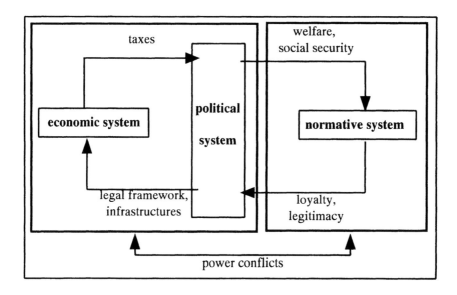

Figure 2.2   A model of the power conflict between political/economic and normative systems

This modification of the Offe-model leads to a daring hypothesis:

Although the 'First World' (the North) pleads for the development of the 'Third World' (the South), it is not really interested in what it calls development.

The reason for this reluctance towards true development is simple: a developed South might threaten the North's dominant position, i.e., its power. Therefore, marginal regions are not only a natural state of things in a dualistic world (every centre needs a periphery, at least as a point of reference), they are also a card in the world-wide power game. As a final consequence of globalization and deregulation, the world will be one huge economic system without political authority of any relevance but with a straightforward dominance of the global actors over the peoples (Figure 2.3).

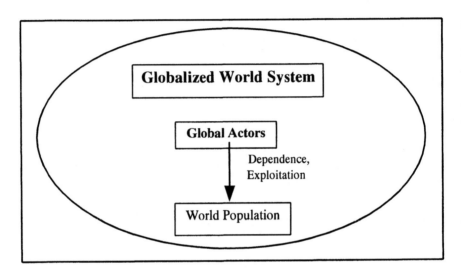

Figure 2.3   The global system of the future

Again we are faced with the problem of scale: marginal regions can be observed on different scales, marginality is no objective phenomenon but is tied to the spatial and temporal scale of observation. A region may be of considerable economic or strategic importance but lose its role due to new circumstances (resource depletion, technological change, new geopolitical situation). On the other hand, a marginal region may emerge from relative isolation and become of great interest (e.g. mountain areas for tourism). Therefore, marginality is not simply a static situation but subject to dynamics, according to the ongoing processes in the respective system (Reynaud, 1981 employs the term 'inversion').

Case studies

Introduction

Following the general considerations, a number of case studies are to illustrate the spatio-temporal dimension of marginality at the end of the second millennium. They have been chosen to represent different scales and topics and are partly based on work done by students in a seminar on marginal regions during the academic year 1997/98.

Africa according to the Human Development Index (HDI)

Marginality can be recognized through a grid of reference, which compares various situations with each other. One such grid of reference is the Human Development Index (HDI) which measures the advancement of human development. It is a quantitative indicator, using qualitative variables, which have to be converted. The search for such an overall index goes back to the 1960s (Tata and Schultz, 1988, p. 582). The HDI (developed by the UNDP in the late 1980s) uses the three qualitative variables health (represented by life expectancy), knowledge (expressed by the rates of alphabetization and schooling) and economy (the level of living, i.e. national income). While data on the former two are not too difficult to be obtained, the third is more delicate to quantify: the monetary income per person is only a truly reliable variable if entire money flows are registered; the existence of a subsistence economy and of the informal sector, however, renders the figures highly unreliable. As a consequence, such an index is very approximate.

As the HDI covers all countries of the world, the choice of indicators is limited in order to ensure comparison between North and South. Development is measured on a scale running from 0 (least developed) to 1 (most developed). It is a composite index which holds good for the population as a whole; in order to assess the specific role played by women in many countries, it has been completed by a genderspecific index and an index measuring women's participation in politics and economy.

By mapping the information furnished by the HDI on country level, the state of development and of marginality of Africa (a continent usually classed as underdeveloped) can be illustrated in a differentiated way (Figure 2.4, simplified after Brechbühl *et al.*, 1998). The overall HDI (Figure 2.4a) shows three 'well developed' regions: the North, a small part of equatorial Africa, and the South. The 'little to weakly' developed part of the continent takes the shape of a crescent round the two countries of Congo and Gabon, with 'very weak' (or truly marginal) confined essen-

14

tially to the Sahara and Sahel region and a part of the south. The old stereotype seems to find confirmation.

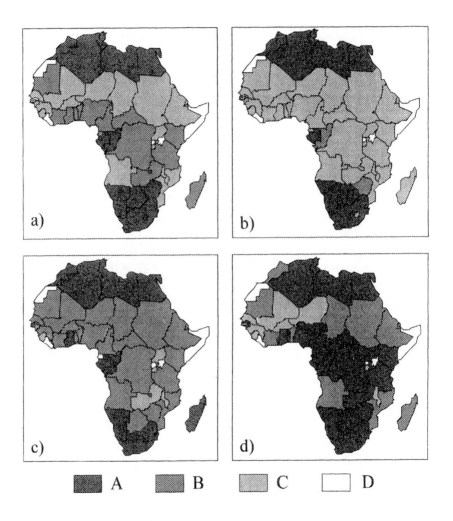

Figure 2.4 **Human Development Index (HDI) for Africa, 1997 (a) overall HDI, (b) national income, (c) health, (d) education**
Legend: A: medium to good development (HDI 0.5 - 1); B: weak development (HDI 0.34 - 0.5) C: very weak development (HDI 0 - 0.334; D: no data

However, a closer look at the three components of the HDI permit us to discover another, maybe unexpected reality. From the point of view of the National Income (Figure 2.4b), Africa is essentially a marginal region ('very weak development'). The belts of 'highly developed' regions as shown by the HDI on Figure 2.4 shrink to some extent, and there are only few countries, which fall into the intermediary class ('weak development'). The overall impression of the HDI repeats itself.

The second component of the HDI, life expectancy at birth, reveals a completely different picture (Figure 2.4c). Very few countries can be called truly marginal ('very weak development'), the situation is for the most part of the continent one of 'weak to good' (index above 0.5). This shows that non-material development efforts are more successful than economic ones, i.e. that health care is making progress. Indeed, the HDI looks at overall life expectancy, although in the case of Africa, infants and children would be a more appropriate group to look at - but this would yield a false picture in comparison with the North.

The current situation is ambiguous: on the one hand, the increase of life-expectancy is certainly a progress, on the other, it can be interpreted as a weakness with regard to the economy: there are more and more hands which could (and want to) work than there are job opportunities available.

Finally, education as another non-material indicator provides us with a third image of Africa, much more positive than we could think of (Figure 2.4d), and shattering our stereotypes even more. Education appears to be a very important field where a lot of effort has been put into. Yet certain countries surprise the observer: Morocco with an alphabetization rate of only 42.1% among adults contrasts remarkably with its eastern neighbour, Algeria (59.4%), as does the rate of schooling (people visiting schools relative to age-cohorts; Morocco 46%, Algeria 66%). A truly marginal region in this domain is found in West Africa only, whereas in most other countries the level of education is appreciably high. This variable has one important drawback: we do not have any indication as to the quality of the training and the use people can get from it in daily life (apart from work). And, a similar comment as above concerning the economic consequences can be added: there may be many well-trained people, but there are not enough job opportunities to apply the knowledge acquired

The case of Africa tells us that this continent is not simply an 'under-developed' unity, a marginal region on the global scale, but that there is considerable variation. We would like to know more, but one of the short-comings of the HDI is the aggregation of data on the national level. This is not likely to change in the near future, but unfortunately it conceals internal disparities, e.g. between regions with varying potential or between margi-nalized social groups (Brechbühl *et al.*, 1998, p. 12).

Despite this drawback, the HDI is certainly a better index than those based exclusively on macroeconomic indicators. One problem remains on the conceptual side: the HDI considers development as a state of things, whereas development is in fact a process. A more elaborate presentation would therefore comprise maps, which show the dynamics rather than a static situation. But for such a purpose, the time of observation is still too short.

Iceland – a marginal country?

A particularly interesting case of a marginal region (if we may call it this way) in the age of globalization is furnished by Iceland (Table 2.1). This country, situated in the North Atlantic in particular environmental conditions, in a way lives a life of its own. Marked by a long period of outside (Danish) domination, it manifests certain reluctance towards the outside world since its independence in 1944. Although it is situated closer to the New World than to the Old, Iceland is both politically and culturally a part of Europe. This is stressed by the country's membership in the European Economic Area (EEA) and in the European Free Trade Association (EFTA). In either case, it lies peripheral to those two trade blocks but finds itself in an intermediary position to the North American market. However, the great transportation routes have always bypassed Iceland because of its northerly location. In a way, the island state (whose EEZ exceeds the land surface seven times) has continually been a marginal region (even during its long history under Danish domination), and it has managed to survive.

Table 2.1   Data on Iceland (1995)

Land surface (sq. km)	103,000
Surface of territorial waters (sq. km)	70,000
Surface of contiguous zone (sq. km)	75,000
Surface of EEZ (sq. km)	754,000
Population (1995)	267,890
Primary sector (%)	10
Secondary sector	25
Tertiary sector	65
Exports (million US $, 1995)	82,534,435
Exports of Fish (% of all exports)	71.9
Exports of Aluminium (% of all exports)	10.6
Imports (million US $, 1995)	80,415,989

Its relatively small population (267,890 in 1995) contains a small potential for defence against aggression that is why, in 1949, Iceland had joined NATO, and in 1951, it concluded a defence treaty with the United States. To broaden the base of its international relations, it became a member of OECD in 1947, of the Council of Europe in 1950, of the United Nations, etc., and it was one of the founder members of the Nordic Council in 1952. It joined EFTA in 1970 and concluded a free trade agreement with the European Economic Community in 1972. Finally, in 1992 it adhered to the EEA.

Given all these various outside relations, it would appear wrong to call Iceland marginal. And yet, on the international scene, it is classed as a weak country (Vallin, 1998, p. 43). Being small, thinly populated, with little industry and a small market, it does not rouse the interest of large-scale investors. Its chief exports are fish and aluminium, the former present in abundance (for how long?) in the Atlantic, the latter thanks to its hydroelectric potential. Iceland is marginal because it lies at the periphery of the international system, but this is to its advantage, given the lack of powerful neighbours. Maybe even its position outside the European Union is to its advantage, because its spatially and economically peripheral situation does not make it a strong partner within the Union. Unlike Switzerland, which is an obstacle on the transcontinental transportation routes, Iceland is of very limited importance as concerns transportation and communication. There is no need to give up independence, but good contacts to all neighbours are nevertheless vital.

The London Docklands – variations in marginality

When the Port of London was closed down from the late 1960s onwards, a vast area of land formerly devoted to warehouses and port installations lost its former role and fell idle. This surface of 22 km², situated between the City and the deprived East End, could not be left redundant but had to be put to a new use. Subsequently, it was to become Western Europe's largest urban redevelopment area (Brownill, 1990, p. 1).

The story of the reorganization of London Docklands is intimately linked to the visions developed by the parties in power. Whereas the Labour governments emphasized social and environmental goals with public investment, the Conservative government after 1979 privileged private enterprise. The Docklands were to become a new financial centre of London, Britain and the whole world, a Wall Street on the Water, relieving the congested City and providing a solution to the space problems many firms in the City were facing with the advent of new technologies. The Greater London Council which used to be a key actor in the redevelopment process, was dissolved in 1986, and planning was essentially left to the free market forces, under the guidance (since 1981) of the London Docklands Development Corporation (LDDC; Brownill, 1990, Imhof-weber, 1994). The underlying assumption was that the economy continued to boom over the next few decades and that there would be a continuous demand for office space.

For a certain period, this worked quite well. Investments were made in the renovation of old warehouses, and in certain dock areas, a new quality of life was created. Heron Quay became a development on the human scale, taking into account both social and environmental considerations. The focus of the whole project, however, was to be Canary Wharf on the Isle of Dogs, a gigantic office area with huge towers and blocks, which Imhof-weber's 1994 report calls an 'office ghetto.' To date, Canary Wharf alone comprises 120 hectares of office space.

Inevitably, where there are ups; there will also be downs, and the assumption of a continuing economic boom provided to be short-lived. By the early 1990s, there was a surplus of office space in London, and at the same time, the ideas about urban development had begun to change: the unsociable monostructures, constructed according to the idea of separating functional areas, were to be replaced by mixed spaces where residential, leisure and work functions existed along each other. In this way, people were to be brought back to town, and offices ought to be converted into apartments, schools, shops etc. This ideal had been anticipated in Heron Quay, but Canary Wharf was planned and built according to the old segregative concept.

As a result, in the early 1990s, the London Docklands appeared to be a gigantic planning and financial disaster (Brownill, 1990), not in the least because the offices were there before an adequate transport infrastructure had been provided. The area, which was thought of as a centre, has become marginalized for several reasons: too expensive, unpleasant architecture, bad link to the rest of London. Far-sighted architects foretell that certain buildings will have to disappear within a relatively short time (Imhof-weber, 1994). The period between the first plans and the disaster is less than a generation!

However, urban development is closely tied to economic development, and the London Docklands are no exception to this. In 1998, the LDDC Docklands Digest Internet site indicated an improvement of the situation (i.e. demarginalization). In particular, it announces that:

The LDDC in its annual report for 1995-96, reports a massive boom 'particularly in terms of housing with this year even better'. In another place, we read that "More than 1.37 million sq. ft (13 hectares) of office space was let in

Docklands during the last year, according to the annual report of the LDDC. The relocating firms added 3,6558 jobs. The LDDC is confident its remaining commercial sites will be disposed off before the quango is wound up in 18 months. The report says the only commercial blackspot is the ill fated Tobacco Dock in Wapping where Kuwaiti owners have failed to announce a redevelopment 'despite rumours' (LDDC, 1998).

While this sounds reassuring, we do not know if this improvement is going to last. This example shows how quickly a region can alternate between marginal and central.

Retirement ghettos – a new type of marginal region?

Retirement migration is a relatively recent phenomenon. It can be recognized as one of the results of the welfare state whose social security system has ensured a certain degree of material affluence to most people retiring from professional activity. A change in surroundings may therefore be desirable at this stage in life.

Elderly persons migrate for various reasons. Affluence can hardly be seen as one, rather is it a supporting factor. The retired may wish to return to his place of origin, join one of the children who has left home, leave an area laden with memories to working life, move to a tourist resort he has known in earlier years or try and settle in a completely new region (Rezzonico and Stuber, 1998, p. 16) – within the same region, inside the country, or abroad.

Retirement migration, however, is not comparable to migration in a person's active years. Elderly people often have specific requirements concerning their new surroundings, which limit the choice of migration destinations. They may want possibilities for easy walking, they often need the proximity of adequate medical care, the climate has to be mild to warm, and they usually want to live in good company, whether they be locals or other retired migrants (Rezzonico and Stuber, 1998, p. 22). Regions with a Mediterranean climate are well suited, but in general, people of the north tend to move south: from Northern England to the South Coast or the South West, from Paris to the Côte d'Azur, from Zurich to the Ticino (Cribier, 1970, Rezzonico and Stuber, 1998, p. 26). Within Europe, such migrations originate, e.g., in the UK, France and Germany (and, of course, in other European countries), and the principal destinations are Italy, Spain, Portugal or Greece (Williams *et al.*, 1997). Marginal regions of Spain and Portugal are particularly favoured by foreign immigrants, i.c. Malaga province in Spain and the Algarve in Portugal – areas with a weak economic potential but a good climate (Williams *et al.* (1997, p. 122).

Considering that retired immigrants are usually fairly well off, the local economy can profit from this movement to some extent. On the other hand, the presence of immigrants from the north puts new constraints on the local society and on the land market, and the presence of elderly people demands new specialized medical services, i.e. new infrastructures. Under these circumstances, a part of the profit may be offset. Retired immigrants are therefore no remedy for demarginalization.

In Switzerland, the region south of the Alps, has become a very popular migration destination also for retired people. One indicator for this process is the language transformation: predominantly Italian speaking, the canton has undergone an important linguistic shift in this century. In 1900, Italian was the mother tongue of 97% of the population, whereas only 2% were German speakers. 90 years later, the situation had changed considerably, and at the local level this process had been even more dramatic (Table 2.2). In particular, the percentage of German speakers has risen from 2.3% to 11.1% in 1970. Although it has fallen slightly to 9.8% in 1990, the absolute number is still rising). Even if we bear in mind that the 1980s were marked by a strong immigration of asylum seekers and refugees from other linguistic areas, the language shift is at least in part a mirror of retirement migration (which, of course, comprises not only Swiss but also other citizens).

Table 2.2   Percentage of Italian speakers in Ticino (Canton, selected districts and communes)

Area	1970	1980	1990
Canton	85.7	83.9	82.8
Locarno District	76.6	74.3	75.0
Ascona	54.9	55.5	61.1
Muralto	71.5	68.2	67.0
Orselina	35.4	38.4	45.3
Lugano District	81.5	80.3	80.3
Carona	70.6	61.3	64.6
Paradiso	69.8	73.8	69.6

In the United States, the situation is somewhat similar (north to south migration), but it is characterized by a new type of settlements which has appeared since the 1960s and for which Sun City in Arizona is an example. Being reserved for elderly people only, such residences risk to become a sort of ghetto, where the old live their life separate from the rest of society. This may be true to some extent, but in 'ordinary' towns, the problem of marginalization and isolation of the elderly is usually more serious. In fact, those run-down urban areas where only old people, students and immigrants can afford to live, are socially (and as a consequence also spatially) very marginal. In particular, they often lack adequate social life and health provisions. Sun cities, on the other hand, offer a wide variety of activities for sports, entertainment and culture, health provisions, churches etc., i.e. a mirror of the current value of 'active old age'. It would be incorrect to call such settlements marginal: the inhabitants live a social life within the same age group, they share similar problems, and new friendships and solidarities (often absent in life before retirement) can develop.

Conclusion

To conclude, we return to the question in the title. Where are we, what has been going on in the course of this century, and what lessons are we to learn from the processes illustrated by the four case studies for our future?

- It has become obvious that at the end of the 20th century, marginality and marginalization continue to be important issues. Despite considerable efforts at all levels (international development aid, regional policy, deregulation etc.), very little has changed: regional disparities have not disappeared and inequality is still a major problem. It is true that progress has been made, but all too often the measures taken were essentially of a technical nature, and this is not enough.
- In his survey of recent research on marginal regions, Scott (1998) concludes that the increasingly globalized economy not only produced higher economic efficiency (and therefore also higher profits and shareholder values) but also 'a growing income inequality, and high unemployment especially among youth'. (p. 16). As we look around us, this assertion is confirmed every day, even if occasionally, unemployment figures go down - they will rise again, and were it only for seasonal variations in economic activities. Deregulation is not the answer to all questions.
- The case studies have shown that marginal regions exist at all scales, but that they are not a static phenomenon. It has become apparent that on the global and continental scales, disparities take more time to be lowered, whereas the local example demonstrates the rapidity with which changes can occur. The last example is linked to the specific conditions created by the economic and social evolution after World War II. In a way it is probably a fashion, and it may lose its importance if the social and economic frameworks change. It is therefore imperative to include the time factor into our reflections.

22

Investigating into marginality, marginalization and marginal regions is therefore a task continuing well into the 21st century. Future challenges may be the problems of global climatic change (Leimgruber, 1998), which will influence the natural conditions for our society, and the question of sustainable development. In both cases, we have to look for more than simply technical solutions and face the challenge of a new attitude of man versus the environment.

References

Andreoli, M. (1992), 'An analysis of different kinds of marginal systems in a developed country: the case of Italy', *Occasional Papers in Geography and Planning, Dept. of Geography and Planning, ASU*, vol. 4, Boone, North Carolina, pp. 24-44.

Beck, U. (1997), *Was ist Globalisierung?*, Suhrkamp, Frankfurt.

Bertrand M. (1994), *Les défis conceptuels de la mondialisation*, Institut Universitaire d'Études du Développement (IUED), Geneva.

Brechbühl, L., Gianferrari, O. and Savioz, D. (1998), *Cartographie de l'Indicateur du Développement Humain*, Paper prepared during a Seminar on marginal regions, Department of Geography, University of Fribourg, Manuscript.

Brownill, S. (1990), *Developing London's Docklands. Another great planning disaster?*, Paul Chapman, London.

Cribier, F. (1970), 'Les migrations de retraite en France: matériaux pour une géographie du troisième âge', *Bulletin de l'Association des Géographes Français*, No. 381.

Grauhan, R.-R. and Linder, W. (1974), *Politik der Verstädterung*, Frankfurt/M.

Imhof-weber, G. (1994), 'London, TV-report for Bayrischer Rundfunk', Munich.

LDDC (1998), *Docklands Digest*, (www.docklands.co.uk/welcome.htm).

Leimgruber, W. (1998), 'From highlands and high-latitude zones to marginal regions', in H. Jussila, W. Leimgruber and R. Majoral (eds), *Perceptions of marginality. Theoretical issues and regional perceptions of marginality in geographical space*, Ashgate, Aldershot, pp. 27-33.

Reynaud, A. (1981), *Société, espace et justice. Inégalités régionales et justice socio-spatiale*, PUF, Paris.

Rezzonico, E. and Stuber, C. (1998), 'Altersmigration - die Entstehung von Rentnerghettos?', Paper prepared during a Seminar on marginal regions, Department of Geography, University of Fribourg, Manuscript.

Scott, P. (1998), 'Development issues in marginal regions', in H. Jussila, W. Leimgruber and R. Majoral (eds), *Perceptions of marginality, Theoretical issues and regional perceptions of marginality in geographical space*, Aldershot, Ashgate, pp. 7-24.

Tata, R.J. and Schultz, R.R. (1988), World variation in human welfare: a new index of development status, *Annals of the Association of American Geographers*, pp. 580-593.

Taylor, P.J. (1996), *Political geography. World-economy, nation-state and locality*, 3rd ed., Longman, Harlow.

Vallin, S. (1998), 'L'Islande, un pays marginalisé?', Paper prepared during a Seminar on marginal regions, Department of Geography, University of Fribourg, Manuscript.

Williams, A.M., King, R. and Warnes, T. (1997), 'A Place in the sun: international retirement migration from northern to southern Europe', *European Urban and Regional Studies*, 4/2, pp. 115-134.

3 Globalization and economic marginalization:
North-South differences

LAWRENCE M. SOMMERS, ASSEFA MEHRETU AND
BRUCE WM. PIGOZZI

Introduction

Vulnerability to economic marginality in the new international division of labour (NIDL) is undergoing a significant shift economically and spatially from its well-documented previous patterns. Economic marginality is changing from distinct general centre-periphery patterns, characterized by uneven development at national and international scales. Relative vulnerabilities to exploitation and poverty were normally sustained in national peripheries in all countries, and in international peripheries in the form of the Third World (Wallerstein, 1992). Although the general patterns and magnitudes of regional inequalities, including North-South disparities, continue to prevail, vulnerability to economic marginality under NIDL is neither restricted to national peripheries in North and South countries at the macro scale nor to the Third World at the global scale (Jessop, 1992; Martinelli and Schoenberger, 1991; Scott and Storper, 1992; Painter, 1996).

There has been a shift in the locus of power to determine the level of world economic locations and interaction from the nation state to transnational corporate (TNC) entities in the NIDL (Dicken, 1992, pp. 120-147; Kegley and Wittkopf, 1989, pp. 159-175; Painter, 1996, pp. 142-143; Shannon, 1996, pp. 1-8; Schoenberger, 1988). There has also been the further disjoining of the space of production from the places where accumulated capital resides (Frank and Gills 1990; Hymer, 1972). These developments of NIDL are producing a more flexible theatre of production giving rise to volatility and capriciousness in marginality with vulnerabilities to economic distress no longer restricted to national peripheries at the macroscale or the Third World at the global scale (Dicken, 1992, pp. 191-225; Schoenberger, 1988; Todaro, 1994, pp. 407-411). The policy implications of marginality under NIDL have therefore become more challenging as economic marginalities within core areas occur even though overall prosperity of the nation rises (Hacker, 1995).

The purpose of this paper is to discuss how globalization impacts more developed and less developed nations (MDCs and LDCs) differentially in economic development and income distribution. The paper has four parts. First, the meaning of globalization with its concomitant processes will be presented. Second, the concept of marginality and its typology will be outlined. Third, relations between globalization and marginality will be hypothesized with some empirical observations. Finally, a case study using General Motors as a TNC and its role as an agent of globalization and differential effects on marginality will be briefly examined.

Globalization

Globalization has been defined as a complex form of internationalization of economic activity which implies a degree of functional integration between internationally dispersed economic activities (Benko and Dunford, 1991; Dicken, 1992, pp. 1-2; Hanink, 1994, pp. 232-238; Porter and Sheppard, 1998, pp. 459-492). The dynamics of the nature, structure, and processes of globalization originate primarily in the 'centres' of economic power and skilled labour in North America, the European Community and the Pacific Rim. With post-industrial needs to reorganize industry, these regions have adopted a more flexible mode of industrial organization and location. Flexible production has become the recent norm which has had made it more economical to operate plants not only less-rigidly integrated vertically but also spatially more footloose. TNCs, taking advantage of this new international division of labour (NIDL) and the new opportunities of comparative advantage it has uncovered, have begun to develop industrial enterprises throughout the world (Hanink, 1994, pp. 212-221; Jessop, 1992).

The functional integration of economic production is organized primarily by large corporations in highly developed economic regions of the North which enjoy a controlling power over peripheries of South America, Africa, portions of East and South Asia, and Oceania (excluding Australia and New Zealand) (Dicken, 1992, pp. 47-88; Friedmann and Weaver, 1980, pp. 163-178; Johnson, *et al.*, 1996, pp. 13-17). LDCs in the global peripheries have been on the receiving end of decentralized industrial enterprise. By virtue of their position as being poor and dependent, LDCs have little or no power to negotiate business deals favourable to the long-term economic development of their respective nations. Industrial enterprises relocated in LDCs, as in the case of export processing zones (EPZs) and tax free zones (TFZs) under NIDL, mirror the conventional mineral and agricultural cash crop estates that developed in the old international division of labour (OIDL) and have had strong export biases and little internal inter-industry linkages. For many LDCs, this sort of TNC-led industrial development did not produce fundamental industrial and technological transformation that is sustainable and developmental for their regions over the long run. There is of course a variety of opinions on the role of FDI and EPZs on LDC economies (Wong and Chu, 1984; Ramachandran and Shah, 1997).

Transnational corporations (TNCs) have been and continue to be the prime agents of economic globalization and the locus of real power. The number of TNCs involved has grown at least six-fold since 1970 from 7,000 to over 40,000. About 90 percent of the TNCs are located in the North with over half found in the U.S., Germany, France, the Netherlands, and Japan. They account for a large portion of the world's productivity. It is estimated that TNCs are involved in over three-fourths of the world trade much of which is between parts of individual corporations headquartered in the North but with productive activity in both North and South countries. The industrial sectors of TNCs cover a wide range of economic activity ranging from manufacturing to capital and banking, technology, trade, raw material processing, entrepreneurship, strategic planning, and management (Barf, 1995; Castells, 1989, pp. 307-347; Dicken, 1992, pp. 47-88; Johnson et al., 1996, pp. 13-17).

The motives of the TNCs are normally three-fold – to increase company efficiency (profitability), gain access to market areas, and assure the availability of cheap raw material sources (Friedmann and Weaver, 1980, pp. 163-180; Wheeler et al., 1998, pp. 64-74). Conventional 'arms length' international commodity exchange continues but intra-firm trade is increasingly based on production by branches and other TNC controlled units utilising the less expensive labour in the South. Foreign direct investment (FDI) by TNCs from the North countries helps to increase the opportunities for international expansion of production and trade. The continued need by TNCs for raw materials found in the South, provides the basis for resource driven extractive enclaves in the South. Enterprise production zones (EPZs) are examples of efficiency driven initiatives supported by the large corporations as they benefit from the increased activity and production.

With the state increasingly deregulated from getting involved in the national economy, and the unions weakened by cost-saving down-sizing and job exports, TNCs have successfully established a new theatre of production and accumulation afforded by the NIDL with cheap and less protected labour pools in LDCs (Jessop 1992; Martinelli and Schoenberger, 1991). By virtue of their financial power, TNCs wield tremendous power in dealings with relatively weak LDC governments, which they co-opt to get access to cheap raw materials and labour (Kegley and Wittkopf, 1989, p. 170). The overall impact of globalization within the NIDL has been to facilitate the potential of TNCs to reap more profits resulting from their motives to achieve efficiency in production, expand markets world-wide, and obtain easy access to raw materials. The modus operandi for TNCs to achieve this has been to practice post-Fordist flexible production, downsizing, and, relocation of production units by scanning the globe and employing market-based foreign direct investment (FDIs) as well as labour based EPZs and TFZs, all at much higher order of efficiency than has been possible in parent countries (Porter and Sheppard, 1998). TNC activity has now penetrated poor rural and marginal areas of both the North and South.

Marginality

Marginality is a condition of poverty and deprivation found in a community or territory that has experienced the adverse affects of uneven development either due to non-competitive conditions in free markets or hegemonic biases in regulated or controlled markets (see also Friedmann, 1988, p. 114; Mehretu and Sommers, 1994; 1997; Mehretu et al. 1997). The character of marginality that pertains to a specific community or territory of a given scale will depend on its political and economic history and the nature of its natural and human resources. Generally, marginal areas occur where there is a convergence of political, cultural, economic and resource problems. However, it is conceivable for regions to experience political and cultural marginality without necessarily showing obvious signs of distress in economic and resource factors. Political and cultural marginality, often insidious and not as visible as economic and physical marginality, occur when groups or individuals associated with the political and cultural elite use hegemonic influence to prevent 'the other' communities from exercising political rights and cultural and economic freedoms (see also Marcuse, 1996). Sometimes such cases are more visible when communities and territories are politically gerrymandered, ghettoized or otherwise contained within spatial margins and result in an abridgement of rights and privileges (see also Benko and Dunford, 1991, pp. 18-23).

One of the main objectives of this research is to differentiate between two counterpoised structural origins of marginality; one based on free markets and the other on controlled markets. In the interest of conceptual clarity, we therefore propose to distinguish between two types of marginality, one resulting from competitive markets and the other from noncompetitive market systems. The first extreme is called contingent and the second, systemic. In reality, a combination of both is often found with differing degrees of dominance of one over the other.

Contingent marginality refers to unequal development caused by competitive inequality within the neo-classical economic framework. Contingent marginality is assumed to be endogenous to the laissez-faire economic system and is considered 'accidental' or a 'temporary and self-correcting aberration' of an otherwise equitable economic framework. It is assumed that such 'aberrations' are expected to be resolved by 'self-adjusting' free market dynamics (Ernste and Meier, 1992, pp. 263-266; Scott and Storper, 1992, pp. 3-24). Contingent margins may, in fact, persist due to what Mingione has referred to as 'malign circuits of exclusion' in which potentially reversible marginality may deteriorate into a state of chronic distress (Micheli, 1996, pp. 41-45; Mingione, 1996, p. 12). When this happens, polarities become too entrenched for market forces to allow effective redressive action. On account of this type of discourse, serious questions are raised about the validity of the assumptions of the laissez-faire system (Ernste and Meier, 1992, pp. 264-265). However, aspects of urban and rural poverty in North countries may be the result of contingent marginality. Practically, it is often difficult to isolate the contingent from the systemic as most marginal communities and territories manifest the effects of both competitive inequality and hegemonic inequity in the resulting political and economic benefits to the region (see also Kuttner, 1997; Marcuse, 1996, pp. 176-216).

Systemic marginality refers to uneven development caused by hegemonic forces of politics and economics that produce inequities in the distribution of social, political and economic benefits. Systemic marginality may originate from forces internal or external to the state but in either case its presence is determined by the degree of bipolar occupational and spatial structures that are present in the national economy (Castells, 1989, pp. 172-197). Unlike the neo-classical framework, systemic marginality does not lend itself to redressive reforms through 'modes of regulation', as in the Keynesian welfare state, to mitigate the deleterious effects of unregulated enterprises (Painter, 1995). In this case, marginality is a deliberate construction of an endogenous or exogenous system which intends to achieve specific desirable outcomes of political control (as in a dictatorship or pseudo-radical regime) or economic exploitation (as in neo-colonial regime) (Blaut, 1993; Mehretu, 1989; Shannon, 1996). This is perhaps the most important source of socio-economic marginality, especially in South countries as in the case of the entire Sub-Saharan region. Systemic marginality is of particular significance in countries that have experienced pervasive inequity under colonial and/or neo-colonial regimes such as Zimbabwe and South Africa. Pseudo radical and totalitarian governments, common in South countries, often aggravate marginality by entering into lucrative compacts with foreign interests thereby reinforcing the exogenous determination of the development process (see also Friedmann, 1988, pp. 108-144; Blaut, 1993, pp. 17-30). This was the case with Zaire (now Congo) in central Africa, a prosperous country whose wealth was immensely squandered by a corrupt regime in collusion with TNC entities.

Globalization and marginality

The functional and hegemonic character of globalization has exposed the world to differential vulnerabilities to contingent, systemic and is termed here as feedback systemic marginality. As indicated earlier, globalization, as dominated by TNC managed trade and transfer of investment resources, is not a neutral process (Friedmann, 1988, pp. 57-80; Kegley and Wittkopf, 1989, pp. 159-173; Massey, 1994, pp. 146-156; Schoenberger, 1988). It has differential impacts for North and South countries. International industrial and trade linkages among North countries have been going on for a long time. They have tended to be dominated by intra-firm linkages. They also take place in a variety of sectors including services. In North countries, these linkages are generally characterized by deals directly between management and management without much use of bureaucratically and hegemonically inclined state authorities. By virtue of what is known as overlapping market theory of international trade (Hanink, 1997, pp. 361-363), most of the world's trade occurs among MDCs which manifest similar demand and preferences for goods and services. TNC-led relationships in overlapping markets are generally functional resulting in contingent marginality for working classes (see Dicken, 1992, pp. 47-87).

On the other hand, TNC-managed trade between North and South countries is based on fundamental endowment differentials that is consistent with the differentiated market theory of international trade of comparative advantage (Hanink, 1997, p. 362). Cheap labour and cheap raw materials form the principal endowments that TNCs seek. In order to access these endowments, TNCs deal directly with state authorities in LDCs who often play comprador functions and expose their endowments with hegemonic control over asset owners and labour pools. Such relationships lead to systemic marginality of LDC peoples. In so doing, TNCs often get involved in politics and, using their immense financial power, they may even make a difference in installing leaders who are favourable to their causes. The most notorious example of this is the role that the International Telephone and Telegraphy (ITT) played in Chile in the early 1970s to prevent a socialist government from being elected, and subsequently trying to help overthrow it in order to protect its economic interests in Chile (Kegley and Wittkopf, 1989, p. 170).

North-South linkages, driven by cheap and unprotected labour pools, could be used by TNCs to undermine MDC labour union collective bargaining. The hegemonic exposure of LDC labour along with post-Fordian flexible production systems, has enabled TNC management in MDCs to 'threaten' job exportation abroad unless significant concessions are made by MDC unions (Barf, 1995, p. 52). Since MDC unions have no protection from the state and have little to no control over LDC labour, they are more likely to sustain what maybe called feedback systemic marginality caused by TNCs. This makes the bargaining position of TNCs even more powerful as they can readily rely on the inevitability of globalization and its union-dreaded downward levelling of wages (Hayter and Barnes, 1992; Martinelli and Schoenberger, 1991, pp. 128-130).

Globalization and the case of General Motors

A good example of corporation globalization is the world-wide economic activities of General Motors. General Motors (GM) is the world's biggest company with revenues of $178 billion in 1997, exceeded only by the GDPs of 24 countries in the world. It has 698,000 employees and a one-company total of 1.2% of the U.S. GDP (Bradsher, 1998; Dicken, 1992, pp. 289-308). GM has production facilities in 51 different countries (including the U.S.) and sales offices in most of the remaining countries. Production of GM parts and assembled automobiles occurs predominately in North America with headquarters in Michigan, and facilities in Europe, South America, E. Asia and minor production in a few African countries. In the early 1990s, over 40% of GM's production and over 60% of Ford's production of passenger automobiles was international and it has been increasing (Dicken, 1992, pp. 289-290). Japanese and European automotive companies are even more internationalized. Since the 1960s, the competition for market share has been tightening. As a consequence, the global as well as the US market share for GM has been shrinking even though it still is the leading TNC in automotive production (Bradsher, 1998; Dicken, 1992, p. 290).

The 1998 GM strike by unions generated considerable debate about whether GM can weather such costly strikes and still hold on to its market share and international dominance (Bradsher, 1998; Greenhouse, 1998). Would such costly strikes force GM to go even more international by taking advantage of cheap labour pools overseas, and by using more outsourcing and subcontracting? Among the 'big three' carmakers in the US (GM, Ford, and Chrysler), GM has been relatively slow in responding to international pressures for increased efficiency. However, future competitiveness may lie in the responding to these challenges: (a) respond to cost containment demands and relocate, downsize or close plants, (b) resolve pressures for 'downward levelling' of wages as a function of cheap labour pools overseas, (c) co-operate with unions to make US labour more efficient, and (d) work with federal and state agencies to help stabilize production costs in order to continue operation in home markets.

The United Auto Workers (UAW) opposes GM moves, which will decrease the size of the labour force or threatens the guaranteed levels of employment and reasonable levels of remuneration. Some of the moves contemplated by GM in 1998 to increase its efficiency were faced with a hostile reaction from the unions concerned about their welfare. Unions have their goals. They want to 'slow and tame' the globalization process, strengthen their collective bargaining, push for 'upward levelling' of wages, and demand a more equitable distribution of corporate wealth to workers (Greenhouse, 1998).

The incompatibility of union and management strategies may result in the increased loss of market share for GM products. If GM chooses to remain competitive, it has to respond to the challenges for cost containment which means reducing its local presence at the risk of creating marginality of the workforce in its wake. Employees laid off in the U.S., often lack skills for other jobs and thus can experience contingent marginality by losing their work to cheaper labour sites and by being forced to take less remunerative occupations. The overseas workers who are not in a position to demand wage or benefit concessions from TNCs, will settle with the going low local wage rates with stiff competition from the vast pool of the unemployed in LDCs. Depending on the role of the LDC elite, such labour pools may be subject to systemic marginality on account of TNC-LDC elite collusion to exploit endowments without appropriate compensation and safeguards. On the other hand, the MDC/LDC wage differential, also has its impact on MDC labour pools by inflicting feedback systemic marginality caused by down-levelling of wages which TNCs may use to improve bargaining positions with MDC labour. The GM example of coping with issues of production, labour, costs, efficiency, competition, and markets can be found in the operating modes of most TNCs, and are major factors in the changing nature of world-wide economic marginalization.

Conclusions

The benefits of globalization that accrue to TNCs are distributed among the TNC management and white-collar classes, investors in stock markets, and national and foreign political elite who position themselves at the interface of the lucrative global linkages. As indicated earlier, globalization marginalizes the working classes of both MDCs and LDCs. In MDCs, globalization makes unions vulnerable to increased pressure by TNCs to accept less than desirable deals on wages and benefits. What has been called the 'declining middle' in the United States over the last decade illustrates the 'polarization' of 'segmented' labour forces with blue-collar working classes losing a share of the national income even though the nation has been experiencing high levels of economic growth by virtue of its dynamic corporate sector. For blue collar workers in LDCs, globalization means loss of rights for collective bargaining as labour is often mortgaged by LDC political and economic elite to accept lower wages, little or no benefits, and more than desirable negative externalities on the social and environmental conditions.

The policy challenges to alleviate the deleterious effects of contingent and systemic marginality brought about by globalization are found in all the three principal actors responsible for globalization (states, TNCs and unions). States in MDCs may use a combination of policies. First, they may apply macro-economic tools of the welfare state to lessen the deleterious impacts of neo-liberal industrial reorganization led by TNCs. Second, as unlikely as it may sound, they may devise ways of controlling the modus operandi of TNCs. Third, MDCs may bring about international coalition for uniform regulatory mechanisms to protect blue-collar workers from excessive exploitation anywhere in the world (like child labour laws, etc.). Such coalitions may also enable them to advance common environmental protection standards, work-place safety and product quality. LDC states, as weak as they may be vis-à-vis TNCs, are within their power to regulate minimum standards in exposing their people and resources to exploitation by outsiders. Finally, advancing free trade zones customs unions and common markets at the global scale with an enlightened approach to an equitable (not equal) sharing of the benefits of globalization may the best long-term objective.

TNCs are an amorphous lot. They are multi-centered and multidirectional in their interaction. Their nature precludes any optimism that they can come to a collective and sensible trajectory for a long-term and viable global relation based on mutual benefits for all concerned. Since short-term profit is the major motive force, long-term viability of home markets (for instance) may be sacrificed. Although they claim to be governed by market functions, they actually manage international linkages, some of which (in LDCs) are hegemonically derived. Although, it is an unlikely prospect, it is conceivable that they may entertain more humane strategies for long-term benefits by making investment in labour and infrastructure, reduce hegemonic links with Third World elite, and reign in what is known as corporate greed.

Unions, especially in MDCs, need to take a more global view of their security. Since globalization is inevitable, and not always bad, unions should have a more enlightened role at home as well as abroad to cope with its impacts. Their challenges will include increased partnership with management in which tolerable limits on wages and benefits can be negotiated along with joint ventures, joint ownership, and other mutually beneficial co-operative ventures. Unions may also devise ways to improve work-place discipline and output efficiency by reigning in unrealistic demands for management concessions which has to cope with its own demands for cost-reduction under the pressures of its investors. Labour should also be involved in the local and national politics in promoting its position as TNCs do working closely with the state apparatus. Finally, MDCs unions may also strengthen co-operation with international unions to afford a more organized process of 'upward levelling' of wages and benefits.

References

Barf, Richard (1995), 'Multinational Corporations and the New International Division of Labour', in R.J. Johnston, Peter J. Taylor, and Michael J. Watts, (eds), *Geographies of Global Change: Remapping the World in the Late Twentieth Century*, Blackwell, Oxford, pp. 50-62.

34

Benko, Georges and Dunford, Mick (1991), 'Structural Change and the Spatial Organisation of the Productive System: An Introduction', in Georges, G. Benko *et al.*, (eds), *Industrial Change and Regional Development*, Belhaven Press, London, pp. 3-23.

Blaut, J. M. (1993), *The Colonizer's Model of the World*, The Guilford Press, New York.

Bradsher, Keith (1998), 'Forget Microsoft: GM is Still the Biggest Kid on the Block', *The New York Times*, July 26, NYT, New York.

Castells, Manuel (1989), *The Information City*, Blackwell, Oxford.

Dicken, Peter (1992), *Global Shift* (Second Edition), The Guilford Press, New York.

Ernste, Huib and Meier, Verna, (eds) (1992), *Regional Development and Contemporary Industrial Response: Extending Flexible Specialization*, Belhaven Press, London.

Frank, Andre Gunder and Gills, Barry K. (1990), 'The Cumulation of Accumulation: Theses and Research Agenda for 5000 Years of World System History', *Dialectical Anthropology*, vol. 15, pp. 19-42.

Friedmann, John (1988), *Life Space and Economic Space*, Transaction Books, New Brunswick, NJ.

Friedmann, John and Weaver, Clyde (1980), *Territory and Function*, University of California Press, Berkeley, CA.

Greenhouse, Steven (1998), 'Strike Force: The Relentless March of Labor's True Foe', *The New York Times*, August 2, NYT, New York.

Hacker, Andrew (1995), 'The Rich: Who are They?', *New York Times Magazine*, A Special Issue, November 19, NYT, New York.

Hanink, Dean M. (1994), *The International Economy: A Geographical Perspective*, John Wiley & Sons, Inc., New York.

Hayter, R. and Barnes, T.J. (1992), 'Labour Market Segmentation, Flexibility, and Recession: A British Colombia Case Study', *Environment and Planning C: Government and Policy*, vol. 10, pp. 333-353.

Hymer, S.H. (1972), 'The Multinational Corporation and the Law of Uneven Development', in J.N. Bhagwati (ed.), *Economics and World Order*, McMillan, London, pp. 113-140.

Jessop, Bob (1992), 'Post-Fordism and Flexible Specialization: Incommensurable, Contraditory, Complementary, or Just Plain Perspectives?', in Huib Ernste *et al.* (eds), *Regional Development and Contemporary Industrial Response: Extending Flexible Specialization*, Belhaven Press, London, pp. 25-43.

Johnson, R.J., Taylor, Peter J. and Watts, Michael J. (1996), *Geographies of Global Change: Reshaping the World in the Late Twentieth Century*, Blackwell, Oxford.

Kegley, Charles W. and Wittkopf, Eugene R. (1989), *World Politics: Trend and Transformation*, St. Martin's Press, New York.

Kuttner, Robert (1997), 'The Limits of Markets', *The American Prospect*, vol. 31, pp. 28-36.

Marcuse, Peter (1996), 'Space and Race in the Post-Fordist City: The Outcast Ghetto and Advanced Homelessness in the United States Today', in Enzo Mingione (ed.), *Urban Poverty and the Underclass: A Reader*, Blackwell Publishers, Oxford, pp. 176-216.

Martinelli, Flavia and Schoenberger, Erica (1991), 'Oligopoli is Alive and Well: Notes for a Broader Discussion of Flexible Accumulation', in Georges, G. Benko *et al.* (eds), *Industrial Change and Regional Development*, Belhaven Press, London, pp. 117-133.

Massey, Doreen (1994), *Space, Place and Gender*, University of Minnesota Press, Minneapolis, MN.

Mehretu, Assefa (1989), *Regional Disparity in Sub-Saharan Africa*, Westview Press, Boulder, CO.

Mehretu, Assefa, Pigozzi, Bruce Wm. and Sommers, Lawrence M. (1997), *Towards Typologies of Socioeconomic Marginality: North-South Comparison*, Paper presented at the IGU Commission on Marginal and Critical Regions, Harare, Zimbabwe.

Mehretu, Assefa and Sommers, Lawrence M. (1994), 'Patterns of Macrogeographic and Microgeographic Marginality in Michigan', *The Great Lakes Geographer*, vol. 1, no. 2, pp. 67-80.

Mehretu, Assefa and Sommers, Lawrence M. (1997), 'International Perspectives on Socio-Spatial Marginality', in Heikki Jussila, Walter Leimgruber and Roser Majoral (eds), *Perceptions of Marginality*, Ashgate, Aldershot, UK, pp. 135-145.

Micheli, Giuseppe A. (1996), 'Downdrift: Provoking Agents and Symptom-Formation Factors in the Process of Impoverishment', in Enzo Mingione (ed.), *Urban Poverty and the Underclass: A Reader*, Blackwell Publishers, Oxford, pp. 41-63.

Mingione, Enzo (ed.) (1996), *Urban Poverty and the Underclass: A Reader*, Blackwell Publishers, Oxford.

Painter, Joe (1995), 'The Regulatory State: The Corporate Welfare State and Beyond', in R.J. Johnston, Peter J. Taylor, and Michael J. Watts (eds), *Geographies of Global Change*, Blackwell Publishers, Oxford, pp. 127-143.

Porter, Philip W. and Sheppard, Eric S. (1998), *A World of Difference: Society, Nature, Development*, The Guilford Press, New York, NY.

Ramachandran, Vijaya and Shan, Manju Kedia (1997), 'The Effect of Foreign Ownership in Africa: Evidence from Ghana, Kenya and Zimbabwe', *RPED Paper 81*, The World Bank, Washington, DC.

Schoenberger, Erica (1988), 'Multinational Corporations and the New International Division of Labour: A Critical Appraisal', *International Regional Science Review*, vol. 11, no. 2, pp. 105-120.

Scott, Allen J. and Storper, Michael (1992), 'Regional Development Reconsidered', in Huib Ernste *et al.* (eds), *Regional Development and Contemporary Industrial Response: Extending Flexible Specialization*, Belhaven Press, London, pp. 3-24.

Shannon, Thomas R. (1996), *An Introduction to the World System Perspective*, Westview, Boulder, CO.

Todaro, Michael P. (1994), *Economic Development*, Longman, New York.

Wallerstein, Immanuel (1992), 'The West, Capitalism and the Modern World System', *Review*, vol. 15, no. 4, pp. 651-670.

Wheeler, James O., Muller, Peter O., Thrall, Grant Ian and Fik, Timothy J. (1998), *Economic Geography*, Third Edition, John Wiley & Sons, Inc., New York.

Wong, K. and Chu, D.K.Y. (1984), 'Export Processing Zones and Special Economic Zones as Generators of Economic Development: The Asian Experience', *Geografiska Annaler*, vol. 66, pp. 1-16.

4 Great Plains settlement: Globalization and deregulation

J. CLARK ARCHER AND RICHARD E. LONSDALE

Introduction

Globalization of the world economy has been gaining momentum for many years, but widespread recognition of its scale and manifestations has occurred only more recently. It involves the spatial reorganization of production and trade, the interpenetration of industries across national borders, the broad extension of financial markets and the diffusion of similar consumer goods world-wide (Mittelman, 1997). Another related phenomenon also gaining momentum has been deregulation, with many governments reducing their role in guiding and controlling the business sectors of their economies.

Although spatial diffusion theory might seem to imply that marginal lands should be less susceptible to the effects of these processes because of their often-peripheral locations away from centres of innovation, the converse may be closer to the truth. Marginal environmental circumstances combined with geographic isolation are apt to restrict the range of alternative resource uses and to increase the level of economic specialization (Hite, 1997). In marginal lands the economic focus is mainly on primary activities, which in turn usually link to a fragile demographic structure indicated by a declining population and the slow death of small towns (Sanchez Aguilera, 1996; Lonsdale and Archer, 1998).

The objective of this study is to investigate the notion that marginal lands are especially vulnerable to changes prompted by the twin processes of globalization and deregulation by examining the effects of these processes in the setting of the U.S. Great Plains. The study area extends over portions of ten states (Figure 4.1). The Great Plains region itself consists of semi-arid grassland of about 1.3 million sq. km and has a present population of about 6.5 million people (16% of the land area of the contiguous U.S. and 2.5% of the population). The ten states, which enclose the Plains, cover an aggregate area of about 2.8 million sq. km with a population of about 35 million people. Unfortunately, the Great Plains has rarely been

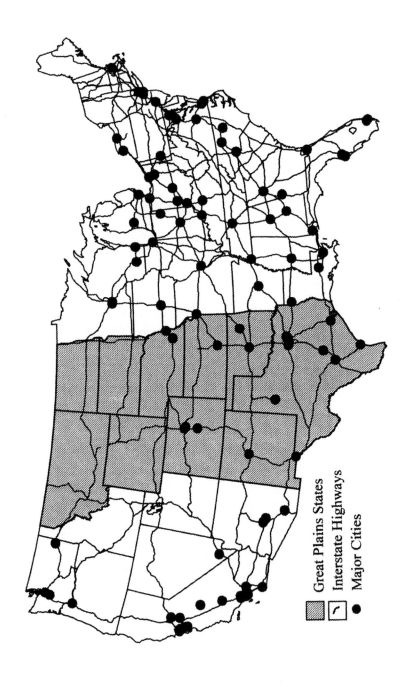

Figure 4.1   Great Plains States

Great Plains States
Interstate Highways
Major Cities

treated as a statistical reporting unit, so it can be necessary to rely on data based upon the ten states.

The Great Plains in comparative international context

It is relevant that a number of the worlds' semi-arid mid latitude grasslands share some of the characteristics and experiences observable in the U.S. Great Plains. Most notably, such areas include (1) Canada, in the drier portion of the Prairies known as the Palliser Triangle, (2) Australia, in the south-east and south-west grasslands transitional between the humid coasts and the arid interior of the continent, (3) Argentina, in the drier western margin of the Pampa and (4) to a lesser extent Russia, in the eastern steppe extending across the lower Volga and Western Siberia regions, and northern Kazakhstan.

The common experiences of these regions have usually included (1) a late 19th century colonisation by Europeans displacing indigenous peoples, usually in conjunction with railroad construction, (2) an emphasis on the market oriented production of livestock and grain, (3) an early reliance on export trade and subsequent emergence as major players in global wheat and meat marketing, (4) a hinterland status wherein the wealth generated helped build major urban centres outside the grasslands or on their periphery, (5) a rather common set of demographic problems in the late 20th century, including low birth rates, population loss through outmigration, and the demise of smaller towns, (6) the initiation of many government programs and regulations designed to aid the rural sector of the economy and (7) a more recent decline in national concern for *lagging* regions and growing dissatisfaction with government regulatory, welfare and support programs.

The early exposure to globalization

About 150 years ago the Great Plains were sparsely populated by Aboriginal Americans who were yet to be incorporated into the world economy. The first European occupiers were cattlemen who temporarily controlled vast tracts of land between 1865 and 1876 (Webb, 1981, pp. 205-69). While cattle could be driven rather great distances, they commanded higher prices when shipped by rail to eastern market centres. Tracks first reached the Plains in the late 1860s. The development of refrigerator units for railroad cars and ships in the 1870s further facilitated shipments to the eastern U.S. and beyond (Gibson, 1976, pp. 458-83). Thus, competition for access to world markets became an intrinsic part of the economic and settlement experience of the U.S. Great Plains early on. Britain received its first shipment of refrigerated beef from the U.S. in 1875; similar shipments to Europe commenced from Argentina in 1877 and Australia in 1880 (Critchell and Raymond, 1969, pp. 13-31).

Beginning in the 1870s a wave of new settlers arrived in the Plains, taking advantage of land grants under the Homestead Act. Many came directly by steamship and then railroad from Europe, where the U.S. railroads maintained recruiting offices. Technological developments also spurred settlement, in particular the steel plow, barbed wire, and later steam powered tractors which made plowing of grasslands more practical. Rail shipments eastward permitted an export oriented agriculture based on wheat, feed grains and livestock, largely cattle. Most of the farms and settlements grew up as integrated peripheral elements of a global economy, and the region never experienced the gradual transition from subsistence to commercial production.

The production of wheat and beef in the Great Plains substantially increased the nation's output of these commodities. U.S. wheat output rose from 7.8 million metric tons in 1869 to 17.9 million in 1899, and then 25.7 million in 1919. In the region which now comprises the ten Great Plains states wheat production rose from less than 163 thousand metric tons in 1869 to over 5.5 million in 1899, and then 11.7 million in 1919 (Figure 4.2). In percentage terms, the Great Plains produced barely 2% of U.S. wheat in 1869, 31% in 1899 and 45% in 1919 (Figure 4.3).

Even with population growth and urbanization within the U.S., agricultural output tended to exceed domestic demand during the late 19th and early 20th century. Thus, an average of nearly 16% of U.S. annual wheat production was exported between 1870 and 1919. However, there was a great deal of yearly variation in foreign demand, leading to substantial and generally quite unpredictable fluctuations in the prices received by U.S. farmers. For example, over 25% of U.S. wheat was exported in the years 1879-81, 1892 and 1915, but less than 5% in 1905-06 and 1911-12. Exports of refrigerated beef, primarily to Britain, increased substantially after 1876, rising to 13% of U.S. production by 1901, but then dropped sharply after 1908 (U.S. Dept. of Agriculture, 1921, pp. 779, 824; U.S. Bureau of the Census, 1960, p. 291). Decreases in wheat and beef exports early in the century were attributable to growing domestic demand, foreign competition and increasing trade restrictions both abroad and at home (Fite and Reese, 1965, pp. 466-69).

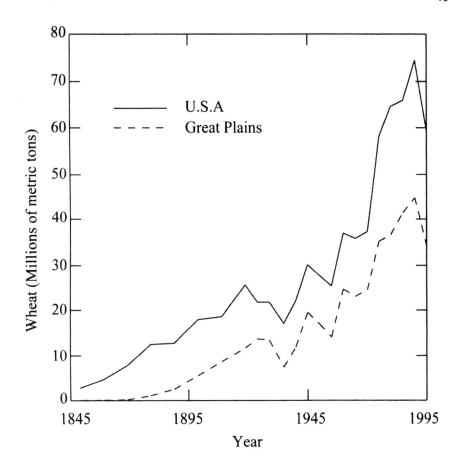

Figure 4.2   USA and Great Plains wheat production

Government involvement in the affairs of rural areas such as the Great Plains dealt mostly with infrastructural improvements. This largely was still an era of laissez faire economics, though Congress did enact legislation concerning trusts and monopolies, trade and immigration. Protective tariffs were instituted in 1922, and in 1929 ineffective efforts were made to support prices, control surpluses and extend credit (Fite and Reese, 1965, p. 564).

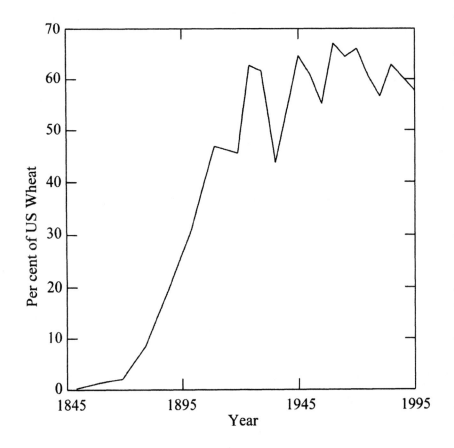

Figure 4.3   Great Plains wheat production as per cent of USA wheat production

The rise of government intervention and regulation

The agricultural sector of the U.S. economy gradually slumped in the 1920s, then things became much worse in the 1930s with the world-wide business recession. Severe drought and dust storms hit the Plains in the four years 1934-37, and the collapse of domestic and foreign markets for grain and meat combined with climatic catastrophe was too much for many Plains farmers. Over a half million people abandoned the land in what had become a dust bowl, and most headed west to the Pacific Coast.

Dramatic changes came after the inauguration of Roosevelt as president in early 1933, and a plethora of *New Deal* programs were quickly enacted. The Agricultural Adjustment Acts sought to restore farming to profitable levels through acreage controls, price supports, crop insurance and mortgage refinancing. Many livestock were destroyed to reduce oversupply and strengthen prices. Government regulation of trade and business practices increased substantially. The Rural Electrification Administration brought power to rural areas for the first time. Several major hydroelectric dams were built, transforming the largely rural regions where they were located, and many other development programs were initiated. Suffice to say, the *New Deal* was and remains controversial, and its overall effectiveness is still being debated. A return to prosperity came with World War II, which brought an increased demand for agricultural goods, higher prices and the construction of many military bases in the Plains states.

The post World War II period saw a general increase in direct and indirect assistance to agriculture. Price supports and commodity loans combined to provide more stability, and several programs were implemented to take land out of production and aid soil and wildlife conservation (Ottoson *et al.*, 1966, pp. 79-115). As a result, government payments to U.S. farmers increased from $283 million in 1950 to $3.7 billion in 1970, with Great Plains farmers consistently receiving between 25 and 29% of this (based on data in U.S. Bureau of the Census, various years). Striking gains were made in agricultural labour productivity with corresponding decreases in farm population. In 1920 it required 32 hours of farm labour to produce 1 metric ton of wheat; in 1930 it was 29 hours, in 1940 17 hours, in 1950 10 hours, in 1960 4.5 hours and in 1970 only 3.3 hours (Archer, 1991). This was the result of a technological revolution wherein mules and horses were completely replaced by tractors and combines by 1950, high yielding hybrid grains were developed, and applications of fertilizers, herbicides and pesticides greatly expanded. While the area cultivated remained about the same (despite set aside programs), the number of farms and farmers substantially diminished. Across much of the rural landscape the result was a net population outmigration and a negative natural population change; this pattern has persisted to the present day (Lonsdale and Archer, 1998).

After World War II the U.S. had large reserve stocks of wheat and was anxious to return to large scale exporting. In the past most wheat exports had gone to Europe, but the Europeans (e.g. the French) were becoming increasingly self sufficient in this regard and later became net exporters. The U.S. turned to the less developed portion of the world, offering them wheat as foreign aid or at subsidized prices. By 1967-68 the U.S. share of world wheat exports had grown to 42%, way ahead of rivals Canada, Australia and Argentina (United Nations, 1968, table 11, p. 16).

The *new* globalization

The latter part of this century, roughly since the early 1970s, has proved to be a transitional period from the post World War II phase to an era of more globally integrated financial markets, deregulation, increased foreign direct investment, trade liberalization and the restructuring of economies and political systems (McMichael, 1994). These developments are all subsumed under the label 'globalization'.

Globalization is not something new to the mid latitude grasslands, as pointed out earlier in this paper. Since their 19th century colonization, these lands have had to deal with large trading firms, ever-larger food processors, a more diverse group of commodity markets, and shifting governmental regulations and tariffs (domestic and foreign). Restructuring has been an ongoing process for agriculture throughout this period. Still, this 'new' globalization is immensely broader in scope and presents the grasslands with another, altered set of challenges.

The significance of globalization for the Great Plains can be ascertained by considering wheat production and export volumes for the U.S. in recent decades (Figures 4.2, 4.4). Although export volumes specifically attributable to the ten Great Plains states are not available, these states have accounted for between half and two-thirds of total U.S. wheat production at every Census since 1930 (Figure 4.3, Table 4.1). Annual figures averaged by decade show a substantial increase in total U.S. wheat production from just under 30 million metric tons in the 1950s to 62 million per year during the 1980s. For the period since 1960 an average of 56% of each year's crop was exported. However, this average disguises enormous variation involving a range as high as over 70% in 1963, 1972, 1988 and 1989, and as low as below 40% in 1960, 1968, 1971, 1985 and 1990 (Figure 4.4).

Using the proportions of total U.S. wheat output in the ten Great Plains states for Census years since 1960 as a guide (Table 4.1), about 55% to 65% of the wheat raised in these states in recent decades has been intended for the export rather than domestic market. The enormous fluctuation in foreign demand for U.S. wheat thus has tended to have a deleterious effect. Demand instability has been one of the factors prompting substantial farm consolidation within the region. While the total area in farms in the Great Plains changed little over the last half century, average farm size increased from 229 hectares in 1950 to 399 in 1990 (Table 4.1). During this same period the farm population fell from 3.7 million in 1950 to under 760,000 in 1990.

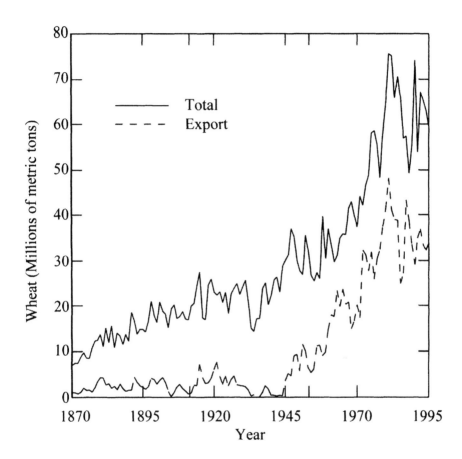

Figure 4.4   USA wheat production and exports

The tendency toward larger and larger scale also becomes apparent when off farm elements of agribusiness are examined. The principle off farm agents of globalization have included the transnational corporations and banks. Because the Great Plains and other mid latitude grasslands have agriculturally oriented economies, of particular significance is the relatively small number of giant corporations who have been the driving force behind restructuring the global food system (Heffernan and Constance,

Table 4.1   Great Plains States: Selected agricultural data

Census year	Total population (1000s)	Farm population (%)	Number farms of (1000s)	Average size of farm (hectares)	Wheat production (metric tons) (1000s)	Wheat production as % of U.S.
1870	1482	NA	121	93	160	2.1
1890	6305	55.2	625	86	2502	20.0
1910	11246	53.9	1187	111	8718	46.9
1930	15077	41.1	1309	140	13438	61.7
1950	17336	21.4	961	229	16902	60.9
1970	23029	7.7	621	355	24604	66.0
1990	31586	2.4	525	399	44886	60.3

Great Plains states: Colorado, Kansas, Montana, Nebraska, New Mexico, North Dakota, Oklahoma, South Dakota, Texas, and Wyoming

Sources: U.S. Bureau of the Census (Various years), Census of Agriculture. Dept of Commerce: Washington, D.C.
U.S. Bureau of the Census (Various years), Census of Population. Dept. of Commerce: Washington, D.C.
U.S. Department of Agriculture (various years), Agricultural Statistics. Washington, D.C.
U.S. Department of Agriculture (1926), Wheat and Rye Statistics: U.S. Dept. of Agriculture Bulletin No. 12. Washington, D.C.

1994). Some of these are grain traders and shippers, some are food processors, some are in the restaurant business and several combine two categories. Among the more notable in grain trading are Cargill (U.S.), Continental (U.S.), Dreyfus (France), Bunge (Brazil) and Andre (Switzerland (Sewell, 1992, p. 127). In food processing it is Nestlé (Switzerland), Philip Morris (U.S.), Unilever (UK and Netherlands), ConAgra (U.S.), Cargill (U.S.) and Coca Cola (U.S.) (Henderson *et al.*, 1998). In restaurants McDonalds and Tricon (both U.S.) are the leaders.

These transnationals have established a world-wide presence through exporting, buying established foreign companies, setting up their own foreign affiliates, gaining access to foreign raw materials and markets, maintaining a global crop and market intelligence network and shifting operations from one country to another to reduce costs and increase sales. Nebraska based ConAgra, with $24 billion in sales in 1997 and 83,000 employees in 32 countries, provides a good example (ConAgra, 1998). When Australia and the U.S. were competing for greater access to Japan's beef market, ConAgra purchased a major presence in Australia's beef industry. Rather than a three way conflict, it became ConAgra vs. Japan (Ufkes, 1993). ConAgra cannot shift beef processing to a low wage less developed country because the available beef cattle are in the Great Plains. They solved that problem by bringing the low wage labour to the cattle, i.e. recruiting and importing labourers into the U.S. primarily from Mexico. The transnationals are seemingly oblivious to national borders; they constitute a kind of supranational entity.

Growing deregulation sentiment

Since the 1970s there has emerged a more vocal public conviction that many government programs are ineffective and wasteful. As Drucker (1993) described it, the *welfare state* with all its social programs and regulations was under attack. After Reagan was elected president in 1980, antitrust enforcement and regulation decreased (Heffernan and Constance, 1994) and deregulation occurred in several sectors including the commercial airlines, the savings and loan associations, the telephone companies and the electric power producers and distributors. Similar sentiment is seen in moves to ease trade restrictions, most notably in the establishment of the North American Free Trade Agreement (NAFTA) and in the ongoing discussions of tariff levels during the GATT Uruguay Round of multilateral trade discussions (Ufkes, 1993).

Of very direct relevance to the Great Plains has been the prospective dismantling of some long established agricultural support programs. After prolonged debate, the Federal Agricultural Improvement and Reform

(FAIR) Act became law in 1996. FAIR replaces support payments with fixed but shrinking annual payments to farmers over seven years, and purports to ease the transition to a genuinely free market unsubsidized agriculture by 2003. However, many are sceptical that in times of crisis in agriculture the government would in fact fail to provide some kind of support.

The use of foreign trade as a 'political weapon' to punish countries with whom the U.S. is unhappy has come under attack. In early 1980 President Carter cut off agricultural exports to the USSR in retaliation for their invasion of Afghanistan. The Soviets were largely unhurt by this; they simply purchased their needs from other sources (Wessel, 1983, p. 101). More recently there has been some clamour to restrict trade with China because of their 'human rights' violations. When India and Pakistan exploded nuclear devices in mid 1998, grain shipments to the two countries were temporarily suspended.

A look ahead

It is hazardous to predict the future course of events in the Great Plains under the impact of globalization and deregulation. Still, two very traditional concerns likely will continue to prevail in agriculture and agribusiness circles, much as they have in the past. As any farmer or rancher on the Plains will tell you, these traditional concerns are 'the weather' and 'commodity markets'.

Climatic marginality will remain an enduring legacy of Great Plains settlement. The droughts of the 1890s and 1930s brought widespread crop failures and substantial outmigration. Significant though less intense periods of inadequate precipitation have occurred since the 1930s. The 'El Niño' of 1998 brought very high summer temperatures and severe moisture deficits in the southern section of the Great Plains, while the spring wheat areas of the Dakotas had too much rain, causing an outbreak of wheat fungus. The politically conservative governor of Texas overlooked his own past market oriented rhetoric to publicly call for relief assistance from the federal government, and Congress indeed passed a $500 million emergency farm aid package (Anderson, 1998). Computer based climate models have suggested that hotter and dryer conditions are apt to become more common in the southern Plains, while the northern Plains, extending into Canada, may see a long term increase in rainfall (Chiotti and Johnston, 1995; and Rozenzweig and Hillel, 1993). However, much uncertainty surrounds such hypothesized models.

Diminished rainfall would likely result in more irrigation. Indeed, the Plains area extending from west Texas to southern South Dakota has already seen an enormous increase over the last four decades in irrigation farming based on the immense 'High Plains' aquifer (White, 1994). Slow rates of groundwater recharge and uncertain energy costs cast doubts on the long-term sustainability of irrigation in parts of the High Plains. There appears to have been a net decrease of perhaps 20% from the 1978 maximum of about 5.2 million irrigated hectares in the 6 states underlain by the High Plains aquifer (Rhodes and Wheeler, 1996). However, the pattern of change is not uniform, and long-term prospects are bright in portions of Kansas and Nebraska where the aquifer is thickest.

The commodity markets represent the second big concern of Plains farmers. Even if moisture remains adequate, whether from current precipitation or ground or surface water, there is no guarantee that the region's agricultural products will be sufficiently in demand to generate high enough returns to make production economically viable. While it seems unlikely that the Great Plains will suddenly cease to be a major agricultural region, there is still a good measure of uncertainty linked to international and domestic patterns of supply and demand.

At global scale, the contribution of the Great Plains to the world supply of food and feed grains has been and likely will continue to be significant but unstable. During the past decade the U.S. usually produced just over one tenth of the world's foreign trade in wheat. Since about 60% of this has been grown in the Great Plains states in recent decades (Table 4.1), it can be inferred that this region produces about 6% of the world's wheat and generates almost one fifth of the international trade in wheat. Such a dependence on export markets makes the Plains' farm economy more vulnerable to variations in demand than any other major U.S. agricultural region.

Unfortunately, it now seems that the 1996 FAIR Act was passed and came into effect just before the U.S. agricultural trade position began to weaken. At the time of the Act, U.S. agricultural exports had risen steadily from a $25 billion low in 1986 to a record $60 billion in 1996. In the buoyant mood of the time, U.S. Dept. of Agriculture policymakers set a goal of $65 billion by the end of the century (Moos, 1996). Great Plains farmers were less vocal than they might have been about the prospect of diminished governmental assistance because the domestic price of wheat reached a record high of $210.58 per metric ton in May 1996 (Allen, 1996). Moreover, the high prices of the mid 1990s spurred increased production in many parts of the world, including even the Middle East and South Asia. Thus, U.S. producers found themselves competing for part of a shrinking international market in wheat. Wheat piled up in U.S. storage facilities as the

1998 crop brought record yields and prices dropped to less than half the 1996 level (Economic Research Service, July 13, 1998).

In summary, the 125 year history of European settlement on the Great Plains has been marked by an emphasis on export oriented agriculture. Dependent on the vagaries of global commodity markets a well as on uncertain precipitation inherent in semiarid environments, wide swings in farm income levels have been the rule. Since the 1930s the Federal government has provided a measure of income stability through several programs, in particular ones providing price supports (subsidies) on certain crops. But the current deregulation trend, already seen in the FAIR Act, threatens to reduce governmental involvement and leave farmers more at the mercy of the weather and the commodity markets. As part of the 'new' globalization, commodity markets are increasingly controlled by a small number of very large transnational corporations, which have little loyalty to any particular region or nation. In the view of Mittelman (1997) this will likely bring a new international division of labour and new tensions and pressures. It is not clear if this will minimize or intensify the current dichotomy between the 'have' and 'have not' regions and nations of the world. But it would seem to more isolate farmers and other residents of marginal lands from centres of authority, and further diminish their already weak powers to redress grievances.

References

Allen, E. (1996), 'U.S. wheat acreage responds to high prices', *Agricultural Outlook*, no. 232, pp. 10-13.

Anderson, C. (1998), 'Special farm aid approved', *Lincoln Journal Star*, vol. 131, July 17, pp. 1A, 8A.

Archer, J.C. (1991), 'Geodemographic restructuring of the American Midlands, 1803-1990', paper read at conference on The Contemporary Social and Economic Restructuring of Rural Areas, London, Leicester, and Birmingham, UK, Aug. 12-19.

Archer, J.C. (1992), 'A medium term perspective on demographic change in the American Midlands, 1803-1990', in I.R. Bowler, C.R. Bryant and M.D. Nellis (eds), *Contemporary rural systems in transition, Vol. 2: Economy and society*, CAB International, Wallingford, UK.

Chiotti, Q.P. and Johnston, T. (1995), 'Extending the boundaries of climate change research: A discussion on agriculture', *Journal of Rural Studies*, vol. 11, pp. 335-350.

ConAgra (1998), *Internent site, Sep. 17, http://www.conagra.com*.

Critchell, J.T. and Raymond, J. (1969), *A history of the frozen meat trade*, Dawsons of Pall Mall, London.

Drucker, P.F. (1993), *Post-capitalist society*, Harper Collins, New York.

Economic Research Service (1998), *Wheat outlook*, July 13, U.S. Dept. of Agriculture: Washington D.C., electronic release via Internet.

Fite, G.C. and Reese, J.E. (1965), *An economic history of the United States*, 2nd Edition, Houghton Mifflin, Boston.

Gibson, A.M. (1976), *The West in the life of the nation*, Heath, Lexington, Mass.

Heffernan, W.D. and Constance, D.H. (1994), 'Transnational corporations and the globalization of the food system', in Bonanno, A. *et al.* (eds), *From Columbus to ConAgra*, pp. 29-51, Univ. Press of Kansas, Lawrence.

Henderson, D.R., Sheldon, I.M. and Pick, D.H. (1998), 'International commerce in processed foods', in D.H. Pick *et al.* (eds), *Global markets for processed foods*, pp. 7-32, Westview, Boulder, CO.

Hite, J. (1997), 'The Thünen model and the new economic geography as a paradigm for rural development policy', *Review of Agricultural Economics*, vol. 19, pp. 230-240.

Lonsdale, R.E. and Archer, J.C. (1998), 'Demographic factors in characterizing and delimiting marginal lands', in H. Jussila , R. Majoral, and C. Mutambirwa (eds), *Marginality in space: past, present and future*, Ashgate, Aldershot, U.K, pp. 129-143.

McMichael, P. (1994), 'Introduction: agro-food system restructuring--unity in diversity', in McMichael, P. (ed.), *The global restructuring of agro-food systems*, Cornell Univ. Press, Ithaca, pp. 1-17.

Mittelman, J.H. (1997), 'The dynamics of globalization', in J.H. Mittelman (ed.), *Globalization: Critical reflections*, pp. 1-19, Lynn Rienner, Boulder.

Moos, E. (1996), 'Exports equal farm prosperity', *Agricultural Outlook*, no. 228, pp. 10-11.

Ottoson, H.W. *et al.* (1996), *Land and people in the northern plains transition area*, Univ. Nebraska Press, Lincoln.

Rhodes, S.L. and Wheeler, S.E. (1996), 'Rural electrification and irrigation in the U.S. High Plains', *Journal of Rural Studies*, vol. 12, pp. 311-17.

Rosenzweig, C. and Hillel, D. (1993), 'Agriculture in a greenhouse world', *National Geographic Research and Exploration*, vol. 9, pp. 208-221.

Sanchez Aguilera, D. (1996), 'Evaluating marginality through demographic indicators', in R. Majoral and R.B. Singh (eds), *Development issues in marginal regions*, Oxford and IBH, New Delhi, pp. 133-148.

Sewell, T. (1992), *The world grain trade*, Woodhead-Faulkner, New York.

Ufkes, F.M. (1993), 'Trade liberalization, agro-food politics and the globalization of agriculture', *Political Geography*, vol. 12, pp. 215-231.

United Nations (1968), *World grain trade statistics 1967/68*, Food and Agriculture Organization, Rome.

U.S. Bureau of the Census (1960), *Historical statistics of the United States*, Dept. of Commerce, Washington.

U.S. Bureau of the Census (1975), *Historical statistics of the United States: Colonial times to 1970*, Dept. of Commerce, Washington.

U.S. Bureau of the Census (various years), *Census of agriculture*, Dept. of Commerce, Washington.

U.S. Bureau of the Census (various years), *Census of population*, Dept. of Commerce, Washington.

U.S. Dept. of Agriculture (1921), *Yearbook 1920*, Washington.

U.S. Dept. of Agriculture (1926), 'Wheat and rye statistics', *U.S. Dept. of Agriculture Bulletin*, no. 12, Washington.

U.S. Dept. of Agriculture (various years), *Agricultural statistics*, Washington.

Webb, W.P. (1981), *The Great Plains*, Univ. Nebraska Press, Lincoln.

Wessel, J. (1983), *Trading the future*, Institute for Food and Development Policy, San Francisco.

White, S.E. (1994), 'Ogallala oases: Water use, population redistribution and policy implications in the High Plains of western Kansas', *Annals of the Association of American Geographers*, vol. 84, pp. 29-45.

5   Southern Patagonia facing globalization

MARÍA EUGENIA CEPPARO DE GROSSO

Introduction

The province of Santa Cruz, located in Patagonia in southern Argentina, has a long sheep farming tradition. This region is currently facing the challenge of the opening up of new markets, and the formation of regional economic blocs. These challenges have generated intense tension, well as territorial and social upheaval, which are reflected in the economy of its peripheral regions (See, e.g., Benitez et al., 1988; Cepparo de Grosso, 1986).

The area is a strongly marginal region. This situation has turned the region into a territory vulnerable to the impacts of globalization. Attempts to confront this situation are subject to a variety of multiple and complex factors. Some of these are of environmental, historical and economic natures. The region is also subjected to measures taken by the state and the community.

The aim of this paper is to show the structural crisis that livestock activities in Southern Patagonia have been undergoing. It also emphasizes the difficulties the region has had to endure in order to cope with the new economic organization, as well as in its attempts to overcome its lower socioeconomic situation.

Factors explaining the recurrent economic crises

Southern Patagonia is a region with unique characteristics. It is a peripheral location, remote from the rest of the country and it is very arid. These problems have a great influence on its spatial organization and the future of this region, not only because of the area it covers, but also because of the economic problems caused by this vastness. The scattered and remote small and medium settlements, separated by large expanses, with a low population density, are a reflection of these natural conditions.

53

Low humidity, strong western winds, poor edaphic conditions and the predominance of natural grazing lands with little nutritional value, make up a natural framework with restricted possibilities for human settlement, and the development of economic activities. Such conditions have conditioned the growth of sheep farming.

Immigrant settlement, since the end of the last century, has had its roots based in commercial gain rather than in attempts to colonize the region. This has given rise to extensive sheep farming and therefore to overuse of the land. The implementation of such techniques, which are not compatible with these delicate arid and semiarid ecosystems, could be considered the foundation of the provincial economic crises. Furthermore, the region's failure to follow national economic development, and the country's uneven penetration into world economic systems, and has made the situation even worse.

Thus, during the Agricultural-Export Period, at the end of the last century, time passed with little development in activities except for the breeding of livestock, placing the region in a decidedly marginal position. The region was not integrated into the National State from the point of view of its population, infrastructure, productive participation and the absence of the internal division of work which characterized the other Pampean regions socio-territorially.

During the period of import substitutes, which arose from the crisis of the 30's, the region started to incorporate itself into the national economy, by expanding its infrastructure and the development of mining exploration, which was necessary for industrial processes in the centre of the country. The role of the State was shown through the political and administrative consolidation of the southern territories. This was the mining boom era, a period, which was characterized by neither large permanent nor dynamic settlements. On the other hand, public administration created many jobs bearing no relation to the province's resources.

The region gradually gained its present sheep farming characteristics, which generated rapid livestock growth, and, the depopulation of its interior regions. The slowness and inconsistency of integrating dynamic decisions, and the absence of a permanent foundation policy congruous to the environment, have also played a role in the formation of the region. Santa Cruz benefited for only a few years during the 50's and 60's by an encouraging policy promoting the stimulation of activities as well as population settlement. Such encouragement did not have the desired results due to irregularities in its implementation. Therefore, the integration was considered fictitious as it was based on the 'export' of its resources, mostly to the domestic market (Cepparo de Grosso and Rodríguez de González, 1994).

For almost a century, measures taken to improve the soil, breeds or to produce fodder have been admirable, but have resulted in depopulation, the depletion of pastureland, overgrazing and livestock weakening. The amount of heads of sheep is dropping dramatically annually. At present, there are 50% fewer animals than there were 40 years ago. In addition to these factors, cyclical droughts, repeated snowfalls and the sudden eruption of the Hudson Volcano, in 1991, which covered two thirds of the province with a thick layer of ash, have resulted in unfortunate consequences.

The drop in the number of productive farms, as well as the decrease in the tonnage of wool produced also show the seriousness of the problem. Since 1969, the number of homesteads with permanent production has started to fall. In 1969, there were 1,400 productive farms. This number fell to 900 in 1991 and 620 in 1997. Among the latter, over 70% have less than 7,500 sheep; the minimum number necessary to maintain a profitable economic unit. The amount of wool produced has also decreased dramatically; the 25,000 tons of wool produced annually in 1990 dropped to 8,000 tons in 1997 (National and Provincial...various surveys).

In turn, the features of its productive circuit, have made this activity vulnerable to the crises of wool and lamb and mutton prices, as well as competition from other products. The main causes are the uneven focus on wool and the lack of integration between the links in the production chain. The international drop in wool prices and the unfavourable fight against subsidized production from Australia and New Zealand are added to the fact that exports of the production to foreign countries continues is done so without processing, due to the absence of equipment to transform raw material on site. Small producers or small landowners (with less than 7,500 sheep or 20,000 hectares) are especially affected by price fluctuations. All these factors have resulted in local capital losses being even more burdened by the livestock breeders' financial debts. A decrease in both production and income has discouraged producers from these more affected sectors to attempt other economic alternatives. The following chart (Figure 5.1) reflects the uneven contrast between areas, action taken by the community and time, which, without great changes, has shaped a strongly conditioned panorama (Cepparo de Grosso, 1986; 1990).

56

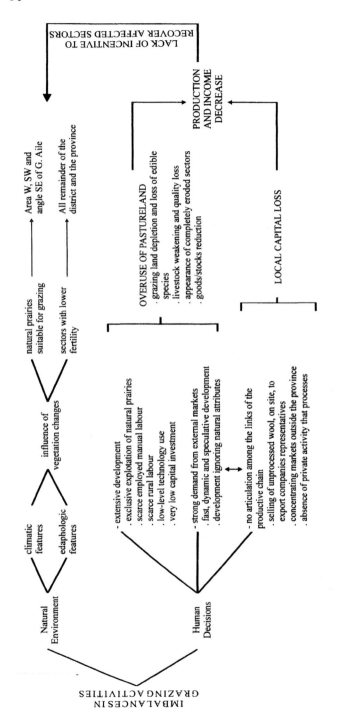

Figure 5.1   Model of the environmental and socio-economic impact of world markets on Southern Pampa, Argentina

Source :   Maria Cepparo de Grosso, 1990.

Perspectives facing a new model

How will globalization affect one of the most important productive processes in the region without causing further social and territorial conflicts? What solutions will the province look for order to escape its structural crisis?

These questions encourage change, which in turn has to include three fundamental and closely linked aspects: technology, economy and politics.

Techno-economic innovations, which are often mentioned within the 'New World Economic Order' framework, are based on a scientific-technological plan; a transformation of the process of technical and work management into a well organized management model. In reality, these ideas have spread quickly, but their impact on the territorial and social spheres have been much slower. In fact, the slowness of technological transformation is an issue, which has been affecting Patagonia for many years, even before discussion about the need to become active in 'global world' had begun. In southern Patagonia, the technological levels applied to development are still elementary due to its vastness, low capital investment and the lack of productive processes involving meat and wool. The marked individuality of producers, the lack of integration and will to organize co-operatives, hinders access to updated information on international economic processes, harming their capacity to negotiate and their access to external markets with better competitive levels. Therefore, changes involving the structural transformation of the society's culture and viewpoints, which are slower and more difficult to alter than technology, are also necessary.

On an international level, techno-economic processes introduce territorial changes, especially in production and trade (e.g., Rofman, 1995; Rofman and Márquez 1996). It is within the industrial process where changes are more easily noticed as there is an effort for their optimization through a new 'flexible specialization and permanent innovation' model. In the case of Santa Cruz, it has not only been unable to move to a superior technological level, but it also does not have all the necessary links required for the productive processing of wool and meat to do so. Therefore, it cannot respond to the changing and selective demands of consumption.

Livestock breeding re-conversion, encouraged by both rural associations and the government, is considered as the only alternative to escape from the current situation in order to reach an improved position in external markets for its still unprocessed raw materials.

The solution lies in diversity that does not only imply merely substituting livestock breeding activities but considers other agricultural activities as well as different alternatives.

The most elementary technique, which consists of controlled grazing in order to give each pasture area a rest, should be the point of departure. This would allow the growth of new plants, the strengthening of desired ones as well as the reduction of undesirable species. Another start could be an alteration in the genetic structure of flocks bred for meat production, or the orientation of livestock production towards bovines, camelidae and dairy sheep in those areas which are more suitable for intensive development. The costs of such ventures may be reduced by consolidating management through the grouping of neighbouring fields through a joint administration, but at the same time maintaining the identity of each farm.

Early and out of season fruit-growing and horticultural activities, with low or no use of agrochemicals, constitute an important alternative in the diversification of plans. These crops include choice fruits or garlic, both of which are in high demand abroad. It has been decided to characterize these products with a regional seal, the same as the one proposed for lamb and mutton. The main aim is to improve profitability by offering products, which are differentiated by their origin as well as their low chemical residue content.

Reform and transformation undergone by the State within a framework of political and economic innovations, promoted by globalization face highly complex challenges in the Southern Patagonia region. It is necessary to face new concepts of development that go beyond comparative economic growth. The features of this region are not the same as most of other Pampean economies. The alternatives for its inhabitants are different. If a proposal for settlement or activities fails, the socio-economic and political consequences are more far reaching, as there are so few options, this being the reason why it is so necessary to change certain parameters. The spontaneous growth which has been characteristic of Santa Cruz throughout its history, cannot continue, in spite of efforts made by breeders, businesses, the military and its inhabitants.

The paradox of Patagonia now faces a new model, one in which the State continues organizing, centralizing and defining macro policies but in conjunction with strategic policies devised by the provinces, municipalities and local communities. New forms of organization, management and development cannot be completely applied in the entire region since the effective presence of the State is still essential. Certain priorities such as the pursuit for territorial equilibrium, social improvement, environmental preservation or the widening and updating of the infrastructure, which serves as a launching pad for strategies and policies of the social agents, cannot be neglected. The exodus of older settlers, forced into leaving their under-productive farms and unemployment or underemployment generated by the transfer of state companies to the private sector, are clear examples of the consequences of incorrect resource and service management.

The change of the State's role is closely related to the centralization – decentralization of its administrative functions. Decentralization may be fundamental for the updating of the present backdrop as it encourages the local governments and the activity of citizens. However, in Patagonia, de-centralization could cause a conflict between the specific interests of the municipalities, the provincial governments, Patagonia as a whole and the country in general. Therefore, more than ever, the role of the different enti-ties is as important as functioning as a whole, through the permanent agreement and negotiation of the parties involved. The management of great land expanses, with a scattered population where it is difficult to have profitable services poses the question of how much does it cost the state to promote or subsidize a service, and, what is the social cost of not doing so?

Conclusion

Southern Patagonia is inserted within a backdrop of conflicts, and accord-ing to its participation in these events, the area can be identified as marginal. It has been seriously affected by economic, political and even cultural mechanisms of segregation.

The space-society-time relationship has built a reality in which limited technological equipment, scarcity of opportunities, and isolation belong to some of the features that can be mentioned. Moreover, human resources related to the dominant productive activity of the province lack the capacity for innovation.

Globalization and integration do not only produce benefits; they also mean costs and risks. For the state, the decentralization of functions and la-bour flexibility causes social conflicts, which are difficult to face. For the private sector, increasing competition demands fast and varied productive projects. For the population, the economic cutbacks and re-engineering processes create important social risks. All the above are consequences that result from this process when changes are not carefully organized and planned. In fact, the profound changes in the economic system have not been accompanied by an even regional development and the already problematic inequalities continue to exist and may become worse.

References

Benitez, J., Liberali, A.M. and Gejo, O. (1988), *La Patagonia: entre el crecimiento y el despoblamiento*, Departamentos de Historia y Geografía, Facultad de Humanidades, Universidad de la Patagonia San Juan Bosco, Comodoro Rivadavia.

Cepparo de Grosso, M.E. (1986), 'La actividad pastoril en Santa Cruz: paisaje homogéneo, estructura invariable', *Boletín de Estudios Geográficos*, Instituto de Geografía, Facultad de Filosofía y Letras, U.N. de Cuyo, vol. XXII, pp. 86-117.

Cepparo de Grosso, M.E. (1990), 'La valoración del pastizal en el extremo sur americano', *Revista Geográfica*, Instituto Panamericano de Geografía e Historia, México, nro 111, pp. 171-205.

Cepparo de Grosso, M.E. and Rodríguez de González, M. (1994), 'La actividad pastoril en la Patagonia Meridional. Un ejemplo de decisiones que reflejan desequilibrios económico-ambientales', *Boletín de Estudios Geográficos*, Instituto de Geografía, Facultad de Filosofía y Letras, U.N. de Cuyo, Vol XXV, pp. 363-374.

National and Provincial Agricultural/ Livestock Registers and Surveys (various years).

Rofman, A. (1995), 'Las economías regionales: un proceso de decadencia estructural', in P. Bustos (eds), *Más allá de la estabilidad*, Buenos Aires, Fundación Friedrich, pp. 161-189.

Rofman, A. and Márquez, N. (1996), 'Las economías extrapampeanas y el desafio Mercosur', in J. Borello and A. Castagna (eds), *Las economías regionales y sus respuestas a los desafíos del Mercosur*, Rosario, Homo Sapiens, pp. 91-111.

6 Managing integration and marginalization for the New Europe

HENRI GOVERDE

Introduction

In order to create 'the New Europe' (Pinder, 1998), the problems of how to manage integration and how to avoid (new) marginalization should be tackled. Therefore, innovations in policies of the EU, particularly the Common Agricultural Policy (CAP), are necessary. How should the EU-CAP policy and the World Trade Organization (WTO)-agreement be integrated? How should the relations between the EU and Central and Eastern Europe (CEE) be developed in order to avoid new marginal regions in the future?

This chapter aims to present a descriptive-analysis about how the EU perceives and manages the common European interests in the context of globalization and the construction of a European polity. Concerned with the common European interests, this chapter focuses on key-issues in the field of agro-food political and economic affairs (the first main part). Special attention has been paid to the CAP as the core policy of the EU since 1958 (second main part). Third and fourth main parts explain the difficulties the EU must cope with, if the CAP should be reformed as a precondition for the enlargement of this European polity with the ten candidate countries in Central and Eastern Europe (CEEC-10). The third main part focuses on the plurality of interests of the individual members of the EU-15 in relation to the CEEC-10. The fourth main part focuses on the EU political administrative system in the case of animal disease crisis, because it shows the differences in the drives of the EU-member states to promote the enlargement. The fifth part focuses on the plurality in agro-political cultures in the EU-members states illustrating how this will probably be of influence in regard to the feasibility of EU co-ordinated Agricultural policies in the future, particularly if the membership of the CEEC-10 introduces the same kind of differences. The analysis has been summarized in the sixth part by using two labels: 'anticipation' and 'resistance'. In conclusion, the last main part discusses various issues for further research, as well as providing some prescriptive aspects on how integration can be managed and how marginalization it can be avoided by the EU.

EU: Its agro-food key challenges in headlines

EU and its political economic context

In the world's political economy, there is a proliferation of regional economic agreements such as the North American Free Trade Agreement (NAFTA -Canada, Mexico and the USA -), Asia Pacific Economic Co-operation (APEC), Mercosur (in Latin-America) and the European Union. The character of these blocks differs tremendously. The EU has created an internal market (1992) and has decided to start a monetary union (1999). However, the EU is not (yet) politically united. Its political power is mainly dependent on the relationship between Germany and France. On the one hand, the non-adultery status of many regional blocks implies that still other groups of nation-states can be of influence in the process of global polity construction. For example, the CAIRNS-group (a mixture of Asian, Australian, European and Latin-American countries) was able to put above the USA power game extra international political pressure which, in turn, helped to finally realize the EU-acceptance of the WTO-regime for agrarian products (1992). On the other hand, the regional blocks have a certain hemisphere. For example, the USA claims political dominance over the Caribbean countries as well as the whole Latin-American continent. The EU suggests its legitimate claim to the CEE countries. Of course, an effective realisation of this claim can create a lot of new marginal and critical regions within the EU.

EU and its agro-food key issues

In a recent historical analysis concerning the evolution of the human activities in the agro-food system, six agro-food key issues were selected as fundamental in the world today (Goudsblom, 1997, pp. 74-83, pp. 89-96; Goverde, 1997, pp. 4-5). These issues are: Biogenetic-engineering; Plant Breeders' Rights; the Uruguay-round and the regime created by the World

Trade Organization (WTO), the EU-expansion to Central and East Europe, Quality Control and Animal Diseases and the Renewal of Rural Areas. Why then were these specific issues selected? The following arguments are of relevance. Via biogenetic-engineering, new types of plants and animals can compete effectively with well-known natural products. However, the seeds of the new plants are perceived as a technological output, which belongs to the biogenetic industry. That is why the saving of the seeds no longer seems to be a fundamental right of the farmer. This Plant Breeders' Right (PBR) issue will cause fundamental changes in the structure of power in many, particularly in the developing, countries. Furthermore, the new WTO-agreement will put an end to the public protection of agricultural activities after some time. Obviously, the EU is trying to anticipate as well as to defend itself in this new global WTO-polity, partly by creating more power via incorporating new members, mainly the Central and East European Countries (CEEC). Throughout the history of agriculture (McNeill, 1976), disciplining the actors involved has been always a matter of concern in diseases of plants and animals such as BSE and the swine fever epidemic prevalent in Europe nowadays. The renewal of rural areas concerns a more cultural oriented and regional as well as local implemented policy of rural innovation, in order to tackle the influence of world-wide agro-food innovations and political-economic developments.

In all selected issues, the EU-institutions are deeply involved. In a certain way, all these issues are interwoven. It is exactly this characteristic which requires the EU to evaluate its CAP.

Reforming the CAP: Between necessity and realism

In order to cope with the challenges mentioned in section 1, the EU seems to have no other choice than to concentrate on the CAP, because this policy claims still circa 45% of the EU-budget. On the one hand, however, the CAP '...lies at the heart of the practical application of the European vision (...). The CAP is the culmination of over one hundred years of state support for agriculture in western Europe' (Ockenden and Franklin, 1995, pp. 1-2). On the other hand, the CAP is not an agenda in itself. The discussion about the future of CAP is related to many other issues e.g. the start of the European Monetary Union (1999), the EU-institutional reforms, the next WTO-round (starts 1999), the review of the EU-Structure-Funds (2000); the image of the agro-food business and the demand for a more integrated approach to the rural areas (multifunctional farming, employment in- and outside the agri-business, environmental policies).

Why is the global context so important for the future of the CAP as well as for the possibilities of the EU enlargement? Grant (1997, p. 14) stated that the US government will '...push for the elimination of all agricultural subsidies' in the next WTO round (starting in 1999). Swinbank and Tanner (1996, p. 34) argued that if the EU fails to offer 'substantial progressive reductions in support and protection' in the negotiations to come (1999), the EU will find itself isolated and the CAP challenged by its trading partners within the WTO. Josling (1997, pp. 192-3) argues in addition to Grant that if the US fails to compel more CAP reform, the prospect of the enlargement to Eastern Europe 'might...in the end turn out to be trigger to overcome internal political resistance against another round of CAP reform' entailing reduced prices.

The EU-CAP has been under reconstruction since 1992. This policy implies (Berkhout, 1996, p. 11): liberalization in order to keep competitive power; transfer payments related to social and environmental targets (cross compliance); programming the rural renewal comprehensively (multifunctional 'farming' and increasing the role of national and regional governance). The EC-proposals in 'Agenda 2000' (March, 1998) follow widely this so-called MacSharry-line. This could have been expected, since this policy seems rather realistic. First of all, it implies a compromise between different opinions in the EU-15. Secondly, it will help to discover a negotiable position in the next WTO-round. Thirdly, more liberalization and lower prices are profitable for the consumers. Still, the incomes of the EU-farmers retain purchasing power. Next, it promotes some convergence to the prices in CEEC-10 agricultural markets. Finally, it also prevents the need for a continuous increase of the EU agro-budget of which the political legitimization is no longer possible. Conclusion: this policy will help the CEEC-10 to get closer to the EU-CAP in the near future. And the more closer these CEEC-10 can come, the less marginal their position will be in the 'New Europe'.

EU political agenda: Three obstacles for the EU-enlargement?

However, when regarding the EU-political agenda as well as the policy, which has been set in motion ever since 1992, it becomes obvious that the management of the European integration process is extremely complicated. In the following sections, a few elements of this complexity will be worked out: the political and economic relationship between the EU-CEE, the management of animal disease crises within the EU and the on-going variety of agro-political cultures in the EU-15 as well as in the CEE countries. All these variables seem to have the power to become serious obstacles for the planned EU-enlargement.

One preliminary remark should be made. It is not our aim to produce a pessimistic picture for the CEEC accession. In all truth, the issue is not if the CEEC-10 will join the EU in the long term. The question is only when and under which conditions. Nevertheless, one should imagine that, because of the mutual interdependence between the EU and the CEEC-10, the whole affair is not only important for Central and Eastern Europe, but for the continuity and the structure of the EU as well. In short, will it be a further integration to a greater Europe or a relative stagnating integration in Western Europe combined with a relative marginalization of Central and Eastern Europe?

The EU-CEEC relationship: Differences in commitment between EU-15

The relations between the EU-15 and the CEEC-10 (Bulgaria, the Czech Republic, Estonia, Hungary, Latvia, Lithuania, Poland, Romania, Slovak, Slovene) have political, economic and security dimensions. According to Grabbe and Hughes (1998, p. 8), the former enlargements of the EU have demonstrated that it is the general feeling about the importance of the political and security dimensions which determines the political will to pass the whole 'acquis communautaire'. The motivations to integrate the CEEC-10 differ widely among the EU-15. This leads to nuances in commitment to the process of enlargement. Although they know to be mutually dependent on the EU, the CEEC-10 have their nuances as well. Why then expand the EU? The EU member states' interests in enlargement vary according to the following criteria (Grabbe and Hughes, 1998, p. 5):

- proximity to potential areas of instability on the peripheries of the EU
- economic integration with the CEEC
- historical links with particular countries
- their view about the EU institutional reformation.

Political dimension

EU countries close to the CEEC area will share more concerns about security and stability. These countries will also probably have closer economic ties to the CEEC (Scandinavian countries, Finland, Germany, Austria, Greece, and to a lesser extent, Italy). However, from the criterion of proximity other countries (e.g. France, Spain, and Portugal) are much more ambivalent to expansion.

Of course, geo-political and economic interests will also influence the views on which are the most important CEE countries. The Scandinavian countries are very concerned about political stability in the Baltic States. Germany is particularly focused on Poland, followed by the Czech Republic and Hungary. Greece has serious security interests in regard to Bulgaria and Romania. The experience of member states suggests that countries which joined the EU primarily for economic reasons (such as the UK, Sweden and Denmark) have experienced greater long-run scepticism about the European integration than those with motives such as affirming their identity as small, independent states (Ireland, Luxembourg and Belgium) or overcoming historical conflicts (Germany, France and Italy). The CEEC arguments for entering the EU are primarily based on 'the logic of historical precedent, geographical position and psychological need'. Economic benefits are only a second argument. Therefore, a heavy burden is put on the process of EU accession to deliver the security and political benefits (Grabbe and Hughes, 1998, pp. 7-8). That is why the conclusion is clear that, in the long run, the CEE countries will support all 'pillars' of the EU-policy system if they can succeed in gaining their political goals. These political goals of the CEE countries are:

1) the re-integration in the world economy and
2) the departure from the Soviet/Russia hemisphere.

This is very relevant for the Baltic States as well as for Poland. Joining the EU and NATO is considered to be the best tool to realize these goals.

Economic dimension

Although the political and security dimensions are perhaps predominant, the economic dimension is an important and rising factor in the EU-CEE relationship. On the one hand, the economic gap between the EU and the CEEC-10 is still wide. The average GNP per capita (1993-1995) in the CEEC-10 was only 48% of the GNP per capita in Greece, 43% of Portugal, 38% of Spain and 36% of Ireland. Only Slovene came close to Greece (88%), but the Baltic States were far behind the wealth of this poorest EU-member state (32%). On the other hand, the CEE countries, particularly the Visegrad-countries, support its agriculture much less than the EU-15 does. For the CEEC this means a more competitive position for liberal world market conditions in comparison with the EU-farmers. Of course, this is, in itself, an argument for the EU-15 to adapt its CAP.

It is true that the EU and the CEEC-10 are interdependent. The EU offers an interesting economic climate for advanced entrepreneurs in the CEEC-region. To the EU, the CEE countries offer a market of circa 100 million inhabitants with potential purchasing power. However, the trade relations are not particularly overwhelming as well as asymmetric yet. The EU has less economic interest in the CEEC than vice versa. To the CEE countries, trade with the EU-15 is more important than trade with any other region, including intra-CEEC trade. However, degrees of trade dependence on the EU vary across the CEEC-10. According to Grabbe and Hughes (based on IMF-figures, 1998: 15), in 1995 the EU-share of world exports to the different CEE countries was to: CEE countries in total 58% (Slovene, 79%; Poland, 69%; Hungary, 67%; Czech Republic, 66%; Estonia, 65%; Bulgaria, 56%; Romania, 54%; Latvia, 45%; Slovak, 44%; and Lithuania, 37%).

Another figure can help us to understand why the EU-15 member states differ rather deeply in their commitment to the enlargement process. Table 6.1 gives insight into the share of the main EU exporters to CEE countries during two particular years: 1989 and 1995. It is obvious that Germany is the absolute market leader and therefore, its commitment is very strong as well. While France and Germany are generally supposed to be the hard core of the EU, it is quite clear that both countries have a completely different interest in the EU enlargement process. When looking at the flow of direct investment (FDI) to Poland, Hungary and the Czech Republic (1990-95) the pattern seems comparable as far as the relative positions of Germany, France and Great Britain are concerned (Grabbe and Hughes, 1998, p. 23). Italy is more an exporter than an investor in the CEEC. The Netherlands and Switzerland are serious investors in Poland, Hungary and the CR (respectively the third and fourth place). According to calculations of the UN and the World Bank (1996), the USA and Germany are the main investors (circa 20% each) in the period 1990-1996.

Table 6.1   **Shares of EU-15 exports to 6 CEEC (BG, CR, H, PL, RO, SK)**

Country	1989	1995
Germany	36.05%	51.43%
Italy	15.53%	11.75%
Austria	9.79%	7.87%
France	9.83%	5.84%
United Kingdom	7.79%	5.47%
Netherlands	5.51%	3.72%
Other countries	15.50%	13.92%
Total	100.00%	100.00%

Source: Grabbe and Hughes (1998, p. 14, revised HG) on basis of IMF.

Balance of power

The balance of power between the EU- and the CEE countries is always supposed to be asymmetrical in favour of the EU. However, the EU-CEEC integration requires adaptations on both sides (Bempt and Theelen, 1996; Nicolaides and Boean, 1997). As the Treaty of Amsterdam (June, 1997) and Agenda 2000 (March, 1998) have demonstrated, much remains to be done concerning the renewal of the EU-institutions, the EU-budget and (mostly in the CEEC) the physical and financial infrastructure. Of course, the EU has outstanding regulative powers: it sets the rules, the procedures and the timing. However, the EU will not receive an economic market of 100 million people free of charge. Thus, a serious re-allocation of the EU-budget is necessary. Of course, the interests, particularly those belonging to the farmers, differ in the EU-member states. Therefore, the EC-proposals in the Agenda 2000 (concerning rearrangement of the priorities in the CAP and the Structural Funds, which include about 80% of the EU-budget) have produced already 'a dance around the billions' which will take several more years. These internal EU-negotiations can imply a rather strong decline in the tempo of the enlargement process. Recently, there was rumour that several CEE countries would have to wait longer (i.e. later than 2005 or even 2007). If this would occur, the EU would lose a tremendous amount of its political credibility, particularly in the Visegrad countries.

EU animal disease management: Disciplinary power versus hinder power

Bovine Spongiform Encephalopathy (BSE or 'mad cow disease') can probably kill human beings. The BSE-disease has caused many doubts about the quality control of meat starting first in Great Britain, and later throughout the EU. BSE was first found in Britain, later in France, Switzerland, Germany, The Netherlands, Portugal and Belgium. The management of the BSE-crisis in the EU could illustrate how today a particular sovereign nation state does not have enough capacity to resist the power of a regional authority such as the EU in the end. Great Britain was not able to continue its domestic politics, after the EU had decided that the export of British meat, not only to the EU but also to third countries, was not to be allowed anymore. Of course, Britain developed some hinder power. Why did Britain not take adequate precautionary measures? A plausible hypothesis concerns a successful lobby of meat manufacturing industries and slaughter houses to deregulate and liberalize this food-sector in the late seventies, early eighties (Kralt, 1997). These suggestions were in accordance with the dominant political ideology at the start of the Thatcher-regime. Therefore, it seems that certain domestic political variables – lobby by non-state actors, being part of a powerful electorate, as well as the ideology of a new political regime – coincided. This created different circumstances for the production of cattle-fodder, which in its turn promoted, regrettably, the optimal conditions for the procreation of BSE in cows. This picture changed in March, 1996, when the British Minister of Health said to the Parliament that BSE was most likely the cause of the Creuzfelt Jacob Disease (CJD) in some (young) people. Nevertheless, in the period May-June, 1996, Great Britain vetoed about 50 EC-proposals in the EU Council of Ministers. At the end of the Florence-summit (June, 1996), however, it was determined that Britain had realized that the political costs of being a non-co-operative member of the EU were too high. By and large, the EU claimed, as an intergovernmental authority, political power successfully against the British hinder power. However, the financial-economic price of the EU anti-BSE measures is high as well. The EU will pay 70% compensation to the British farmers. Although this percentage falls regularly under the EU-CAP policy, it is still a high price, particularly because both the British government and the agro-sector had clearly neglected to follow advice on taking measures to combat BSE for almost 10 years.

The BSE-case demonstrates that in the beginning the EU Agencies could not implement and maintain their regime in a specific nation state for a long time. Only when the farmers and consumers continued to worry about the possible impacts of the BSE disease, did the politicians and administrators come under political and economic pressure to solve this problem, or at least to control the effects by disciplining one member state. The international press spelled out the BSE-case much more than the swine fever epidemic, which harassed the Dutch pig-breeders during 1997. However, this animal disease made clear as well that the EU and national authorities have great problems disciplining the branch (breeders, transporters, entrepreneurs of slaughter-houses, and meat-exporters). Altogether it is estimated that this swine fever catastrophe has cost the EU more than one Billion ECU. The management of this type of crises will always require much administrative energy, perhaps even more after the enlargement of the EU in the next century. Therefore, it can be expected that countries which have relatively little interest in the CEEC-market and which can count on a higher risk of contracting animal diseases, will not contribute to the acceleration of the enlargement process.

Domestic agro-politics: Obstacle for EU enlargement?

Although the MacSharry Line seems to break with the history of the EU-CAP, still an important question remains; is the EU 'farm lobby' no longer powerful enough to block the road to liberal reform and will this prevent domestic agro-political resistance from hindering further enlargement of the EU? Keeler (1996), a US specialist in this field, has explained that the institutional and political bases of agricultural power in the EU have been eroded somewhat in recent years, but the pillars of support for the CAP – and resistance to liberal reform – remain formidable. The French model (an almost classic principal-agent system: unpopular policies are slowly or imperfectly, if at all, implemented) as well as the Italian model ('autogoverno' or 'autogestione' of the agricultural sector, parallel to a lot of corruption and abuse of power) are still in operation (Keeler, 1987; 1997). In Britain, the agricultural policy based on the paradigm of 'policy community' (Smith, 1993) has not yet been challenged. The recent change in the Dutch agro-political subsystem (abolishment of the 'Landbouwschap', a public-corporatistic institution with much formal policy-discretion) is not a representative example for Western Europe (yet). In sum, the power of the organised agriculture remains sufficient to fend off anything radically approaching liberal reform in the EU-15 and should continue to frustrate reformers in the coming era of EU enlargement to the East.

The argument is based on two separate lines (Keeler, 1997, p. 5 and p. 8): one line of argument concerns the impact of the Uruguay-round agreement, another line is based on an institutional analysis in the CEE countries. First, empirical studies have proven that the GATT/WTO agreement (1993), which included agro-food products, 'did not itself spur liberalization to a great extent' (Grant, 1997a, p. 196). In general, there seems little in the 1993 WTO-Agreement to enforce rapid or radical CAP reform. Secondly, efforts to promote rapid agricultural modernization in Eastern Europe are likely to be impeded by two related institutional factors: the power of organized agriculture and the weakness of the state. The dynamic of state intervention in the agricultural sector tends to generate a 'corporatist' pattern of policymaking. This pattern empowers farm organizations and thus, limits how far and fast a government can go in e.g. a reduction of subsidies that is viewed as problematic by the agricultural population. Furthermore, when examining models of agricultural modernization from post-war Western Europe, the dominant national farmers' unions do not simply 'lobby' state officials, but instead they tend to 'co-manage' the affairs of the sector. Moreover, when explaining why, given not only the clout of the farmers but also the relative weakness of state machinery in the CEEC, one should expect modernization programs – in Poland and elsewhere in other CEE countries – to reflect a model which is certain to disappoint proponents of reform.

The recent developments in the Polish and Hungarian agro-political arenas seem to verify Keelers' hypothesis. Being the most agricultural country of the CEE (25% employed in farming), Poland has to reduce employment in the agro-sector dramatically to raise efficiency (agro production is only 7% of the GNP). The newest strategy for political and economic reform, designed by the Polish Minister of Finance (Leszek Barcerowicz), implies for the rural areas a decline in employment in the primary sector with tens of thousands of jobs. The cabinet wants to create new jobs in those areas (small industries, housing, services, education, and health care). Selling public owned firms will derive the money. However, the Polish Farmers Party is a relevant political variable. Being a partner in coalitions of the pre-1991 communist regime and joining several coalitions after 1991 as well, the Farmers Party became part of the opposition since October, 1997. This is a sign that the government-farmers connection is no longer a core relation in the political arena. Recently on July the 10th,

1998, the farmers staged a demonstration in the capital, for the most part to keep power on the local level after the September municipal elections. They want higher subsidies for their products (because these subsidies are much higher in the EU!) and they want import tariffs as well as import quota. In fact, the Polish farmers suggest that they are ready to give up their relative advantageous position to world market-prices and to prevent the Polish market from 'cheap' (= heavy subsidised) EU-products. After the new cabinet was born in Hungary (June, 1998) the same approach pressed the new government to higher subsidies there, also. In sum, this trend in the CEEC will probably have negative impacts not only on the process of integration for the 'New Europe' but also on the process of European accommodation to the WTO-rules. Higher subsidies in the CEEC as well as import tariffs and -quotas will not stimulate the CAP reform in the EU.

EU management of integration and marginalization: Juggling between anticipation and resistance

Based on the analysis as it stands up till now, this section will focus on the EU opportunities to legitimize its activities in the near future. Dividing the EU efforts up into anticipation and global integration and resistance and European integration can illuminate the EU policy discretion.

Anticipation and global integration

The EU single market programme and liberalization under the regime of the WTO have generally improved access conditions for the EU trading partners and increased the exposure of the EU economy to international competition and structural change. The Trade Policy Review Body (TPRB) of the WTO was positive in its interim review (Nov., 1997) about the progress made by the EU in these fields, particularly by imposing further limitations on farm subsidies. In the Agenda 2000 proposal, the EC argued also why the EU should anticipate the next round of WTO-negotiations by reforming its agriculture sector (EC DG VI, 1998, p. 3). 'First of all, with this reform the Union has to lay down the agricultural policy that it intends to carry out in the years ahead in a way that satisfies its own interests and takes a realistic view of developments in the international context. This needs to be done before the opening of the WTO negotiations so that the Union can negotiate on a solid basis and knows where it wants to go. Secondly, it must be made quite clear to all that the reform to be adopted will outline the limits of what the Union is able to agree to in the forthcoming international negotiations'.

Thus, according to the EC, the CAP reform is mainly a management instrument of mega-steering. First, it helps to create external political credibility and political legitimacy for the positions the EU will take among nation-states and trade blocks involved in the coming world trade negotiations. Secondly, vice versa, it should produce internal political legitimacy to enhance an agricultural model that cannot be resisted by the EU-member states, their agricultural interest groups and the CEEC negotiators. A positive effect of the second argument is that the EU can speak with one voice in the WTO which is important in order to give political weight to its economic power.

In conclusion, from an ideological point of view, the EU remains committed to the fundamental WTO objective of progressive multilateral liberalization, which is based on the non-discrimination level. The EU sees a clear need to tackle the task of further liberalization and wider participation by all countries in the global world, in a comprehensive, global way (WTO, TPRB, 1997, p. 17). In fact the EU is organizing a meta-management of integrating itself (i.e. the EU-15 and the EU-CEEC-10) into the world economy of the 21st century.

Resistance to European integration: CEE marginalization as an impact?

The legitimacy of the EU has been challenged in different ways during the last decade. The Treaty of Maastricht (Dec., 1991) was accepted by the EU-12 only after a heavy political battle during the referenda in France, the United Kingdom, Ireland and Denmark. The EMU is not joined by four EU-member states – DK, GB, GR, and S – (May, 1998). In the last parliamentary election campaigns in France (1997) the social dimension of the EU was blamed and the French Social Democrats were brought to power again. In the Netherlands and Germany (1998) the position of these countries as net payers to the EU were quite seriously contested. Neither the EU-member states nor the EU seem to be able to create continuous political credibility for further European integration.

In regard to the CEEC-10, the EU prefers that the CEE governments spend their scarce public money on innovations in farming instead of on price or income subsidies to the farmers. Therefore, the EU instruments are oriented to help the CEE agribusiness and farming to adapt to EU-standards (transport infrastructure, education, animal registration, certification of production processes, etc.). Although some facts should not be disregarded, the CEE-5 countries (the first group which will negotiate for accession: Estonia, the Czech Rep., Hungary, Poland, Slovene) interpreted the blame of 'Der Spiegel' (in July, 1998), that some countries – particularly Poland – were not working seriously enough to fulfil the EU-demands in the accession negotiations, as the expression of anti-enlargement lobby in the EU. Thus, in the pre-opening era of the EU-CEEC negotiations the parties started sharpening their swords. However, this approach is not only an autonomous process which can be related to the negotiations, but it is fed by domestic political (agricultural) movements in different EU-countries as well as by nuances in the general interests in the enlargement. Large sections of the agro-political cultures in many EU-member states (particularly in E, F, GR, P and I: section 5) will resist the CAP reform for as long as possible. Here, not only conservative radicals like the cattle-farmers in Italy (Comas) or the Pig Breeders Union in the Netherlands (NVV) are relevant, but far more important is the on going interwoven networking between the governments and the agro-sector organizations (the Neo-corporatist system). Further, some governments prefer a fast CAP reform, because they expect it will help to diminish its net payer's position (D, NL). These countries require for some re-nationalization of agricultural policy, because it will allow them to enhance the sector's preparation in anticipation of new future WTO-rules. This dichotomy between EU-member states confronting the CAP reform could split the EU-voice in the WTO-arena, which may diminish the political weight of the union. The different approaches to the CAP resulted, recently (25 June, 1998), in the Council of EU-Agriculture Ministers in a new package of price supports related to quota for products. In this way, many countries still prefer short-term benefits from the CAP, rather than to reform ('read' to diminish benefits) for long term goals in a global perspective. The EU policies are the result of a complicated process of policy-making. In this context the EU-institutions are like jugglers who have to keep many balls in the air at the same moment.

Conclusion and discussion

The position of the EU is not a comfortable one. Although the EU has been founded on the belief that integration helps to keep peace and security in Europe, there is some doubt as to whether this belief-system can survive under conditions of ever-growing complexity (and perhaps instability). The global political and economic situation forced the EU to accept the GATT/WTO-regime based on the free market ideology. This regime pressured the EU into reducing its traditional neo-corporatistic system of agrarian production- and income subsidies. In fact, the EU has to adapt from being a rather politically left-oriented, bureaucratic interventionist way of governance to being a right wing-oriented reductionism of governance activities.

With reference to this process of transformation, the following conclusions appear to be of relevance. First of all, the interests of the EU-15 concerning the enlargement differ particularly to matters of security and cultural identity, the economic agenda, and electoral politics. These domestic obstacles will retard the process of enlargement. Secondly, the EU-management of the BSE-disease and the swine fever epidemic has made clear how vulnerable the internal market is to catastrophes. Many consumers felt affected in their very basic needs. This causes another obstacle, which will give more political credibility to the enlargement. Thirdly, in the process of enlargement the EU mainly sets the conditions. However, this approach increases the feelings of the authorities and the people in the CEE countries that they have become politically deprived as well as colonized or marginalized by the EU-polity and policies. Finally, the networking between governments and agricultural interest – and pressure groups in the CEE countries demonstrates the characteristics of Neo-corporatism in the field of agricultural policies. The more this networking results in higher subsidies to products, import quota and income transfer payments in the CEE countries, the less EU-15 farmer organizations will be ready to accept CAP reform. Finally, this can erode the EU position in the next WTO-negotiations.

Of course, the best way to tackle the relevant dangers has not yet been found. From the theoretical point of view, Helen Wallace (1996, pp. 11-12) was right when she explains her interest in the EU level of analysis. She wrote '...that modern governance, at least in western Europe, involves efforts to construct policy responses at a multiplicity of levels, from the global to the local....'. However, the total result of this challenging process of governance is an unplanned one. Let's hope that in the EU and in the CEE all actors will understand that further integration is a better response to the different dilemmas than CEE and/or EU marginalization.

76

References

Bempt, Paul van den and Greet Theelen (1996), 'From Europe Agreements to Accession', *Trans European Policy Studies Association, Series European Policy*, no 11.

Berkhout, Petra (1996), 'Met MOE en WTO het nieuwe millenium in Gemeenschappelijk Landbouwbeleid ter discussie', *Spil*, nr 141-142, 1996-3, pp. 11-18.

European Union (1998), *Agenda 2000*, Commission proposals Explanatory Memorandum, The Future for European Agriculture, DG VI, (03/20/98, 1-18).

Goudsblom, Johan (1997), *Het regime van de tijd*, Meulenhof, Amsterdam.

Goverde, Henri J.M. (1997), *Diffusion of Power in Agro-Food Policy Networks*, IPSA, XVIIth World Congress, August, 17-21, Seoul.

Grabbe, Heather and Kirsty Hughes (1998), 'Enlarging the EU Eastwards', *(Chatham House Papers) The Royal Institute of International Affairs*, London.

Grant, W. (1997a), *The Common Agricultural Policy*, Basingtoke, MacMillan.

Grant, W. (1997b), *The CAP in the Global Agricultural Economy: Prospects for the 21st Century'*, IPSA, XVIIth World Congress, August, 17-21, Seoul.

Josling, T. (1997), 'Can the CAP survive enlargement to the East?', in J. Redmond and G. Rosenthal (eds), *The Expanding European Union*, Lynne Rienner, Boulder.

Keeler, J.T.S. (1987), *The Politics of Neo-corporatism in France: Farmers, the State and Agricultural Policy-making in the Fifth Republic*, Oxford University Press, New York.

Keeler, J.T.S. (1996), 'Agricultural Power in the European Community: Explaining the Fate of the CAP and GATT Negotiations', *Comparative Politics*, January, 1996, pp. 127-149.

Keeler, J.T.S. (1997), *Agricultural Power in an Expanding European Union*: IPSA XVIIth World Congress, August, 17-21, Seoul.

Kralt, P.J. (1997), 'Opening van een Policy Window: BSE-crisis', (masters thesis), Wageningen Agricultural University, Wageningen.

McNeill, William (1976), *Plagues and People*, Garden City, New York.

Nicolaides, Phedon and Raja Boean, Sylvia (1997), *A Guide to the Enlargement of the European Union*, European Institute of Public Administration, Maastricht.

Ochenden, Jonathan and Franklin, Michael (1995), *European Agriculture, Making the CAP Fit the Future*, Chatham House Papers, London.

Pinder, David (ed.) (1998), *The New Europe*, John Wiley & Sons, Chichester etc.

Smith, Martin J. (1993), *Pressure, Power and Policy, State Autonomy and Policy Networks in Britain and the United States*, Harvester, Wheatsheaf, New York, etc.

Swinbank, A. and Tanner, C. (1996), *Farm Reform and Trade Conflict*, University of Michigan Press, Ann Arbor, (cited in Keeler, 1997).

Wallace, Helen (1996), 'Politics and Policy in the EU: the Challenge of Governance', Helen Wallace and William Wallace (eds), Policy-Making the European Union, Oxford University Press, Oxford, New York, etc., pp. 4-36.

World Trade Organization, Trade Policy Review Body (1997), *European Union*, Report by the Secretariat, Summary Observations, Geneva.

Part 2 – Policies and politics of change

7 A Northern dimension for the European Union:
Background and proposals

TOIVO MUILU

Introduction

The northward expansion of the European Union that took place when Finland and Sweden joined it at the beginning of 1995 added many entirely new features to its geography: the existing densely populated member countries in Central Europe suddenly found themselves with a wide, sparsely populated northern periphery with harsh natural conditions and a remote location and with regional problems paralleled only by those observed in Scotland and the mountain regions. The total area of forest within the EU doubled, for example. In addition, the new eastern border of the European Union was the 1340 km frontier between Finland and Russia, which not only concealed behind it enormous natural resources but also represented perhaps the most striking difference in standards of living of any border in the world. It is very likely that the global importance of the north will increase in the next few years, for as Heikkilä (1998, p. 5) points out, the Arctic area provides a link between Europe and America, making the EU, Russia, Canada and the United States neighbours.

This paper will discuss the Northern Dimension initiative proposed by Finland to the European Union and approved as part of the EU Luxembourg agenda in December, 1997. The point of departure in the initiative and in this paper is the enormous opportunities offered by the north and the at least equally conspicuous unsolved problems that exist. The paper also sets out from the assumption that the EU will in any case have to take its Northern Dimension into consideration either in the proposed form or in some other way, preferably sooner rather than later.

The north as a concept

The north cannot be regarded as an exact concept but like many of the definitions employed in regional geography, as a parameter, which is dependent on the criteria and viewpoints, employed. Its definitions are also intertwined with the concept of arctic areas (see e.g. Naukkarinen, 1989). Physical geographical criteria are employed in a number of investigations concerned with northernness. Among these, however, the +10°C limit for July temperatures and the southern boundary of the permafrost zone, for example, do not extend to the current EU area.

It is thus quite reasonable that the northernness aspect should be approached from the point of view of human action by describing the features in terms of which northern areas differ from the core areas of Europe. First of all they are characterized by harsh natural conditions and a resulting short growing season, reducing the minimum growing season in the EU from 220 days before Sweden and Finland joined to only 130 days. In addition, the north is extremely sparsely populated, the population density of the northernmost two provinces of Finland and Sweden being only 2 inhabitants/km², whereas the average for the EU countries is 115 inhabitants/km². Since 80% of the inhabitants live in towns and built-up areas, this means very long distances between centres. These factors place special demands on building, heating, overall technical maintenance and winter traffic etc. The majority of Finland's export trade in particular takes place by sea throughout the year, despite the fact that the northern parts of the Baltic Sea are covered by ice in winter (OPINION adopted by the Committee of the Regions...1998; The European North – Challenges and Opportunities, 1997, pp. 2-3).

The north has to be delimited in terms of regional geography if any concrete content is to be attached to it. There are a number of definitions, of which just two will be discussed here that are most essential from the point of view of the EU. According to the Polar Committee of Finland, the European North comprises the following regions: the North Calotte, the Barents Euro-Arctic Region, the Komi Republic in Russia and the sea areas around Scandinavia and Northern Russia (Figure 7.1). The resulting region comprises approximately 1.6 million km², i.e. an area almost equal to that covered by France, Germany, Italy and Spain combined but which still has only some 6 million inhabitants. Approximately 1.3 million km² of this area and some 4.8 million of its inhabitants are located in Russia, so

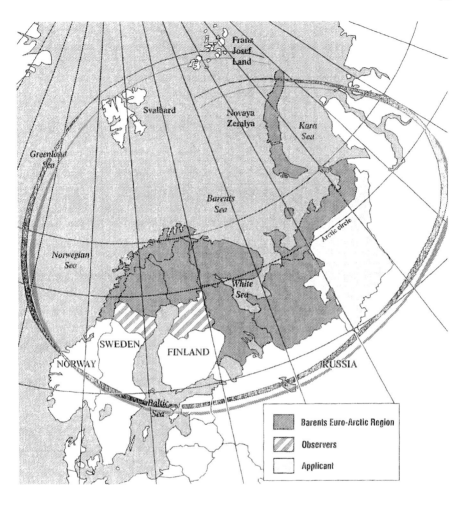

Figure 7.1   The European North

Source: The European North - Challenges and Opportunities, 1997.

that Russia can be said to occupy a very important position in the context of northern areas (The European North - Challenges and Opportunities, 1997, p. 6).

In Finland's EU initiative the Northern Dimension is defined more broadly, as in a speech by Prime Minister Paavo Lipponen (1997, p. 2):

Geographically, we include in it the region from Iceland in the West across to North-western Russia, or from the Arctic Ocean in the North to the southern coast of the Baltic Sea. Thus not only countries around the Baltic Sea, but also all the other Nordic counties, Great Britain, the United States and Canada are more or less directly involved in the Northern region, particularly in the circumpolar North.

It is thus essential to realize that the Northern Dimension in the initiative does not refer to European areas only.

The 'Northern Dimension' as a Finnish initiative

The Northern Dimension as such is not a new thing, for questions connected with Northern Europe, Russia and the Barents region have been to the fore in a number of research projects, seminars and political discussions for a long time (e.g. Jussila *et al.*, 1993; Heininen and Langlais, 1997a; Heininen and Langlais, 1997b; Saarela *et al.*, 1997; The Nordic Countries..., 1997; Tykkyläinen and Jussila, 1998). According to Heikkilä (1998, p. 5), the isolation, which prevailed in northern areas throughout the Cold War era, ended with the co-operation initiatives proposed by Mikhail Gorbachov in his speech in Murmansk on 1.10.1987.

The Northern Dimension has also been contained in the EU vocabulary for some years, although that organization has admittedly shown little interest in northern matters so far. The northernness aspect began to assume a more concrete content in the EU only after Finland and Sweden joined. A statement submitted by the Committee of the Regions on 12.6.1996, for example, is concerned with the Northern Dimension and the development of a policy of co-operation between the EU and Russia and in the Barents region (OPINION adopted by the Committee of the Regions..., 1998).

The roots of the Northern Dimension as Finland's official EU political initiative are usually considered to go back to the speech given by Prime Minister Paavo Lipponen in the 'Barents Region Today' conference in Rovaniemi on 15.9.1997 (Lipponen, 1997, see also Heininen and Langlais, 1997b). The initiative is thus so new that any search for new information will largely have to resort to newspaper articles, official EU announcements and WWW pages. As a rule, even in the last-mentioned the keywords 'Northern Dimension' or in Finnish 'pohjoinen ulottuvuus' yield only speeches and news items. These usually content themselves with repeating the same themes, those on the basis of which the content of the initiative will be outlined in more detail below.

The European Office of the Ministry of Foreign Affairs has defined the Northern Dimension in the following manner (EU ja Pohjoinen ulottu- vuus, 21.11.1997):

> The Northern Dimension is an overall concept used to develop EU policy and to de- fine its interests in the changing situation in northern Europe in order to promote the objectives of Finland and the European Union. It contains measures for safeguarding stability and social and economic development in our neighbouring areas. Its corner- stones are cooperation between the Barents region and the areas surrounding the Baltic Sea, cooperation between Nordic neighbours and cooperation under the Arctic Coun- cil. Cooperation pursued by different countries with their neighbouring areas and bilateral relations serve to add to the scope of the Northern Dimension.

The overall content of the concept is described in Table 7.1, which is based on the statements and announcements mentioned here, the speech given by Prime Minister Lipponen and certain other sources (listed below the table). It can be concluded that the initiative can be regarded as a 'lucky dip' at this stage, in that it covers a large number of issues con- cerned with different fields of human activity and the environment. Although it largely sets out from the natural resources of Russia and the safeguarding of peaceful development in the area, the initiative does not involve any traditional security policy aspects in the form of military co- operation, for example. The initiative was on the agenda at the EU summit in Luxembourg in December, 1997, so that it now enjoys the status of an official EU initiative.

One point made in Prime Minister Lipponen's speech was that the EU already has a 'Southern Dimension', i.e. it is engaged in Mediterranean or so-called Euro-Med co-operation which involves most of the countries lining the Mediterranean Sea (see e.g. Cole and Cole, 1997, pp. 338-340). It is thus interesting to note that the initiative has received high-rank politi- cal support from the southern EU countries in particular, at least from the Portuguese Prime Minister (Helsingin Sanomat, 3.3.1998) and the Spanish Minister of Foreign Affairs (Kaleva, 21.5.1998). According to Joenniemi (1998), this is thus quite logical, for it is also beneficial for the countries of southern Europe that attention should be paid to north and south as the ba- sic attributes of Europe rather than emphasizing the east-west axis.

Table 7.1   Content of the EU Northern Dimension initiative

Sectors	Objectives and opportunities	Problems	Measures
Position of Russia	Increased co-operation between the EU and Russia, safeguarding of peaceful, stable development	Position in terms of military policy, the legacy of the Cold War, (regional) administrative confusion in Russia	Russian membership of major international organizations (e.g. WTO) and bilateral agreements between the EU and Russia
Natural resources and energy networks	Utilization of the vast natural resources available in NW Russia	Undeveloped infrastructure in NW Russia	Construction of oil, natural gas and electricity transmission networks, investments, long-term loans
Transport Networks	Development and linking of transport networks and telecommunications in Northern Europe and Russia	Long distances, harsh natural, conditions, high building costs	Technical assistance, investments, loans
Environmental protection and nuclear safety	Supervision of agreements, improving nuclear safety, contract-based environmental co-operation	Obsolete and dangerous nuclear power stations, military nuclear waste, insufficient monitoring of the state of the environment	Creation, implementation and supervision of international environmental standards in Russia, environmental co-operation
Commerce and economic co-operation	Linking of Russia to international economic co-operation	Poorly developed basic economic structures, legislation and institutions, border co-operation	WTO and EU (?) memberships, venture capital

Table 7.1 continues ...

Internal affairs and legislation	Principles of constitutional government, security of national borders	Organized crime, drug trafficking	Improved border supervision, mutual recognition of judicial decisions
Co-operation in research and training	Prevention of environmental damage, environmental technology, research into northern areas	Lack of co-ordination	Expansion of EU and other international research programmes to Russia
Other sectors	A functioning democracy, a civic society, labour policy, cultural and regional policy, indigenous peoples etc.	Lack of institutional development and stability (a Soviet legacy)	Humanitarian co-operation, cultural exchange, 'grass-roots' co-operation between citizens etc.

Sources: Heininen and Langlais, 1997b; Lipponen, 1997; The EU and the Northern Dimension, 1997; The European North - Challenges and Opportunities, 1997; OPINION adopted by the Committee of the Regions..., 1998; newspaper articles.

Perhaps the most important points in the initiative are connected with its implementation and costs. It should be noted that *it does not propose the forming of any new organizations or the making of any new investments*, but rather underlines better co-ordination of existing actors and resources. According to Lipponen (1997, pp. 4-5):

Cooperation in the Northern regions is already organized well enough to make major new institutional arrangements unnecessary. Nor do we need a new financing regulation for this purpose. A review of the present Union documents on the region should be conducted with the aim of devising a better coordinated policy, with clear priorities, making the Northern Dimension an integral and generally recognized part of the Union's relations with Russia and the association countries.

The most important co-operation forums in the north are the Council of Baltic Sea States (CBSS), the Barents Euro-Arctic Council (see Figure 7.1) and the recently founded Arctic Council. The Union participates in the two first-mentioned ones but is not a member of the Arctic Council.

Regarding the organization of funding, Prime Minister Lipponen had this to say (1997, p. 6):

Financing cooperation in the Northern Dimension should mainly come from national governments, bilateral donors, international financing institutions and Union programmes. We emphasize coordinated efforts, now lacking in many projects. In the financing framework for 2000-2006, sufficient funds ought to be directed to the Northern regions through TACIS and PHARE programmes and Interreg funds. It is most important to improve TACIS and PHARE regulations in the coming review. Proposals for new guidelines for PHARE financing are included in the Commission's Agenda 2000 papers. The funding of TACIS should be secured, but better coordination with Interreg and funding from international financing institutions is needed. Better commitment to part-financing from the recipient country can be expected. The IMF, the World Bank and EBRD channel substantial funds to the Baltic States and Russia. The EU must become more active in getting these institutions to better coordinate their activities. To supplement country-specific strategies, a regional approach is necessary. We also encourage the European Investment Bank to consider financing programmes in Russia according to priorities set by the EU. Nordic financing institutions, notably the Nordic Investment Bank, also should get more closely involved in Northern Europe.

The Northern Dimension initiative can hardly be said to be explained fully on the basis of the above, but it is gradually being given a more concrete content, as a programme of action is currently being prepared by the Office of the Council of State under guidance from the EU Commission and based on the preliminary programme approved by the Finnish government in February, 1998. The aim is to present an interim report at the EU summit in Vienna in December, 1998 (Kaleva, 19.4.1998).

Critical observations

Although the Northern Dimension has thus attracted increasing 'official' attention, it has also aroused criticism. The major problem so far has been that the initiative is based solely on political speeches and declarations, so that its concrete content and the use made of research data and theories have remained in the background. Heininen (1998), for example, has demanded that a comprehensive strategy should be created for northern research, but the low level of co-ordination of research is in a way quite understandable bearing in mind that the initiative was only proposed recently.

Finland's active role in this matter has aroused suspicion in the other Nordic countries, particularly regarding the possibility that it was intended only to serve Finnish interests. It is true that Finland has major national interests at stake, but it has continuously been emphasized in the preparation of the project that peaceful development in the north and sustainable utilization of natural resources are in everyone's interests, at the EU level and in global terms. It has been estimated that by the year 2005, for example, the European Union will already have to purchase approximately 60% of its natural gas from outside Europe, at which point Russia will be the most economic alternative (Helsingin Sanomat, 20.1.1998).

Norway, a non-EU country, has been worried about its opportunities for influencing northern policies in Europe. Norway and Russia are in fact the only European countries which have direct access to the Barents Sea, and they also share a long history of utilizing the regional resources, so that it is quite understandable that there should be concern about being side-tracked. The Barents Regional Council is in practise the only forum where Norway can present its views. Norway has nevertheless been consoled by the fact that the Northern Dimension covers co-operation with all countries and actors in the area and not only the interests of the EU countries (Helsingin Sanomat, 20.1.1998).

Critical opinions have also been raised about the fate of the indigenous peoples of the north and of the northern environment. Massa (1998) emphasizes that the Europeanization of areas inhabited by indigenous northern peoples has either destroyed their cultures completely or transformed them into crisis cultures struggling on the periphery of the global economy. In addition, the European world economy has caused extensive ecological damage in the north and has led to the partial disappearance of the original, sensitive natural environment. The real challenge faced by the EU Northern Dimension is to ensure that when the initiative assumes concrete form the same negative trends will not occur.

Conclusions

The Northern Dimension is so far only an obscure concept, for it was only in autumn 1997 that it was expressed as an official initiative. The points of departure are ecologically sustainable utilization of the natural resources in NW Russia in particular, peaceful and stable development in the area and clarification of the role of the EU as a northern actor. Lying behind the initiative is not only Finland's national interest but also the idea that northern areas will increase in importance in the Europe of the future.

So far the initiative has aroused more questions than it has answered. Its purpose is to link numerous issues and actors in a controlled manner even though their objectives and interests may be contradictory. Historical experiences of reconciling the exploitation of natural resources with safeguarding the position of indigenous peoples have not been encouraging. Although the population of the north is small, all the topics within the proposed Northern Dimension will inevitably mean changes in human activities. How will it be possible to guarantee that these changes will be for the good of both the natural environments of the northern periphery and human life there?

We are in the end faced with the question of whether we are able to see into the future of northern areas. We are often still inclined to view the north as a periphery, a marginal region that marks the last habitable land area. As globalization proceeds, however, even remote, isolated areas will be integrated into the global economy, in either a controlled or an uncontrolled manner, through technological development. Despite its defects and incompleteness, and despite the criticism that it has aroused, the Northern Dimension initiative can be regarded as the first comprehensive attempt to create a systematic pattern of action for safeguarding the future of the northern periphery of Europe.

References

Cole, J. and Cole, F. (1997), *A Geography of the European Union*, second edition, Routledge, London and New York, p. 395.

EU ja Pohjoinen ulottuvuus, 21.11.1997, publication in Internet at the Finnish Government site, at http://www.vn.fi/vn/um/euinfo/julkaisu/pohjoine.html.

Heikkilä, M. (1998), *Arktiset visiot*, Pohjoinen, KL-paino, Ylivieska, p. 160.

Heininen, L. (1998), 'Kansalliseen pohjoisen politiikkaan', newspaper *Kaleva* 18.3.1998.

Heininen, L. and Langlais, R. (eds) (1997a), 'BEARing the European North: the Northern Dimension and Alternative Scenarios', *Arctic Centre Reports* 23, University of Lapland, Rovaniemi, p. 196.

Heininen, L. and Langlais, R. (eds) (1997b), 'Europe's Northern Dimension: the BEAR Meets the South', *Publications of the Administrative Office of the University of Lapland* 39, University of Lapland, Rovaniemi, p. 284.

Helsingin Sanomat 20.1.1998 (newspaper article), 'Norja huolestunut EU:n pohjoisen politiikasta'.

Helsingin Sanomat 3.3.1998 (newspaper article), 'Portugalilta vahva tuki pohjoiselle ulottuvuudelle'.

Joenniemi, P. (1998), 'Pohjoisen uusi tuleminen', newspaper *Kaleva* 27.4.1998.

Jussila, H., Persson, L.O. and Wiberg, U. (eds) (1993), *Shifts in Systems at the Top of Europe*, FORA, Stockholm, p. 181.

Kaleva 19.4.1998 (newspaper article), 'Pohjoista ulottuvuutta linjattu'.

Kaleva 21.5.1998 (newspaper article), 'Espanja tukee aloitetta pohjoisesta ulottuvuudesta'.

Lipponen, P. (1997), 'The European Union Needs a Policy for the Northern Dimension', 15.09.1997, *http://www.vn.fi/vn/english/speech/970915e.htm*.

Massa, I. (1998), 'Kenen ehdoilla pohjoista kehitetään?', newspaper *Helsingin Sanomat* 10.6.1998.

Naukkarinen, A. (1989), 'Arktinen vyöhyke ja sen asukkaat', *Duodecim* 105, pp. 399-405.

'OPINION adopted by the Committee of the Regions on 12 June, 1996 on the Northern Dimension of the European Union and Cross-Border Cooperation on the Border between the European Union and the Russian Federation and in the Barents Region', 27.7.1998, *http://www.kemi.fi/jorma_virtanen/eu/cor_en.html*.

Saarela, A., Planting, T. and Lausala, T. (1997), 'Financing of projects in North-West Russia', *Studies and Reports* 30/1997, Ministry of Trade and Industry, Finland, Helsinki, p. 179.

The European North - Challenges and Opportunities (1997), Ministry of Trade and Industry, Helsinki, p. 31.

'The Nordic Countries and the New Europe: an anthology' (1997), *TemaNord 1997:553*, Nordic Council of Ministers: Copenhagen, p. 114.

Tykkyläinen, M. and Jussila, H. (1998), 'Potentials for innovative restructuring of industry in Northwestern Russia', *Fennia 176:1*, pp. 223-245.

8 Rural Northern Finland and EU-membership

MATTI HÄKKILÄ

Background

Finland joined the European Union together with Sweden and Austria on January 1st, 1995. Since Norway did not, Finland became EU's northernmost member country and at the same time its most predominantly rural country (see OECD, 1993, Table 2). The rural population in Finland was by and large against the idea of becoming a member of the union, and the farmers in the north of Finland in particular were doubtful whether it would be sensible to join.

What is normally understood by 'northern Finland' is a region which is constituted of the administrative provinces of Oulu and Lapland and comprises 48% of the area of Finland as a whole, and where just under 13% of the population live today. About half of this area lies north of the Arctic Circle.

From the point of view of regional development, however, regions more important than the administrative provinces in EU-Finland are the historical provinces (Figure 8.1) which constitute the NUTS 3 level of Finland in the regional system of the EU. The main part of northern Finland is historically divided into three provinces: those of Lapland, Kainuu and Northern Ostrobothnia. The southernmost part of the administrative province of Oulu belongs to the historical province of Central Ostrobothnia.

Northern Finland is a sparsely populated area where rural settlement is particularly scattered (Rusanen et al., 1997, Figs 3a-3d). According to the tripartition of the Finnish countryside (Malinen, 1993, pp. 113-115), the main part of northern Finland belongs to the isolated countryside where the occupational structure is non-diversified and the problems are the biggest. Only the coastal municipalities can be considered as part of the rural heartland where the structure of rural industries is more diversified.

91

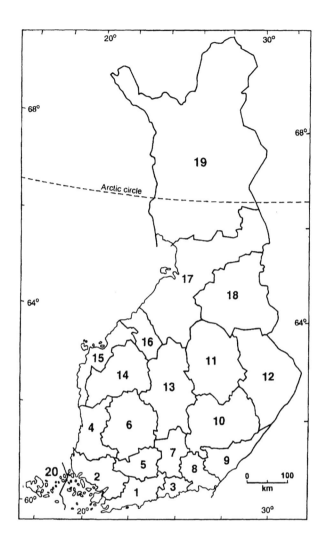

Figure 8.1   Historical provinces (NUTS level 3 regions) of Finland
1. Uusimaa, 2. Varsinais-Suomi, 3. Eastern Uusimaa, 4. Satakunta,
5. Häme, 6. Pirkanmaa, 7. Päijät-Häme, 8. Kymenlaakso, 9.
Southern Karelia, 10. Southern Savo, 11. Savo, 12. Northern
Karelia, 13. Central Finland, 14. Southern Ostrobothnia, 15.
Ostrobothnia Swedish, 16. Central Ostrobothnia, 17. Northern
Ostrobothnia, 18. Kainuu, 19. Lapland, 20. Åland.

Rural development

In the well over 50 post-war years, settlement of the Finnish countryside has undergone two phases, or two developments in completely different directions (e.g. Häkkilä, 1986). These phases emerged in Northern Finland on average later than in Southern Finland, and even within Northern Finland the point of their emergence is later when moving from south to north.

Up till the 1960s, the settlement policy practiced at that time caused rural settlement to expand to previously unpopulated areas and new farms were set up (Palomäki, 1960; Smeds, 1963). At the same time, the big post-war forest working sites received labour. In the early 1960s when the rural settlement was at its height there were approx. 60,000 farms of over 1 field hectare in northern Finland, of which some 15% had been established as a result of post-war settlement operations (Häkkilä, 1986, table 1). The majority of the farms were small, however, comprising only a few field hectares.

The culmination phase of rural settlement remained nonetheless very short-lived. The need for labour in industry and other trades typical of population centres attracted people from the countryside. Similarly, the agriculture and also forestry were mechanized and needed less labour. Sufficiency in foodstuffs had already been achieved in the 1950s, and steps to restrict overproduction had to be taken as early as the 1960s. The field reservation system (Jaatinen and Alalammi, 1978) that was launched in 1969 gave a particular boost to the trend of small farms abandoning agriculture. This system was initiated concurrently in the whole country, but it 'worked particularly well' in the north of Finland where the farms had not yet had time to achieve capability of surviving (Häkkilä, 1984). At the same time, many other factors unfavourable from the point of view of living in the North-Finnish countryside emerged (Häkkilä, 1988) with the result that rural settlement began to thin out with increasing speed.

What most recently further accelerated the rate of giving up agriculture in Finland as a whole as well as in northern Finland in particular was our country's EU-membership. This has aroused speculations about the collapse of agriculture especially in the more remote areas. However, no alarming changes are foreseen (Kettunen, 1997, p. 2).

Structure of agriculture

After a farmer family gives up agricultural production the farm is seldom sold, especially not in northern Finland, but it remains in the possession of the family or the estate. Hence, the decline in the overall number of registered farms is slower than the decrease in the number of farms that still practice production (Häkkilä, 1984). By 1995 the total number of farms in northern Finland had dropped to 33,000, but only a third of these were active (Farm Register, 1997). Consequently, the number of farms has fallen almost to a half, and the number of farms practicing production to a fifth of the corresponding figures for the early 1960s. Only a very small number of the farms still in the register continue to be active, especially in Kainuu and Lapland. Naturally, those farms that have remained active have the largest acreage of arable land. However, the size structure of the farms in the north of Finland and particularly in Lapland and Kainuu is disadvantageous in comparison with that in the country as a whole and especially in southernmost Finland (Figure 8.2).

On the EU scale, the arable areas of Finnish farms are small. Even those for active farms are on the average only about and in northern Finland clearly under a half of the mean for farms in most EU countries. It is only in the Mediterranean countries that the arable areas of the farms are smaller than in Finland (Maatilahallitus, 1992). In principle, the arable areas of Finnish farms should be at least double compared with those in the central EU countries, for the yields per hectare in our country are only about a half of theirs.

The location of northern Finland and the consequential climatic conditions limit the agricultural production to grass fodder cultivation and, in some degree, to feed grain cultivation. The crops are utilized first and foremost in dairy farming, which is the dominant branch of agricultural production in northern Finland. Of all active farms in northern Finland about a half are dairy farms and some 10% other cattle farms (Farm Register, 1997). In the south-western part of the province of Oulu agriculture is more diversified.

Nearly all farms is Finland have a forest area, which has a considerable significance for their livelihood, especially in northern Finland where the forest areas of the farms are large. The average growth of forest per hectare in the north of Finland is, nonetheless, only a third or a quarter of the mean growth of forests for southern Finland (Häkkilä, 1977, pp. 42-46). In Lapland as well as in northern Kainuu many farmers practice reindeer herding in addition to agriculture, although the majority of those practicing reindeer husbandry do it as their sole source of livelihood.

94

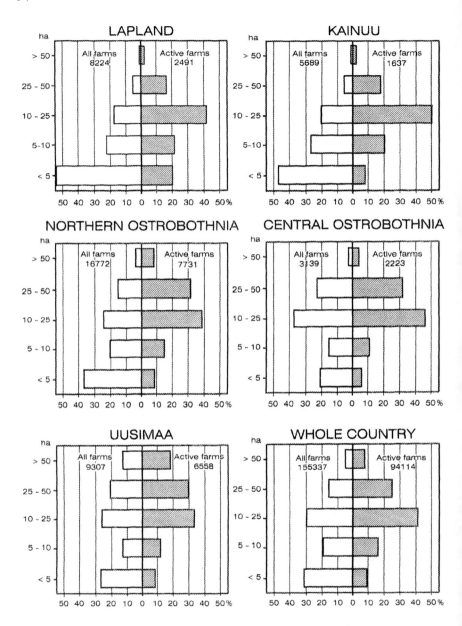

Figure 8.2   Size structure of all farms and active farms in some
NUTS level 3 regions and in the whole country

Impact of EU-membership on the agriculture

During the national agricultural policy, Finnish agriculture was subsidized by means of a complex support system in which the main emphasis lay on various, mostly regionally graded price supports. The producer prices were even double compared with those in the EU countries (e.g. Kettunen, 1994, p.12). When Finland became a member, the producer's prices plummeted. The decrease in the value of the stocks were compensated, however, so that in the first membership year the farmers had hardly any loss of income. In the membership negotiations it had been agreed that for the five-year transition period Finland is granted an annually lowering national support package, with the aid of which our country has to fully adapt to the union's agricultural policy, CAP, by the end of 1999. This means that the structural development in Finnish agriculture continues to be intense.

The membership in the union has clearly increased the area under cultivation in Finland (Kettunen, 1997, p.13). The farms that have continued to practice agriculture have leased fields from abandoned farms, and also remote patches of arable land that have been uncultivated for a long time have again been taken into cultivation. This is due to the fact that subsidies in the EU's support system are for a big part paid according to field area. Today there are also in northern Finland, especially in the south-western part of the province of Oulu, some farmers who cultivate arable areas of 100-200 hectares.

Until recently, the prevailing assumption has been that dairy farming has the best possibilities to survive in Finland, also in the present conditions of EU-membership. The Agenda 2000 projections have undermined this view, since 15% cuts in average support prices by 2006 will be counterbalanced by a yearly payment for dairy cows. The dairy farms in northern Finland are often small, but the agricultural subsidies in the future will be based more and more on the arable area or the number of livestock. The fact that the amount of yield will become less significant applies to dairy farming in particular for the reason that the mean yield for North-Finnish dairy cows is of the same order as elsewhere in the country and competes fully even on the scale of the whole European Union (see Commission, 1990, Maatilahallitus, 1992).

The trump card of Finnish and particularly North-Finnish agriculture may in the future well be foodstuffs that are free from various kinds of pesticide remnants. In 1996, an average of only 0.7 kg of effective agents of pesticides were used per field hectare in Finland. In Germany the corresponding figure was 5.7 kg and in Holland as much as 21 kg of effective agents were spread per field hectare (Helaakoski, 1998, p.5).

In organic cultivation, pesticides or artificial fertilizers are not used at all. Organic farming has become common very rapidly in our country during the past about ten years, and in the 1990s Finland has spurted among the top countries in the branch.

The authorities started to subsidize natural production already during the national agricultural policy in 1989, but the EU-membership has further increased the interest in the trade, since, as has been stated above, the agricultural subsidy from the EU is mainly bound up with the acreage or the number of livestock, which means that the amount of crop or yield is not decisive for the subsistence of the farmer. This favours a more extensive method of production. In addition, organic farming, being a labour-intensive branch, is well suitable for northern Finland suffering from unemployment.

As a matter of fact, organic cultivation has increased the most in Northern Ostrobothnia over the past years, and it has had a notable increase also in Kainuu and Central Ostrobothnia. In northern Finland, the proportion of natural farms of active farms was approx. 5% in 1996, whereas the corresponding figure for the country as a whole was 4.7% (Yearbook of Farm Statistics, 1997).

In this respect, the chapter on rural policy in the Agenda 2000 communication seems promising from the point of view of Finland. In the communication it says, among other things:

Growing demands for a more environmentally sensitive agriculture coinciding with the increasing use of the countryside for recreation create new obligations and opportunities for agriculture. The commission favours giving a more prominent role to agri-environmental measures, especially those which call for an extra effort by farmers such as organic farming, maintenance of semi-natural habitats. Other aspects of sustainable rural development will be pursued by a reorganization to make existing structural policies more targeted.

Be it a question of conventional agricultural production or natural production, the farms that practice cultivation grow bigger and their number declines all the time. It has been predicted that by 2005, along with the membership, the number of active farms will drop in Finland till even less than a half of the present figure (Niemi and Linjakumpu, 1996, p.134). The official objective is along the same lines. If these predictions will materialize and if the reduction in the number of active farms will take place in the same proportion as in the whole country, the number of active farms in northern Finland will fall to 5,000-6,000 farms, that is to say, to a tenth of the figure for the culmination period in the early 1960s. Those farms that continue to be active are, of course, far larger than 40 years ago.

According to the Agenda 2000 communication, area-based compensations will also be used in the future, which will probably mean that as large a part as possible of the field area in northern Finland will continue to be cultivated, in the near future at least, despite the decrease in the number of farms. This view is supported by the fact that the Cardiff summit of the leaders of the EU countries in 1998, where the Agenda 2000 program was discussed, confirmed the earlier accepted principle that agriculture is practised everywhere in the area of the union including the unfavourable regions. In a longer time perspective, it remains to be seen what the impact of the union's possible expansion to the east might be. The possibility is that it would increase the EU's agricultural land area by 50%.

Diversification of the rural sources of livelihood

The basic subsistence of the rural population, even in northern Finland, comes still from agriculture, but since the number of active farms continues to decrease, agriculture can only sustain quite a small number of people. New jobs have to be found. Therefore, the development of various kinds of small-scale entrepreneurship is an essential means to secure substitutive and new jobs in rural areas.

To start a new type of rural enterprise is, however, no simple matter, at least not in the more outlying districts of northern Finland. The remote location as such along with the long distances and harsh natural conditions restrict the possibilities and options of entrepreneurship. The small population means limited local markets and entering the markets farther away is often restricted by the small size of rural enterprises. The distances and the hard winter cause extra costs.

In northern Finland, there is no significant entrepreneurial tradition, either. It is true, agricultural farms are enterprises as well, but they have, for example, hardly any experience of marketing the products, for earlier the farm products sold well without effort. The dairies bought the milk, the butcheries the meat and the forestry companies the timber, the prices having been agreed in the incomes policy agreements or in the timber price agreements on the level of central organizations. Wage work was available, say, in forest economy. The new rural entrepreneur, on the contrary, has to know not only how to make his product, but also how to sell it.

It could be seen as early as the 1970s that the countryside will not remain populated solely with the aid of agriculture, and ever since then various kinds of development activities aimed at the diversification of the industrial structure in the countryside have been practiced. Programs for rural development have been prepared nationally, provincially and locally, and innumerable projects for the development of the countryside have been initiated (e.g. Hautamäki, 1985, Katajamäki and Kaikkonen, 1991, Malinen, 1993, Uusitalo, 1995). Just before the Finnish EU-membership became a fact, the country changed over to program-based rural policy. Positive results have certainly been achieved, but it has not been possible to put a stop to the depopulation of the countryside with help of the programs and the measures taken.

With Finland's joining the union, rural development was granted considerable extra resources. In accordance with the community's treaty of foundation, the regions that are the most poorly developed and regressing are supported with measures of regional and structural policy. They are united to programs which structural funds of the community partly finance.

To target subsidies in the period of 1994-1999, the union agreed upon six common Objectives (1, 2, 3, 4, 5a and 5b) that the structural funds support. In the membership negotiations Finland and Sweden managed, due to their special conditions, to push through a new Objective 6 which more or less corresponds to Objective 1, in other words, the support program for the most poorly developed regions. It includes subsidies for the structural development of the countryside and agriculture, the Objective 5b program being especially designed to subsidize the rural development. Objectives 1, 2, 5b and 6 are regional (Figure 8.3), while Objectives 3, 4 and 5a can be implemented throughout Finland outside the area of Objective 6. Nearly all of northern Finland belongs to Objective 5b or 6 regions, outside which remains only the well-developed Oulu region. The programs for the development of the countryside are specific for the various historical provinces (NUTS 3 regions).

Half of the subsidies received by the structural funds in Finland are channelled to the regional Objectives, and Objective 6 obtains a little less than a third of all the EU subsidies. About 90% of the resources of the structural funds are used to provide capital for the Objective programs and nine per cent have been reserved for community initiatives. Of these, LEADER is the most important from the point of view of rural development since it provides additional resources and realizes the plans of local activity groups in the rural development projects.

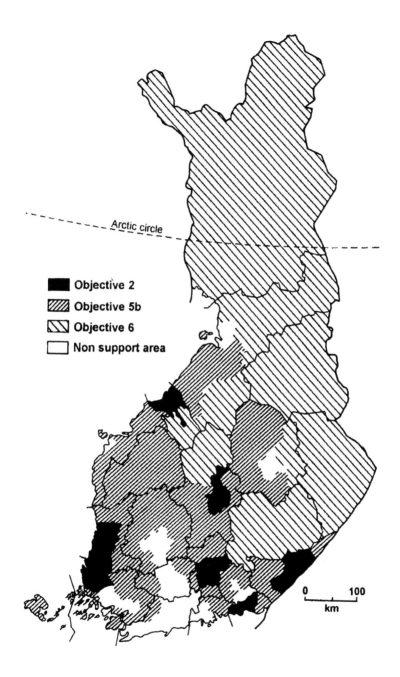

Objective 2
Objective 5b
Objective 6
Non support area

Arctic circle

0   100
km

ıre 8.3   Objective areas of EU 's development programmes

Some observations

The membership in the European Union has brought about many kinds of changes in the life of Finnish farmers. One of these is having to continually write various kinds of applications and reports. If Finland's national agricultural policy was complicated, that of the union is far more complex and bureaucratic, the farmers spending a lot of time filling out different types of forms.

Finnish farmers are also irritated by the many detailed regulations and schedules. Especially the schedules used in the EU are not suitable for the Nordic conditions in Finland (Kettunen, 1997). Sowing reports, for example, should have been filed by May 15, but a deadline like this is very early even in normal years. The Spring of 1995 was exceptionally late whereas the spring of 1998 was very rainy, for which reason the fields were so wet that it was not possible to finish sowing everywhere in Northern Ostrobothnia, not even by the end of June. The union did grant an extension of time, it is true, but a few thousands of field hectares had to be left completely uncultivated owing to the wetness. All in all, it has to be noted that the Finnish farmer population has begun to adapt to EU bureaucracy and EU agricultural policy, even surprisingly well.

As far as other rural industries are concerned, activities of all kinds seem to have increased also in rural northern Finland. Today, far over a thousand EU-projects are going on in the northern half of the country. Plenty of investments have been made for example in the entrepreneurship based on nature and natural resources. Yet however, the migration from the countryside to the population centres and from the north to the south continues to be heavy, which means that the authorities have not managed to arrest the regression of the countryside, at least not of the remoter areas.

The tourist trade is one important object for development in northern Finland. Although the summer is short and the mosquitoes a nuisance to the tourists, the bright summer nights along with the vast wilderness areas, numerous lakes and rivers attract tourists from the densely populated areas of both Finland and the rest of Europe and the world. Northern Finland has hundreds of kilometres of common borderline with Russia, and so when the conditions there become more stable it is also possible to develop tourist services across the border. The union's Interreg and Tacis programs provide economic resources for this. Winter tourism will also win popularity when, for example, the cross-country skiing becomes more popular. In the future, the position of northern Finland may get even better in this respect, for due to progress of the greenhouse effect the winters may become too mild for skiing even in southern Finland. In the north of Finland there is hardly any fear of this.

In terms of surface area, the greater part of northern Finland belongs to the region of the Objective 6 program. According to the Agenda 2000 communication the number of structural funds is proposed to be reduced from seven to three, in which case the Objective 6 program, for example, would discontinue to exist. The regions of Objective 6 could be transferred to Objective 1, if they fulfil the tightening criteria of Objective 1. Lapland, for instance, does not meet the criterion 'that a region's per capital gross domestic product must be below 75% of the EU average'. Now however, the Commission has presented as one of the 'special arrangements' included in the Agenda 2000 that Objective 6 regions exceeding the GNP criterion will be included in Objective 1. This is important for Finland, since this is how the countryside can continue to be developed also in a region which is the most scarcely-populated and which has the highest unemployment rate in the country.

References

Ahvenjärvi, H. and Häkkilä, M. (1997), 'Luonnonmukainen maatalous läntisessä Euroopassa (Organic farming in Western Europe)', *Terra* 109:4, pp. 198-207.

Cole, J. and Cole F. (1997), *A Geography of the European Union*, 2nd edition, London and New York, p. 395.

Commission of the European Communities (1990), *The agricultural situation in European Community, 1989 Report*, Brussels-Luxenburg.

Farm Register 1996 (1997), *National Board of Agriculture*, Helsinki.

Hautamäki, L. (1985), 'Maaseudun kehitys ja omatoimisuus', *Tampereen yliopisto, Aluetieteen laitos, Tutkimuksia Sarja B* 35/1985, p. 97.

Helaakoski, L. (1998), 'Maaseutu yrittää', *Turveruukki Oy:n tiedotuslehti Suopursu* 2/1998: 3-5, pp. 3-5.

Häkkilä, M. (1977), 'Geographical aspects of forest returns on Finnish farms', *Fennia* 152, p. 86.

Häkkilä, M. (1984), 'The recent development of agriculture with special reference to Kainuu, Finland', *Nordia* 18:2, pp. 123-134.

Häkkilä, M. (1986), 'The expansion and retreat of agricultural settlement in Northern Finland after World War II', *Nordia* 20:1, pp. 27-39.

Häkkilä, M. (1993), 'Perspectives of Finnish Agriculture in the Integrating Europe', *University of Oulu, Research Institute of Northern Finland, Research Reports* 114, pp. 51-78.

Jaatinen, S. and Alalammi, P. (1978), 'The field reservation scheme in Finland 1969-1977', *Nordia* 12:1, pp. 15-30.

102

Katajamäki, H. and Kaikkonen, R. (1991), 'Maaseudun kolmas tie (The Third Way of the Rural Society)', *Helsingin yliopisto, Maaseudun tutkimus- ja koulutuskeskus Seinäjoki, Julkaisusarja* A:1, p. 174.

Kettunen, L. (1994), 'Finnish Agriculture in 1993', *Agricultural Economics Research Institute, Research Publications* 73a, p. 61.

Kettunen, L. (1997), 'Finnish Agriculture in 1996', *Agricultural Economics Research Institute, Research Publications* 82a, p. 64.

Maatilahallitus (National Board of Finland) (1992), *EY-tietoa*, Helsinki, p. 8.

Malinen, P. (1993), 'A New State Policy for Diversifying Rural Areas', *University of Oulu, Research Institute of Northern Finland, Research Reports* 114, pp. 93-121.

Niemi, J. and Linjakumpu, H. (1996), 'Regional Structural Development of Finnish Agriculture until 2005', *Agricultural Economics Research Institute, Research Publications* 81, pp. 123-142.

OECD (1993), *What Future for our Countryside? A Rural Development Policy*, Paris, p. 80.

Palomäki, M. (1960), 'Post War Pioneering in Finland, with special reference to the role of the Settlement areas', *Fennia* 84, pp. 43-96.

Rusanen, J., Naukkarinen, A., Colpaert, A. and Muilu T. (1997), 'Differences in the spatial structure of the population between Finland and Sweden in 1995 – a GIS viewpoint', *Statistics Finland, Research Reports* 221, p. 46.

Smeds, H. (1963), 'Förändringar i Finlands jordbruksgeografi under efterkrigstiden', *Nordenskiöld-samfundets tidskrift* 23, pp. 3-31.

Uusitalo, E. (1994), *Maaseutupolitiikan keinot, Elinkeinojen edistäminen maaseudun kehittäjäyhteisöissä*, Jyväskylä, p. 269.

Yearbook of Farm Statistics 1997, National Board of Agriculture, Helsinki.

9 The Tuscany observatory of rural society development:
A policy tool against spatial and information marginalization

MARIA ANDREOLI, FRANCESCO DI IACOVO, HEIKKI JUSSILA
AND VITTORIO TELLARINI

Introduction

This paper aims to demonstrate how an initiative based on network approach is able to cope with the problems of rapidly changing space of economic and rural development. The paper introduces a method for rural development based òn innovation development approach that incorporates a network approach toward regional development.

The structure of the paper is the following. At first, some of the concepts behind the idea of the Observatory for rural development are presented. Secondly the paper discusses the role of the Observatory for integrating different aspects of rural and economic development, and provides an analysis of the ability, readiness and capacity of the authorities and organisations to promote innovative rural development methods. Thirdly, a discussion of the spatial dimensions and aspects of the 'rural reality' of Tuscany with a special emphasis on some of the (experimental) regions of the Observatory is presented. However, the Observatory for rural development does not only deal with special areas, but it encompasses the entire whole of 'the rural society'.[1] This in turn makes it possible to analyse the ability of developers with different 'backgrounds' to communicate between each other (between regions) and with authorities.

Methodology and theory

The idea of the Observatory for rural development embeds inside a second idea of network economy and network theory. From the methodological point of view, this Observatory can be regarded as both 'an observer' and an 'active participator'. The double role of the Observatory does not have an equivalent in the literature dealing with the 'network economy' or the 'network approach' toward regional, economic and social development. However, from the theoretical point of view the ideas put forward by regional economists about co-operation (e.g., Cappellin, 1992; Snickars, 1989) give basis for the analysis of the Observatory and its role.

From a methodological point of view this paper aims to describe the ideas of rural development and the need to increase the awareness of the role played by communication of the methods of rural development. This approach is similar to the one used by small firms when building either spatial and/or economic co-operation (e.g., Vatne, 1990).

The general methodological approach within the Observatory is to integrate economically oriented and based development with social or 'the human aspect' of regional development. In this sense the Observatory's work approach and the theoretical methodology in spatial sense are close to that presented by Brown already in 1981 about the development approach of innovation diffusion.

About rural development in Tuscany – a short description

One of the main features to be taken into account when analyzing Tuscany situation is that of distribution of population, which is shown in Figure 9.1. It does show that population has concentrated, on the more fertile lowlands along the coast and on the axis drawn by the Arno River. From Figure 9.1 it is possible to see the higher concentration of inhabitants in the municipalities that are capitals of the provinces. In summary, the most populated areas are the ones of Versilia coast, Livorno[2] municipality and the territories between Florence and Prato, the newest province capital of Tuscany.

In this paper, we have also made an attempt at mapping rural and urban areas in Tuscany. There are several problems that face this attempt; the most fundamental of which is that of 'changes in time'. While it is possible to construct an index of rurality, this usually is 'time-specific', since features of rural and urban areas evolve in the time, as it is changing in the time data availability. Two other main reasons make it not an easy task:

1) There does not exist a 'universally accepted' definition of what is urban and what is rural, especially in an area as densely populated as Tuscany where already 15-20 years ago researchers were speaking about 'urbanised countryside'. Besides, some researchers put the stress more on economic features of rurality, while others emphasise cultural aspects;

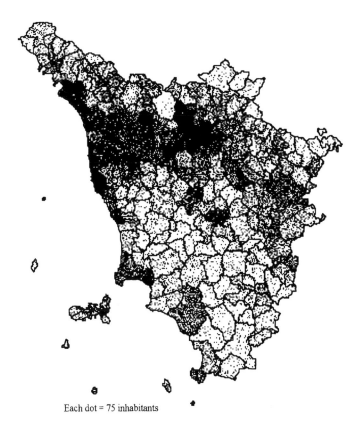

Each dot = 75 inhabitants

Figure 9.1   The density of population in Tuscany in 1996

2) Also in the case that a 'definition' of rurality and urbanity does exist, it is not always possible to find data for measuring and mapping it, especially if this definition includes cultural and other similar features that are not easily 'measurable'.

The attempt to map the urban and rural areas in Tuscany has been based on the following set of variables:

Var1) density of population 1996,
Var2) population living in built-up areas [3] in 1991
Var3) value of real estate in 1996, in Billions of ITL/sq. km
Var4) percentage of agriculture and forestry land 1990 on total surface 1991,

Var5) percentage in agriculture of total active population under 55 years in 1991,

Var6) 'farms 1990 - families 1991' ratio, and

Var7) percentage higher educated on population above 24 years in 1991.

The above variables were not supposed to be describing urbanity/rurality per se, but to be linked to their manifestation. They have been used for performing a Principal Component Analysis (PCA) and the first factor resulting from it has been taken as a 'proxy of rurality/urbanity' in Tuscany municipalities. Table 9.1 shows the correlation between variables and between variables and the first factor, which is accounting for 51% of the total variance. The first unrotated factor has been mapped in Figure 9.2.

Table 9.1   Correlation between variables and the first unrotated factor resulting from PCA

	Var1	Var2	Var3	Var4	Var5	Var6	Var7	1 Factor
Var1	1.000							0.807
Var2	0.440	1.000						0.738
Var3	0.910	0.380	1.000					0.767
Var4	-0.316	-0.276	-0.339	1.000				-0.476
Var5	-0.378	-0.540	-0.296	0.321	1.000			-0.707
Var6	-0.433	-0.600	-0.369	0.248	0.572	1.000		-0.765
Var7	0.439	0.406	0.446	-0.131	-0.435	-0.538	1.000	0.691

While Figure 9.2 shows our attempt to map the urban/rural continuum of Tuscany, Figure 9.3 shows the area covered by the 10 Local Action Groups (LAGs) created under LEADER II. This area is not exactly corresponding to Objective 5b area since several municipalities excluded (or only partly included) in 5b Objective have been included in LAGs' areas. This should be kept in mind when examining the main features of Tuscany LAGs, shown in Table 9.2. A particular emphasis is given to demographic characteristics of LAGs, which are compared with those of Setteponti, with those of the rest of Tuscany and with the average score for the whole Region. Setteponti is a rural area chosen as one of the case studies by the Observatory and it is partly included in the LAG of Appennino Aretino.

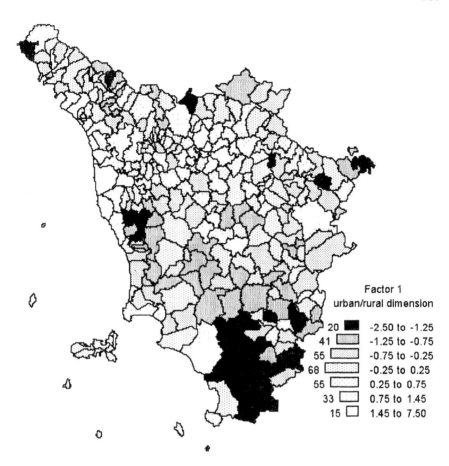

Figure 9.2   An image of the continuum of 'rural-urban' Tuscany

From Table 9.2 it is possible to see that while all the areas currently included in LAGs suffered a strong out-migration during the 1950s and 1960s (-11.77%) and even stronger in Setteponti (-21.94%), the rest of Tuscany experienced a strong increase (21.45%).

Afterward the trend slowed down, and in the 1970s and 1980s the total rate of out-migration from all LAGs was only -0.41%. In the so-called 'rest of Tuscany', too, the immigration/growth rate slowed down being only about 2.36%. The situation was the opposite during the early 1990s, when LAGs areas showed an increase of population (+0.82) while the 'rest

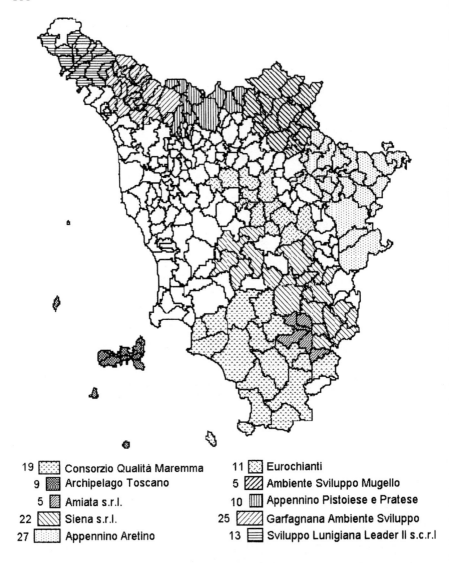

19		Consorzio Qualità Maremma
9		Archipelago Toscano
5		Amiata s.r.l.
22		Siena s.r.l.
27		Appennino Aretino

11		Eurochianti
5		Ambiente Sviluppo Mugello
10		Appennino Pistoiese e Pratese
25		Garfagnana Ambiente Sviluppo
13		Sviluppo Lunigiana Leader II s.c.r.l

Figure 9.3   Areas of LEADER II Local Action Groups in Tuscany

of Tuscany' had a decreasing population (-0.55%). It is important to note that, while the first two rates refer to a 20-year period, the last one refers only to a five-year period.

A more careful analysis of the Table 9.2 could highlight the strong difference in situation and trends existing among the ten LEADER II Tuscany LAGs. It is important to notice that the economic features (e.g. rate of unemployment, but also per capita income) could be affected by the population age structure (unemployment tends to be lower when elderly people make a large share of the population).

Table 9.2   Main features of Local Action Group areas and the area of Setteponti compared with the rest of Tuscany

C o d e*	Area km² 1996	In- habitan ts 1996 (000)	Den- sity Inhab./ km² 1996	Popu- lation change 1971/ 1951 (%)	Popu- lation change 1991/ 1971 (%)	Popu- lation change 1996/ 1991 (%)	100 Young/ Elderly in 1996	Unem- ploy- ment in 1991 (%)	High edu- cation >24 years (%)	Per capita income in 1993 € ***
1)**	3,513	164.9	46.95	5.32	0.53	1.04	52.97	13.07	25.93	10,497.64
2)	266	30.3	114.30	-5.81	1.39	6.38	63.51	17.17	23.27	11,481.82
3)	338	14.3	42.19	-24.05	-17.53	-2.98	31.94	11.88	23.54	9,942.41
4)	2,361	81.1	34.34	-26.82	-3.18	0.40	43.54	8.75	21.89	10,769.78
5)	2,506	215.0	85.78	-8.78	2.70	0.56	58.52	8.45	29.76	11,964.70
6)	1,209	89.2	73.83	-18.06	7.54	4.11	61.73	7.34	22.66	10,991.44
7)	1,562	97.2	62.26	-22.82	11.06	2.54	61.70	9.31	23.33	10,692.93
8)	805	128.9	160.23	2.74	-7.30	-1.07	48.62	10.13	26.73	12,044.32
9)	1,133	82.5	72.87	-16.53	-8.32	-1.60	52.50	14.43	19.52	10,011.20
10)	792	48.5	61.24	-26.51	-6.59	-0.17	37.61	12.39	23.01	9,738.04
11)	14,483	952.0	65.73	-11.70	-0.50	0.83	53.14	10.44	25.15	11,067.99
12)	278	28.6	103.01	-21.94	15.98	5.48	68.39	9.30	20.15	10,744.94
13)	8,405	2,558.6	304.43	21.47	2.40	-0.55	55.82	11.57	30.53	11,655.47
14)	22,997	3524.7	153.27	9.95	1.64	-0.17	55.08	11.27	29.04	11,493.52

*   1=Consorzio Qualità Maremma, 2=Arcipelago Toscano, 3=Amiata S.r.l., 4=Siena S.r.l., 5=Appennino Aretino, 6=Eurochianti, 7=Ambiente Sviluppo Mugello, 8=Appennino Pistoiese e Pratese, 9=Garfagnana Ambiente Sviluppo, 10=Sviluppo Lunigiana Leader II s.c.r.l.., 11=Total of 10 LAGs, 12=Setteponti, 13=Rest of Tuscany, 14=Tuscany total/average.

**   In 1999 the regional composition of the Local Action Groups of Consorzio Qualità Maremma (1), Appennino Aretino (5) and Sviluppo Lunigiana Leader II s.c.r.l (10) has been changed. However, the information given in the table – and in the whole article – refers to the situation as it was in August 1998.

***   The official irrevocable transfer rate (31.12.1999) to ITL from € is 1936.27.

110

Figure 9.4 shows how the active population was distributed among the main economic sectors in 1991.

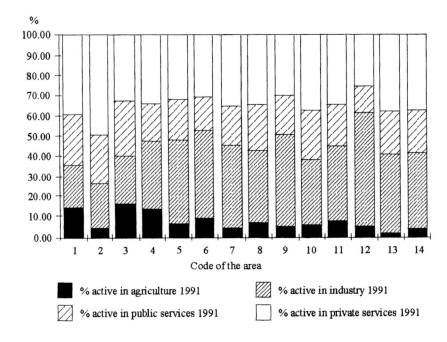

Figure 9.4 **Sectors of employment of the residents in Tuscany by LAGs (1 to 10), the average of LAGs (11), Setteponti (12), the rest of Tuscany (13) and Tuscany average (14)**

For additional information regarding names of LAGs see table 9.2

Source: Census of Population, 1991.

A new approach toward rural development: An Observatory-network

The experiences obtained during LEADER programme regarding the top-down and bottom-up approaches to local development have influenced rural development actions. These programmes were initiating many new approaches for rural development. Especially the emphasis put on networking and co-operation between people, enterprises and local communities have provided valuable information for the issue of rural development today.

The first LEADER era has caused changes in rural development. Due to this programme the questions and actions for developing entrepreneurial activities in rural areas are under an active development, although the 'traditional subsidising' of entrepreneurial activities in least favoured regions still has importance in some regions. This change in the scope of 'development' has meant that especially small firm and small enterprises are seen as essential factors for development. It is this which has changed the images and visions of development and marginalization both in the 'centre' and in the 'rural regions' (e.g., Oksa and Rannikko, 1996; Sommers and Mehretu, 1996; Susiluoma, 1996).

The Observatory-network approach

When economic development in rural regions was seen as being a part of the 'global' economic development progress, there was no apparent need to create special policies for rural regions. The general regional policy measures, which had the aim to alleviate regional disparities, were often deemed to be enough. However, the industries and services within traditional core regions where not able to diffuse their wealth and development potential to the most distant regions and consequently regions depending heavily on rural occupations started to suffer. The reason for this was, and is, the issue of accessibility. This refers to the ease with which people are capable to obtain (i.e. gain access to) goods and services that they desire (e.g., Robinson, 1992).

Since the European Union policies for the general regional development did not have enough effect on rural regions it was imperative to look for new types of development approaches. This asked for better knowledge and understanding of rural economic and social development. It was not anymore enough just to describe general trends of rural development, e.g., rural decline. It became evident that a closer and more active approach for revitalising rural regions was necessary (see, e.g., CEMAT, 1992). This need has been the catalyst for creating various bodies, which have the aim to promote rural development and to advance the understanding of rural regions.

It is in this light that the initiative put forward by the Tuscany Agency for Development and Innovation in Agriculture and Forestry (ARSIA) about the creation of an 'Observatory' for rural development in Tuscany needs to be viewed. The agency is mostly interested in innovation and innovation diffusion on rural regions, and, consequently, the development of an 'Observatory' for rural society was not enough. The main emphasis was on the innovative methodological aspects underlining the construction and functions of the Observatory. Thus, at the end of 1996, ARSIA issued an open competition to present projects for the methodology and implementation of an observatory for Tuscany rural society and for the actions and activities able to promote its development (B.U.R.T., 1996).

The project presented by the Department of Agricultural Economics of the University of Pisa won this 'competition', and it proposed to implement an Observatory-network for the rural society in Tuscany (Di Iacovo *et al.*, 1997). The reasons for the decision to implement such an Observatory-network were the following:

- To provide a tool for improving the visibility of the actions, the attitudes and capacity for making projects, and the ongoing dynamics in the rural areas of Tuscany.
- To individuate the activities and the competencies of the subjects who operate in the rural society; to implement informative supports and connections between the various regional, national and international rural 'realities', trying to make activities and competencies to circulate and to activate them in a synergetic way.
- To implement a structure through which subjects could converse, coordinate their requirements, increase the critical mass and the quality of the initiatives that will be set up in the Tuscany rural society. This asks for actions of social and economic animation for rural areas in Tuscany.

An Observatory is usually a (privileged) point of observation of a certain phenomenon. In the case of development of rural society, an Observatory-network should:

1. Be an element capable to catalyze participation (stimulation of collaborations) and the exchange of knowledge and experience, which is the network logic;
2. Support and channel development and co-operation activities among actors and areas.

This with the aim at:

a) Acting as a starter of co-operative activities;
b) Increasing outside visibility (inside each area and among areas);
c) Increasing the weight inside the EU.

Since the focus is not any longer on the farm but on the area, it is necessary to adopt a consistent development logic. Thus, it is necessary to pass from a farm system logic, which has vertical and (substantially) hierarchical relationships, to a network logic of spatial development, which has horizontal and (substantially) more 'equal' relationships. The use of network logic of development and communication makes it possible to manage clear relationships, to improve exchange flows and to amplify the effect of development actions.

The second reason for network logic is that information technologies might provide tools (and competence and a new cultural approach) that enable to bridge the (traditional) physical and cultural barriers to communication. Barriers that even today are present and that represent a serious element of hindrance for development within disadvantaged local systems (e.g., Andreoli and Gouérec, 1996).

The Observatory-network: Structure and functions

The Observatory includes four 'structures' (for more information about the Observatory, see http://www.osservatorio.arsia.toscana.it/index.html/):

1) Research structure, whose members are researchers from several Italian Universities (Pisa, Florence, Campobasso, Perugia and Trento) besides foreign partners from Finland, France, and Republic of Ireland;
2) Concerting structure, whose members are - besides the responsible of the project - Tuscany Region, ARSIA, the Italian Institute of Agricultural Economics (INEA), representatives from the main professional organizations of farmers and from the 'case-study' areas;
3) Experimental structure, based on three 'case-study' areas; 1) a LEADER area, 2) natural park and 3) a rural area that is partly excluded from objective 1, 2 or 5b areas; and
4) Technical support system provided by the Department of Computing and Information Science of the University of Pisa.

The research structure, with its articulate and interdisciplinary composition, constitutes the 'engine' of the project, although it is supposed to confront dialectically with the concerting body and with the experimental structure. While adjusting the methodology and during the actual implementation (experimentation) of the Observatory, the research structure will have:

- to specify the information to be gathered for the analysis;
- to evaluate the indications provided by the bodies of concertation and by the experimental structure;
- to indicate the contents to be assigned to the network;
- to verify the attainment of the pre set objectives.

The concerting body represents the 'practical' approach toward rural development and it aims:

- to interact with the research structure in order to provide operative indications for steering the project,
- to contribute to make the Observatory as capable as possible to understand the complexity of the phenomena that will be monitored and evaluated, and
- to act as a 'strap of transmission' with the specific territorial realities, contributing to transmit to the local level the suggestions agreed at the level of concertation body.

The structure of technical support has the task:

- to analyze and to face the technical problems of implementing a network spread over the territory,
- to implement the network, and
- to train the staff who will be involved in the operation of the network.

The experimentation structure constitutes a 'field laboratory' in which the methodologies individuated during the research will be experimented. The following three areas of: Garfagnana (Comunità Montana totally included in 5b areas), Setteponti area (rural area partly excluded from objective 5b, 1 and 2 areas) and Parco di Migliarino (protected area) form the so-called 'field laboratory'.

First results – the networking point of view

Developing a network based on co-operation does not always bring results as fast as people expect. The case of the rural Observatory for Tuscany proves this point quite clearly. A network idea needs to develop and foster a culture of openness, co-operation and mutual assistance and besides 'human cultural issues' there is a need to develop a 'technical' culture that gives the necessary infrastructure for the work. This asks for some fundamental changes in the way people work.

During the initial stages of the Observatory the regulations regarding rural development financing were partly open and partly under the decision process. This meant that, 'leaders and/or directors' of the LAGs and other rural development agencies were waiting. In order to fill the 'gap' created by the institutional delays and to try to provide 'first hand' information a series of seminars (whose list could be found on the web site of the Observatory) were organized by the Front-Office of the Observatory.

These seminars were the starting point for building a functional network of people interested on a common agenda. The typescripts of the speeches of the seminars and of the following debates have been sent to all the LAGs, for improving the effectiveness and usefulness of the seminars and for trying to involve those who have not participated.

These seminars served also as a first step for building the Observatory-network. Initially, it was thought to use the Internet instead of seminars, etc., to disseminate 'first-hand' information. However, at the beginning only one LAG was connected and used Internet services, and consequently one needed more traditional ways for building networks, e.g., fax and telephone. The process of network-building has proceeded relatively well, since there has been a willingness to make everybody to share the knowledge by putting both questions and answers on the 'net'. However, due to the above-mentioned difficulty from the side of the LAGs to access telematic services, the Observatory has used a 'newsletter' for spreading information.

Perhaps from the network-infrastructure point of view and from the dissemination point of view the most concrete result has been the construction of a WWW-site: http://www.osservatorio.arsia.toscana.it (see Authors note) This site has been developed as the channel for information dissemination regarding rural development in Tuscany. This site is promoting the Observatory, but it also gives space and access links to the case study areas (Garfagnana, 'Parco Naturale di Migliarino' and Setteponti) as well as to various other information sources. The WWW-site is thus used not only for making rural areas more 'visible' from outside, but it aims to promote the experiences of rural development among other LAGs in Tuscany and outside.

The Observatory has used Garfagnana as a 'pilot' area, since it was the first LAG to have an Internet connection and an already started programme for the implementation of a 'telematique pole' for the region (Andreoli and Jussila, 1998). Since all the other LAGs have the implementation of telematic projects in their Local Action Plans (LAP) and the Observatory is guaranteeing them space and technical assistance for home page development, there is the hope that other LAGs would decide to exploit this opportunity.

Problems of network approach

The network approach towards rural development, especially in the form of an Observatory-network, which is aiming to be an active partner in rural development, is not an easy task. When this idea of the network approach was at first put forward most of those responsible for rural development welcomed this idea. It was seen as a method to stimulate common actions and common 'spirit' for rural development.

The problems that have been met when building and developing the network 'philosophy' can be divided into three groups. These groups are:

1. Technical problems when constructing network connections,
2. Institutional problems due to the different level of experience, ability and available resources, and
3. The 'human' dimension problem for co-operation.

The questions dealing with the 'technical' possibilities of the LAGs to develop networking capabilities were to a large extent 'out of the hands' of the Observatory-network, since the LAGs had to use their financial resources for buying the required hardware and software. These financial resources were available very much later than the starting of the Observatory and not always there existed the ability and the willingness or the capabilities to use them immediately for this purpose. The Observatory, too, had resource availability problems and consequently at the beginning the WWW-site was hosted by the Department of Computing and Information Science, which was one of the Observatory partners. This was, however, a temporary solution, and currently ARSIA, the Observatory promoter has taken care of the Observatory's WEB-site on its own server. This move was also necessary for data security and 'look and feel' requirements of the site.

The second set of problems stemming from the institutional setting of the LAGs is equally important. The fact that some LAGs had previous work knowledge about rural development under LEADER I gave them a head start in the process. Secondly, other LAGs had more financial, human and other resources available when the work started. This comes evident when going through the various documents of questions that the LAGs have channelled through the Observatory. Also the fact that some LAGs did not put any question at all shows that some groups did not have a focused plan on how their work should be organized.

These two sets of advantages over the other Local Action Groups make it difficult to work on equal bases and discuss about problems on an equal footing. It is probable, although not certain, that these types of differences might hinder the work of an Observatory based on an idea of a network. This is due to the theoretical fact that at some point 'partners' should have an equally based interest and willingness for working together. Thus, the institutional setting in the case of Tuscany could be an obstacle to this kind of network development.

From institutional point of view it is important to note that the passage from LEADER I regulations to those of LEADER II has some important and fundamental implications for networking. The fact European Union structural funding (also those included in LEADER II) are under the rules agreed by the Italian Government and the Commission can create problems. Currently the agreement between Italy and European Union says that by the end of 1998 55% of structural policy funding needs to be 'committed'. The programmes that have not met this target are then under 'a remodification' of the financial resources. The aim of this 'remodification' is to increase the effectiveness of the usage of the available funds (see INEA-MiPA, 1998, pp. 105-107). This approach towards the use of funds may lead to a more effective and 'higher quality' use of the money provided by the Community. Nevertheless, at the same time, it may hamper the development aims, because regions might not any more be on an equal footing due to this possibility of remodification of disposable resources. Consequently, it is possible that regions that do not meet the 'standards' could have fewer resources than others could, and so the programme would be creating disparities between regions instead of bridging them. It is in this scenario that a 'beggar thy neighbour' strategy could become a successful one, and make harder to create the culture of co-operation that a network approach asks for.

The human dimension aspect of co-operation is closely linked with the institutional question about the possibilities of co-operation between LAGs. This factor is in many network studies (e.g., Lundqvist and Persson, 1990) found to be an important (see Jussila and Tykkyläinen, 1990), but often forgotten 'variable', especially in the regional economic development. The studies on business co-operation, however, frequently stress the importance of the 'human' aspect for successful co-operative networks (e.g., Vatne, 1990; NordREFO, 1994).

The co-operative nature of the Observatory-network does require that people responsible for the day-to-day affairs of the LAGs do co-operate with each other. At this point it is, however, not possible to estimate issues of 'personal' relationships. However, the fact that some of the LAGs' leaders have been working much longer than others can be seen as a positive aspect for the network. It is a positive aspect when these people are willing to share previously acquired information and knowledge. It is in this connection that the roles of the Observatory and of the Front Office are important. To disseminate all available information obtained means that all LAGs would be on the same level of information, although the availability of the information does not guarantee that it will be used. However, the Front Office and the Observatory do have made an effort to provide a 'user-friendly' interface for the information.

The future of networked co-operation

At the time of this writing the Observatory-network has been operational for 13 months. Although this could seem quite a long time, it is not enough for giving an in-depth evaluation on the Observatory's achievements. This because the idea of the Observatory, when proposed, was new and in many ways 'unclear', and, consequently, this idea has evolved during this time.

However, this process of observing with 'an active' touch is a very positive attempt to create co-operation and to revitalize and re-activate the economies of rural areas in Tuscany. The fact that many different types of areas have been included into the programme of research and active intervention, does suggest that this type of approach is fruitful in attracting and encouraging new kind of actions for rural development. However, at the same time one should remember that very often new things create resistance of some sort, and, consequently, this idea of a network might produce some resistance. In order to avoid this, the Observatory-network has been built with an 'open door' approach that should guarantee that all those that are participating feel that there is an advantage in being 'networked'.

Rural regions are in many cases quite conservative and thus there is a resistance to accept new modes of work and methods of co-operation. When glancing through the literature about how 'eagerly' rural regions have been changing their development methods or attitudes, one usually quite often finds statements like the following 'a true Garfagnino checks and double checks before committing himself to a new thing' (see Andreoli and Gouérec, 1996). However, this 'statement' has been proved very wrong as Garfagnana is perhaps the most active of the regions involved. This, however, after very difficult times during the 1950s through the 1970s, when all indices showing the capacity of development were on 'red'. People there do remember and do not want to go back to that, and consequently, the case of Garfagnana proves an other important issue, i.e., only those in the region can turn the tide (e.g. Andreoli and Jussila, 1998; Jussila and Tykkyläinen, 1990).

The Tuscany Observatory for rural development is aiming to create a 'culture' of co-operation and mutual assistance, which in turn will prevent the emergence of new problems. The process of learning networked co-operation on the 'root-level' has only started, and there is a long and probably 'bumpy' road ahead. The lessons of the first round of rural development under the Objective 5b and LEADER programmes, however, do support the hypothesis that 'networking' is the future method of rural and regional development. In this respect the Observatory for Rural Society in Tuscany is probably proving to be a fruitful and innovative approach for development. As the urban system is building increasingly complex systems of networks, it is imperative that also the rural regions use the 'modern' methods of networking when promoting the development of these areas, whether the 'development' is economic, social or cultural by its nature.

Authors' note

At the end of December 1999 ARSIA took the direct operative responsibility of the Observatory and its Web-site (http://www.osservatorio.arsia.toscana.it). The server experienced a major disk crash around the change of the millennium, and up until now (August 2000) the server has been down and the URL of the observatory does not respond.

Notes

1 The Italian word 'mondo rurale' has been translated with the significance equal to the concept of 'rural society'.
2 The English name for Livorno is Leghorn.
3 For more information see Census of Population 1991.

References

Andreoli, M. and Gouérec, N. (1996), 'Tradition and modernization in the agricultural development of a Tuscany (Central Italy) marginal area: The role of advisory and extension services', in R.B. Singh and R. Majoral (eds), *Development issues in marginal regions – processes, technological developments and societal reorganizations*, Oxford & IBH Publishing Co. PVT. LTD, New Delhi, pp. 193-209.
Andreoli, M. and Jussila, H. (1999), 'Marginal regions and new methods for development in the EU: Comparing Garfagnana in Italy and Koillismaa - Kuusamo in Finland', in H. Jussila, R. Majoral, and C. Mutambirwa (eds), *Marginality in Space — Past, Present and Future: Theoretical and methodological aspects of cultural, social and economic parameters of marginal and critical regions*, Aldershot, Ashgate, pp. 205-226.
Brown, L.A. (1981), *Innovation Diffusion – A new perspective*, Methuen, New York, p. 345.
B.U.R.T. (Bollettino Ufficiale Regione Toscana) (1996), *Metodologie e costruzione sperimentale di un osservatorio sull'evoluzione delle necessità del mondo rurale Toscano e delle attività e degli interventi atti a promuoverne lo sviluppo*, Firenze.

120

Cappellin, R. (1992), 'Theories of local endogenous development and international cooperation', in M. Tykkyläinen (ed.), *Development issues and strategies in the new Europe*, Avebury, Aldershot, pp. 1-20.

CEMAT (1992), *European Regional Planning Strategy*, Council of Europe, Publishing and Documentation Service, Strasbourg.

Di Iacovo, F., Francesconi, L., Tellarini, V. and Ulivieri, E. (1997), Paper presented at an international meeting of the European Network for Information Technology in Agriculture (EUNITA), http//www.inea.it/eventi/workshen.htm.

INEA - MiPA (1998), *Le politiche strutturali e di sviluppo rurale in Italia: Analisi della spesa e problemi di attuazione nel quadriennio 94/97*, Osservatorio sulle politiche strutturali, Roma, pp. 109.

Jussila, H. and Tykkyläinen, M. (1990), 'Periferins framtid - nya vägar behövs de?', in L. Lundqvist and L.O. Persson (eds), *Nätverk i Norden*, Industridepartementet – ERU, Ds 1990/78, pp. 237-258.

Lundqvist, L. and Persson, L.O. (eds) (1990), *Nätverk i Norden*, Industridepartementet – ERU, Ds 1990/78.

NordREFO (1994), *Småföretagens internationalisering – en nordisk jämförande studie*, NordREFO 1994:7, p. 224.

Oksa, J. and Rannikko, P. (1996), 'The changing meanings of rurality challenge rural policies', *Finnish Journal of Rural Research and Policy*, English supplement, vol. 3, pp. 3-14.

Robinson, G.M. (1992), *Conflict and change in the countryside*, 2nd edition, Belhaven Press, London, p. 482.

Snickars, F. (1989), 'On cores and peripheries in the network economy', *NordREFO* 1989:3, pp. 23-35.

Sommers, L.M. and Mehretu, A. (1996), 'Micro-marginality in Michigan: Recent patterns and trends', in R.B. Singh, and R. Majoral (eds.), *Development issues in marginal regions – processes, technological developments and societal reorganizations*, Oxford & IBH Publishing Co. PVT. LTD, New Delhi, pp. 233-239.

Susiluoma, H. (1996), 'The immaterial somersault: a covenant between reason and emotion', *Finnish Journal of Rural Research and Policy*, English supplement, vol. 3, pp. 158-164.

Vatne, E. (1990), 'Hvorfor er nettverk mellom foretak viktig ogh vilke implikasjoner kan dette ha for den regional utvikling', in L. Lundqvist and L.O. Persson (eds), *Nätverk i Norden*, Industridepartementet – ERU, Ds 1990/78, pp. 15-26.

Acknowledgements

This research has been funded under the University of Pisa's project for the implementation of the Tuscany Observatory for rural society, promoted by ARSIA.

10 The deep rural context and micro-regional changes in Southern Portugal

LUÍS MORENO

Introduction

The Algarve region, Southern Portugal, has some of the common history of other regions under gifted about power to make a fair control of their resources through public policies with regional/local basis. The consequences were out-migration and relative deprivation in human resources, which has the greatest evidence in the rough upcountry: the Caldeirão mountains, known as 'Serra do Caldeirão'. However, not only the Algarve has particular regional features that change any presumable 'poor destiny' but also the overall context of decentralization since the seventies of 20th century did have an important role on the process of social and economic restructuring, which made people in the deep rural mountainous upcountry areas the 'target' of a continuing dynamics of social and territorial intervention directed to the furtherance of the endogenous potentials, in the pursuit of the strengthening of a self territorial identity.

On the one hand, this paper is intended to present just a diachronic synthesis of this somewhat complex process, linking the distant and the recent past to provide the understanding of the context of human agency for rural development of Algarve inland at the present time. On the other hand, there is an attempt to perspective the positive and perverse outcomes of that agency, with unequal expression, due to interest conflicts between: 1) the goals of the project which has a perspective of 'integrated rural development' or 'local development' and (up to what extent?) environmental protection; 2) the goals of 'regional development', which imply both the territorial integration 'coastland - upcountry' and the achievements of private agents who operate sometimes in an intrusive way which calls in question local positive externalities.

121

The exposed purpose of this paper, dealing with an embracing subject, leave as the only option to direct the reader for larger works on which this is based (references).

Historical-structural conditions of the Portuguese internal disparities

Mainly until seventies, Portugal revealed the traces of a country strongly dependent of both external resources and centralist political conduction. Since the 15th century, the history of the Portuguese discoveries is also the construction of a process of progressive 'veneration' of external realities and relative neglect of domestic affairs, which was driven by the political power established in Lisbon. For this small country, with restricted natural conditions for intensive farming, in early times the political/cultural conditions made appear to be easier to get distant resources by trade or spoliation than to build a solid economy based on the factors of regional development. The practice of colonialism has extended both the dependence and the regional unbalance, but the international context has also supported the situation, as the country worked as an intermediate level in the process of unequal exchange after the Industrial Revolution. Indeed, placed in a (semi) peripheral position in the international division of labour, Portugal got more and more the main two coastal cities (Lisbon and Oporto) as the poles of both upcountry (and some colonial) resource drainage and concentration of opportunities for economic and social promotion. We may even add that Lisbon played the role of the only national centre of political power and the only producer of structuring decisions (macrocephaly).

The situation above is consistent with a cultural feature that we may link with the prevailing functionalist paradigm in the context of democratic deficit and low educational levels: until the *coup d'état* in 1974 the centralism maintained the myth of superiority of urban-centred and formalist values, which was accepted as the use of elitist and diffusionist procedures controlled social life and kept several relations of dependence.

The macrocephaly and the international capitalist relations made also propitious a paternalistic State that was suitable to keep both the low wages and the 'social peace', elements of a strategy of successful 'outward directed industrialization' mainly shaped by the 'labour intensive' feature (Murteira, 1979).

This overall context allows us to point out the following articulated conditions of regional underdevelopment. At different scales of territorial insertion, the dependence is related to the exercise of a deficient and top-down planning, poor structuring public investment, weakness and unevenness on the distribution of infrastructures and equipment to support activities, poor empowerment (from individual to social), social, economic and territorial exclusion, poor fitting of external products and/or solutions to the real conditions, poor productivity and a feeble economy.

The case of Algarve: From fifties to seventies

As a region framed in the national context but in a higher level in relation to the 'subregion' of Serra do Caldeirão (Figure 10.1), the situation of Algarve is worth to outline, in evolutive terms, because it is an intermediate step to explain the development of the regional unbalance that lays the mountains in a marginal position.

In the fifties, the seashore of Algarve is 'discovered' by some English tourists (Cavaco, 1983). As the environment was agreeable, related with the light sand, clear sea waters, warm air and the increasing fashion of tanning the skin at the seaside in summer, the tourism has increased enormously until the beginning of the seventies, making 1955-72 the 'golden age' of mass tourism (Lewis and Williams, 1988).

Thus, in the sixties the 'coastal Algarve' is the target of a selective investment: exploitation of the resource sun/sea for tourist purposes. Meanwhile, the only public investment worthy of note is the Faro airport (1965) and some subsidies for hotel construction. Notwithstanding, this is enough to allow immediate high economic profits in the private sector, giving the tourism sector an advantageous position in intersectorial competition. So, the seashore – with increasing concentration of unimodal tourism enclaves – and the coastal urban tissue gain a 'sucking effect' and it became very difficult to allocate resources (time, space, workmanship) for other activities. The poor industry further declines, the agriculture, already with a legacy of serious structural problems, loses competitiveness (selective losses in the regional economic tissue) and there is a relative public and private disinvestment in the upcountry, causing a strong demographic loss there (Moreno, 1996).

In the early seventies, this 'picture' of Algarve shows a double polarization: temporal (seasonal) and spatial. About this latter, as any researcher about planning knows, the demographic amount is mostly the essential criterion for the allocation of public services and equipment. However, within

124

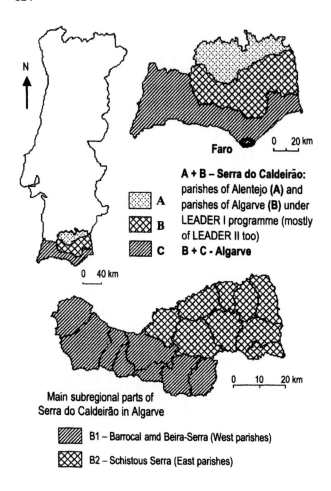

A + B – Serra do Caldeirão:
parishes of Alentejo **(A)** and
parishes of Algarve **(B)** under
LEADER I programme (mostly
of LEADER II too)

B + C - Algarve

Main subregional parts of
Serra do Caldeirão in Algarve

B1 – Barrocal amd Beira-Serra (West parishes)

B2 – Schistous Serra (East parishes)

Figure 10.1   LEADER I zone of 'Serra do Caldeirão' in Portugal and sub-regional parts in Algarve

these public fields there was a considerable lack of means to restrain the deep environmental stress, among other right measures of country planning. So, cities grew disorderly and dispersed houses appeared here and there (most for seasonal use), even in sensitive areas of the coast. In the rough inland, the relative lack of both endogenous high-profit means and public investment induced lasting and seasonal emigration, ageing and the acceleration of environmental degradation. This latter had origins on serious mistakes about the inadequate agricultural use of thin schistous land (a past political campaign to produce wheat almost everywhere), instead of the practice of a combination of forestry, pasture and agriculture, appropriate to the Mediterranean mountainous environment (Guerreiro, 1977; 1987).

The broad context of rural development in the inland of Algarve

The crisis of 1970's and the beginnings of democracy

In Portugal the 1970's, economic crisis had mixed its consequences with the changing of political regime. Indeed, in the context of the building of the democracy, since 1974, the economy was weakened, due mainly to: 1) big dependence from oil, which became much more expensive; 2) escaping of some capital; 3) the loss of the advantageous colonial trade; 4) the influx of returnees from colonies, with little economic means; 5) high economic costs of the social instability, wage and (retiring) pension rising and shortening of the working hours (Lopes, 1996).

Besides the national problems, in the Algarve we must add the negative effect of international crisis, which had deeply reduced the afflux of tourists.

In the democratic context, the solutions to escape from the deepest consequences of crisis implied the extended opening to foreign influences. From these, we may put in relief the EEC countries, and the request Portugal made in 1977 to be a member of European Community has to do with it. The functional and organic decentralization processes Portugal selected were no more than the following of similar procedures already taken in other European countries, an effort for administrative reform and higher efficiency suitable to receive resulting help in order, in turn, to a successful integration in EC.

The decentralization as the dawning of rural development processes

As suggested before, the functional and organic decentralization was measures induced by the EC integration process (1977-1986, period of adjustments until the statute of full EC member). The former consisted of the implement in Algarve (as in other Portuguese regions) of the regional services of central government (deconcentration); the more relevant examples for our subject are: the Commission of Regional Co-ordination (CCR) and the Agriculture Regional Services (DRA). The 'organic decentralization' may be considered the genuine decentralization in the sense that it brought to the Algarve some power to get regional/local decisions; it concerns the municipalities and the university (UAL). However, while the former have got a Law of Local Finances to allow the assumption of all the new responsibilities in the opening of the eighties, the UAL only got an Autonomy Law in 1988. Nevertheless, it is a component of our next reasoning to illustrate that UAL had some power and autonomy before, in terms of potential to take part in the process of answering to social, economic and territorial needs.

In what concerns to the outcomes of local government, we can state at once the positive action in the promotion of the quality of life of rural population (Henriques, 1990; Costa *et al.*, 1993), though the role in the process of long term development (namely by the improvement of both employment and economic conditions) has only begun at the end of eighties and is still uneven (COSTA, 1993).

The Algarve University (UAL) came into the world in the end of 1970's but was still in installation process when some of its teachers and researchers collaborated with the CCR in the survey of the north-east of Algarve (schistous serra) to prepare the first Portuguese 'Integrated Programme of Regional Development', as EC-PIM's image. In fact, that upcountry area was recognized as one of the most neglected in the whole country, and some pioneer work was made in the scope of French-Portuguese co-operation. One of the UAL's teachers had experience of adult education in the context of United Nations (UNESCO), with acquaintances in several UN branches of different countries (mainly EC), which would be decisive for the dynamics further explained. Open-minded by the research in the scope of PIDR-NE studies, he created an educational university project in 1985: RADIAL (Network to Support the Integrated Development of Algarve). As an ambitious project, it was intended to practice 'education for development' with an Action Research methodology. Though it was supported by an institution whose funds were reserved for children aid (Bernard Van Leer Foundation), it was understood that children could only be properly aided if the whole of their social environment were improved. That's why RADIAL has begun with several ways to induce Integrated Rural Development (IRD) in the mountains, resorting to both fieldwork – to get permanent feedback from the families and communities – and partnerships – to engage different agents for specific works and resource allocations (Moreno, 1996).

Think globally, act locally: A lemma for a long-term project

From 1985 to 1988 the members of the RADIAL project managed to connect some resources and competencies of: a) the pertinent regional departments and services of central government (ex: Ministries of Labour, Education, Planning, Agriculture); b) municipalities; c) other agents, including teachers and pupils from the UAL. The results were: 1) the constitution of kindergartens (CAI), where children are under care of ladies who receive concomitant educational training; 2) self-employment of women (including those in the scope of Local Employment Initiatives - OECD), assisted by 'sandwich courses' of vocational training; thus women could hold down a more profitable work than poor farming, while children stay at CAIs. The bias towards women support has to do with a peculiarity in the Serra do Caldeirão: men are seldom there, except those who cannot (by any reason) get a job in the littoral or in other region or country, which makes generally the women the main real and potential agents to modify the local social and economic life, and also the group which can 'transmit' more easily to descendants the new induced values of self-respect and self-development.

The contextual failure of other former initiatives 'for rural development' made propitious the prolongation of RADIAL action. Indeed, the rural extension (since 1977) was a fiasco and the agricultural extension had serious limitations (Moreno, 1993); other instruments had no specifics for rural development; even the regional programmes (continuation of the logic embodied in the PIDR-NE), condition to get the co-partnership of the EC funds, are included in this latter limitation. However, the RADIAL project had insufficient budget to carry on its purposes and its legal statute implied little possibilities to get other resources. Therefore, in 1988 the members of RADIAL and some more persons established the 'Associação In Loco' (association for local development), which embodies the RADIAL and extends its action far beyond the 'educational' scope, adopting the lemma in title.

Rural and local development using LEADER programme

Since the In Loco association became much more than an university project, it got the possibility to stand as a candidate for several programmes (national and EC), which has been done in the course of time. As it was successful, the team enlarged (from 12 founders to 30 members in 1991) so that it presents different qualifications (people in the fields of psychology, sociology, geography, economy/management, law, informatics, local development, etc.).

The national and international contacts of In Loco's president were advantageous to access information, in order to reach EC funds (through programmes managed or participated by In Loco agents), making himself a good protagonist in the local, rural and even regional development.

The first big EC programme managed by In Loco with some structuring effects was the LEADER I (1991-93), through the 'local action plan' (PAL) called ARRISCA (acronym that means Support to Integrated Rural Reanimation of Serra do Caldeirão – Algarve/Alentejo; but it is also a Portuguese word meaning 'taking the chance'). The main distinctive feature of ARRISCA is its rely on the (home/field) work of agents (animators) which have the role of 'extended arms' of the central In Loco team, 'handling' the Serra social environment, but with the advantage of an autonomy only tempered by a multiple evaluation process (including self-evaluation), inherent to the Action Research methodology. The animators are young people who kept on living in Serra do Caldeirão and are paid and trained to mediate the process of IRD or local development.

During the ARRISCA, several actions were carried out to create a sustainable social and economic dynamics in the Serra do Caldeirão. The concerned fields may be grouped as: promotion of Serra's image and publications; realization of fairs ('Feiras da Serra'); promotion and betterment of 'home technology' and 'home-made products', including 'Farm Products'; Rural Tourism; implement and advancement of information and communication technologies; training for self-employment and development (Moreno, 1996).

The LEADER II programme, through the PAL ARRISCA II, followed the general methodology of its predecessor, in spite of several changes due to a new arrangement on the institutional mechanisms to allow bigger participation and control of decision-making by partners committed in different branches of agency, jointly in the Local Monitorship Commission (CLA). Anyhow, In Loco is inevitably the most influent part of CLA and its members' state that the great finality of LEADER is always to be an instrument to reach the empowerment at the individual and community level, as a process to encourage and improve the participation of people in social, cultural, economic and political dimensions of development. Of course, this includes the involvement in the processes of (local/country) planning (to feed the bottom-up component). While people don't show to be prepared, the animators themselves, but mainly the In Loco central team, have fulfilled that 'citizenship duty' through the (inter) Action Research, in contact with the local government and local/regional planning leaders, to solve problems from short to long term scope.

Participation on planning is well paid with multiple resources

Besides the resources allocated to LEADER (I and II) and to other EC programmes (NOW, HORIZON, etc.), the help for the social and economic improvement of inland after the PIDR-NE sure relied also on the resources from the Support Community Boards inherent to Regional Development Programmes 1986-89, 1989-93 and 1994-99. Particularly this latter has a separate item concerned to the local development (besides the recurrent 'rural'), revealing the previous results of lobbies on which we may include In Loco and *animar* (the national association for local development in rural areas, in which foundation and direction In Loco had/has a fundamental role). The same may be perceived if we read the main document of the great planning guidelines for the Algarve region (CCRAlg, 1993), where we can find for the first time the inclusion of the regional strategic thinking of In Loco's president, persuasive, putting the Serra as a subregion, so deserving particular attention.

As the In Loco has got a past and an advantageous curriculum about rural and local development in the mountains, this means specific competencies and all the contracts or partnerships with the different governmental departments, municipalities and other entities became normal and expected.

Positive outcomes and problems in the 'Serra do Caldeirão'

Despite most of In Loco activity have had the best overall results, on account of its 'comparative advantages' among the other potential agents that could eventually do a work for rural/local development in the Serra (unknown entities, besides local governments), some of the performance was restrained by the resistance of both a political leader and some more people whose interests were felt to be threatened. There are reasons to think that the untimely loss of mandate of the president of Alcoutim municipality (before the 1991's suffrage, due to some irregularities), giving place to an opponent from other party (open to IRD dynamics), was backed by some In Loco informal investigations (Moreno, 1996). Of course, some hindering never disappeared but took the form of (or was embodied in) cultural, political/ideological arguments.

The kind of obstacles suggested above is normal part of the agency for rural/local development and has some influence on some problems pointed out forward. However, it never hindered the main positive effects of In Loco agency in the Serra do Caldeirão (Moreno, 1996), first presented here as a summary:

- Creation of self-employment, closely followed by ongoing vocational training
- Increased access both to informatics and telematic equipment
- Improvement of the self-representation and strengthening of cultural identity (Serra Newspaper, Serra traditional songs, Serra agro-food ...)
- Transfer of responsibilities to local entities / agents (notably animators and local associations)
- Increasing of number and range of interactions / social intercourse among the people of Serra do Caldeirão, through the regularisation of Serra Fairs, promoting festivals and meetings of thematic specifics (e.g. arbutus-berry brandy, goat breeding)
- Promotion of women's statute through animation, vocational training and economic emancipation
- Induction of the emergence of local/municipal offices to support social, economic and rural development
- Increasing contribution to planning and development through partnerships among public and private entities, from the local to the regional level and even to the national level.

Problems of recent dynamics: West Caldeirão versus schistous Serra

In order to present the broad territorial differences in terms of qualitative conditions, after the dynamics of IRD, we must pay attention to the fact that those conditions resulted both from structural factors (closely dependent from natural and cultural history) and recent social, economic and territorial restructuring. Concerning this, there are considerable differences between the two main sections of the Serra do Caldeirão in the Algarve, and that is the reason why they are used as units to be compared (Table 10.1).

In the Algarve inland, the west parishes (see Figure 10.1 – B1) have generally moderate natural conditions for agriculture (Barrocal), except where hard limestone is too dense to allow arable soil. But a narrow zone between Barrocal and the schistous Serra (Beira-Serra) has very rich sedimentary soils and the most important inland villages of the whole Algarve

Table 10.1   Some recent issues: West Caldeirão and schistous Serra

	West parishes (Figure. 1 – B1)	East parishes (Figure. 1 – B2)
Planning and Public Investments	Resource concentrations in poles like Salir, Alte and S. B. Messines. The weight of scattered settlement gives birth to 'hunger' of infrastructures considered non-urgent on the perspective/ scale of regional planning.	Investment concentrated in the 'Guadiana axis' (frontier with Spain), mainly for touristic purposes, after a time when roads had top priority. Great expectations around two projects: 1) R&D in the 'economic rank' of goat (indigenous breed); 2) Trans frontier co-operation for integrated and tourist development.
Private investments	Greater innovation and larger diversity of initiatives on, handicraft but also on little factory/ repairing and commerce. Rural tourism diversified, including 2 'model-farms'(innovative and preserving practices and pluriactive integration). Easy agriculture where water is accessible but there are big problems where/when it becomes scarce.	Cultural-based and systematic lack of private investment. Decline of some activities previously supported by development programmes (spicy/medicinal herbs; some handicraft). Forestry and cattle breeding (goat and sheep) very dependent on subsidies. Large projects (exogenous investment), induced by big rough areas (tourist and environmental purposes), have very slow execution, at the rhythm of public subsidies. The most questionable appears as a strange enclave (5 stars hotel, golf-cources, and palm-trees...)
Households	A significant number of parents and children suffering from some stress: economic life implies the active ancestors that commonly flow to/from seashore towns (household	The male element is often (in general) working out (weekly commuting, seasonal or long-term migration), Women are the only real or potential agents for continued

Table 10.1 continues ...

	effects of economic integration ...)	social, economic and territorial improvement (aided by RADIAL, NOW, etc. projects.)
Major conflicts	About environmental problems – some reveal the differences between rural and 'service class' (neo-rural) values... Other are the result of disagreement between functionalist (roadway) planning and environmentalist perspectives... The latter often endanger the municipality sources of income, as it is usually understood...	The EC and national support to develop forestry creates more and more difficulties to those who live from cattle raising (also supported by funds) – incompatible land uses, except on a traditional farming-grazing- forest. The municipality does not discourage some strange enclaves (source of a rare income), and there is little opposition because of the lack of alternatives as source of potential employment inward...

appeared there and have still significant importance (e.g., Silves, S. Bartolomeu de Messines, Alte, Salir, S. Brás de Alportel). The west parishes are also intersected by reasonable roads and have a fairly good accessibility in relation to the littoral.

On the contrary, the east parishes (see Figure 10.1 – B2) are badly provided with roads, the villages are smaller and poorer than in the western Caldeirão and the physical accessibility is worse too. This has a historical/cultural relation with the small productivity and incomes extracted from the thin and misused schistous land. Nevertheless, some commercial tradition exists in Martinlongo (in the crossroad of Alentejo – Algarve) and Alcoutim, close to Guadiana river (along the frontier Portugal – Spain), target of some new tourist demand (Moreno and Ramos, 1996).

It must be said that the whole Serra is promoted, to a certain extent, for urban consumption, once several efforts are being made to attract people from outside to visit and to live in the inland, mostly by the municipalities. Of course, this has been completed with a double promotion (external image and the self-promotion), mostly by the IRD agency, in the sense that only the rise of a self territorial identity – in parallel with the enlargement of economic endogenous potentialities – makes indigenous people stay, instead of using the (improving) roads to increase both commuting and migration.

Conclusion: Problems of Caldeirão 'diluted' in the regional questions

At the moment, there is a conflict – and also competition – that opposes IRD agency to: some 'tourist snipers', which use to carry people in jeeps to 'jump and to see the Indians' and ignore several territorial products which illustrate history, culture and biophysical resources (old villages, old mines, gastronomy, museums, fauna and flora, etc.); some (deep) ecologists who would like to make the Serra do Caldeirão as a 'Natural Reserve'; some investors on tourism sector to make 'islands' of golf-courses in a peaceful and 'exotic environment' (Table 10.1); measures of general country planning which may include the highway Lisbon-Algarve crossing the Serra do Caldeirão on environmentally sensitive areas just to get functionalist advantages or the construction of a regional sanitary waste embankment without the construction of an alternative way to avoid dust-trucks crossing regularly some calm villages.

The 'road to the future' seems to be the already existent but still in progress movement to join increasingly citizens and politicians at 'courts' of discussion and planning. It happens, in a certain way, when we consider (for example, among other ways of partnership) the integration of In Loco (perhaps as the main mobilising agent) in the Regional Development Agency of Algarve – *Globalgarve* (more than 20 public and private entities), which has got competencies to manage some instruments of public policies (Moreno, 1998).

References

Cavaco, Carminda (1983), 'Turismo e desenvolvimento do Algarve', *Seminário 'O papel da Universidade no processo de regionalização e de desenvolvimento regional'*, Faro, Universidade do Algarve, pp. 233-262.

CCRAlg (1993), *Enquadramento estratégico para a região do Algarve 1994-1999*, Faro, CCRAlg, p. 145.

Costa, João Casaleiro (1993), 'A promoção do desenvolvimento local', *Desenvolvimento Local*, Nº 3, Abril/Junho 1993, CGD, pp. 2-5.

Costa, M. da Silva and Neves, J. Pinheiro (coord.) (1993), *Autarquias Locais e Desenvolvimento*, Actas do Colóquio em Braga (Nov. 1991), Porto, Editorial Afrontamento.

134

Guerreiro, M. Gomes (1977), *O Algarve do futuro na perspectiva ecológica*, Lisboa, Secretaria de Estado do Ambiente.

Guerreiro, M. Gomes (1987), 'O Algarve mediterrâneo no contexto nacional', in *Seminário 'O Algarve na perspectiva da antropologia ecológica'*, Lisboa, INIC, 1989, pp. 361-382.

Henriques, José Manuel (1990), *Municípios e desenvolvimento*, Col. Estudos Locais nº 2, Editorial ESCHER Publ., Lisboa.

Lewis, J.R. and Williams, A.M. (1989), 'No longer Europe's best kept secret; the Algarve's tourist boom', *Geography*, vol. 74, nº 323, pp. 156-158.

Lopes, José da Silva (1996), *A economia portuguesa desde 1960*, Lisboa, Gradiva, p. 331.

Moreno, Luís (1993), *Informação na agricultura algarvia: os anos oitenta*, Univ. Lisboa, Faculdade de Letras, p. 192 + p. 64 annexes, (master thesis).

Moreno, Luís (1998), 'Desenvolvimento rural e ordenamento na Serra do Caldeirão: entre a acção local e a visão regional', in *V Encontro Nacional da APDR, Emprego e Desenvolvimento Regional*, Coimbra, Fac. Economia, s. paralela 6.

Moreno, Luís and Ramos, A. Sampaio (1996), 'Mobilização turístico-recreativa na Serra Algarvia: um olhar 'de costas para a costa', in *Colóquio Internacional 'Territórios do Lazer'*, Lisboa, CEG-NeTEL.

Moreno, Maria do Rosário (1996), *Da indução do desenvolvimento rural à gestão multiparticipada*, FCT-UNL, (unpublished masters thesis), p. 273.

Murteira, Mário (1979), *Desenvolvimento, subdesenvolvimento e o modelo português*, Lisboa, Editorial Presença.

11 Unforeseen regional effects as a result of corporatization of government administrative bodies

PAUL OLAV BERG

Introduction

This article represents a tentative and preliminary attempt to discuss a group of problems that has so far attracted little attention in literature concerning local and regional development. So far there is little empirical documentation on which to build. The aim of this paper is to present a background and discuss various approaches to further analyses of local and regional consequences of the reorganization of the public sector, that is currently taking place in the OECD-countries. Briefly these consequences relate to:

- Changes in the geographical distribution of employment and population
- Changes in the delivery of public services
- Changes in price policy – differentiation of prices of public services
- Competition as opposed to monopoly in the services' market.

Approach

In the course of the last 10 - 15 years a lot of central government administrative bodies responsible for infrastructure, public administration and the supply of public services have been given a freer position in relation to central government. This implies that they have been transformed from central government administrative organizations (e.g., directorates) to more autonomous state-owned bodies like public corporations, public limited companies or joint-stock companies. This reorganization has in Norway been implemented against a background of changed domestic political conditions, at the same time as it has been inspired by recent international administrative policy trends ('New Public Management' - dogmas).

It is too early to form a clear picture of how successful this reorganization has been, judged on the basis of the arguments that were put forward to substantiate the changes. Research that has been made at the LOS-Centre at the University in Bergen suggests, however, that at the same time as the corporatized bodies and institutions face an intended pressure to improve their efficiency, unforeseen consequences may be that the possibilities for the public to influence the supply of public services through democratic bodies have been impaired (Grønlie and Selle, 1998; Christensen and Lægreid, 1998). More autonomy seems to mean less democracy!

To the extent that this has happened, what are the consequences? Do consequences differ between centrally and peripherally located regions? To what extent have the new autonomous institutions been instructed to take into account societal and social considerations? These questions may be illustrated through an example: It would probably be generally agreed upon, that the postal services should work as usual, also after having been given a more autonomous position. Further this should also apply in areas where the population base is so small that the income from postal traffic does not fully cover its costs. To what extent has the recent corporatization changed this institution's possibilities to observe societal considerations like this?

Background

Internationally, Norway has, together with other Scandinavian countries, gone relatively far in defining the provision of infrastructure and welfare services as public responsibilities. There are several causes for this. One obvious cause is that geographical and distance-related characteristics, together with an earlier shortage of private funding alternatives, have made governmental commitment necessary. Another reason is that a public engagement has been seen as a necessary condition for securing the provision of a basic supply of infrastructure and welfare services in all parts of the country.

The way the public sector has been organized has gradually changed over time. At first the various public services were an integrated part of the central government administration. Over time the operative responsibility has been transferred to more free-standing units like directorates. At the same time there has been a decentralization of tasks which were previously attended to at the central level, partly to central government agencies at regional and local levels, and partly to county and local municipalities.

The central government's provision of services has increased over the last 50 years, during a period in which the public sector has gone through an enduring expansion, parallel to the development of the welfare state. Within the central government administration, directorates and state-owned institutions have over a long time wanted a position as free from their owners as possible. This matter came up for discussion in the 1950's. At that time the discussion centred around the degree of independence for the main state-owned communication companies; the postal services, telephone and telegraph services and the state railway. The government, however, at that time wanted to retain control over their operations, as these institutions were considered to play an important role as instruments in welfare policies and in regional equalization policies. A unanimous Storting wished in the 1960's to go no further than to grant these bodies status as independent directorates with special authorities (Grønlie, 1998).

After an interlude, when this debate was absent from the political agenda, it reappeared in the 1980's, - this time inspired by the new climate for administrative policies which had developed. An ideological shift took place, internationally as well as nationally, characterized by a scepticism in the growth of the public sector, and by the desire for a slimmer and more efficient state. These market liberalistic trends gave less legitimacy to the idea of a still expanding public sector. At the same time they promoted and facilitated the endeavours for corporatization. After years marked by optimism on behalf of public planning a reaction set in.

At the same time the efficiency of the performance of the public sector came to be questioned. It was alleged that the organization of the central government service supplies was not sufficiently adapted to new competitive conditions. A topical catchword was 'the competitive state'. It was claimed that the public sector was both too expansive and too costly.

Active influence from OECD

From the 1980's and onwards, a series of doctrines and dogmas named under the collective term of 'New Public Management' arose. The basic ideas are that the public sector may be made more efficient by adopting organizational structures, originally developed in the corporate sector. Greater efficiency may be obtained by exposing the public sector to more competition. The main components of these trends are efficiency improvements, public and market orientation, privatization, corporatization, outsourcing and the use of user charges, internal markets and contracting out the provision of social services. In general it involves the introduction of management-principles developed in the private and corporate sectors. The aim has been to contribute to a slimmer, more flexible and a more cost-effective public sector.

These 'management'-dogmas imply that traditional public administration through laws, administrative rules and negotiations should be replaced by 'target-to-effects' incentive systems. More emphasis is to be put on results than on the ways by which results are achieved. There should be a clearer division between politics and administration. This implies that political decision-making authorities should concentrate on policy-making and strategic planning, whereas it should be left to the operative units to run their activities as efficiently as possible within the political frames that have been set.

The 'New Public Management'- doctrines may seem to have made a considerable impact on Western industrialized countries. These countries' own interest organization, OECD, has to a considerable extent acted as a trend-setter through its comprehensive 'PUMA'-programme, by actively influencing its member countries (OECD, 1995).

What impact have the 'New Public Management' dogmas had in Norway?

Recent research shows that the impact of the 'management-dogmas' on Norwegian public administration has generally been limited so far. This applies to the introduction and implementation of 'target-to-effects' incentive systems, out-sourcing and above all privatization, in which Norway has shown more restraint than most other OECD-countries.

In one field, however, the 'management'-dogmas may seem to have had a full breakthrough. This applies to the phenomenon of corporatization within central government. Former directorates, government services and other administrative bodies have on a large scale been converted into state-owned enterprises, public corporations and state-owned joint-stock companies with a more autonomous status. The number of former central government bodies that have been converted into state-owned corporations and companies is at present between 15 and 20 in Norway.

What is the background for this comprehensive corporatization? Recent research shows that the Storting and the Cabinet have had a rather retracted role in this process, whereas the administrative bodies themselves have by far dominated the process (Lægreid and Roness, 1998). In particular the leaders of the various administrative bodies have led the way, in order to achieve a maximum free position on behalf of their respective government services. These endeavours have regularly been supported by the trade unions, as more autonomy would carry the prospects of a freer wage structure.

This situation may be compared to the similar discussion that took place in the 1950's and 1960's. At that time the government wanted to retain possibilities for political direction and control, in order to ensure an equalization of the social and geographic distribution of infrastructure and government welfare services.

Under the new political conditions of the 1980's and 1990's, the Storting and the Cabinet have apparently not to the same degree been preoccupied with such objections. In addition, the efforts to gain a more independent status could this time draw support from the winds of change that were blowing - the 'New Public Management' dogmas.

Among the political parties, especially the Conservative Party (Høyre), which has for a long time been a strong spokesman for a 'smaller and more retracted state', has supported these efforts for autonomy. The Labour Party has also supported these efforts, governed by a different set of motives. In a period in which the public sector has faced a pressure for downsizing, corporatization has been seen as a more favourable alternative (Grønlie, 1998).

However, these questions have been only marginal on the political agenda. The reform work that has taken place, has through the 'management'- dogmas been introduced as a universal, non-political technique, - as a method of obtaining better efficiency and a better service supply for the general public. Political implications and consequences connected to the corporatization process have largely been absent.

Inadvertent consequences of the corporatisation process?

The corporatization process was based on arguments that more local autonomy would at the same time ensure a more efficient superior political direction. When political decision making units are relieved of having to deal with detailed matters related to running operations, they should allegedly be more able to deal with more strategically important matters.

It has thus been a clear condition that more local autonomy in running operations should be combined with necessary strategic political steering and control. In such a process, goals were to be determined and external conditions were to be defined in accordance with societal and social considerations that the government as owner wanted to give priority to. The extent, to which this has happened so far, is debatable. So far, knowledge on consequences of the corporatization that has taken place is limited. Recent research suggests that democratic direction and control of the new autonomous bodies may have been weakened. It is warned that the 'target-to-effect' incentive systems that have been introduced, as well as the corporatization process itself, may impair the political-democratic leadership, in spite of the fact that this process was introduced as a means of strengthening democratic control (Lægreid and Roness, 1998). To the extent that this is the case, it will also include 'user democratic' aspects. Consumers and the general public will lose possibilities of influencing on democratic decision-making processes that decides the supply of public services in their local areas.

Regional and local consequences of the corporatization?

The opponents of the corporatization process have feared that it would result in changes in the social and geographical distribution of public services that would be unacceptable. The most sceptical feared that this process, in addition to leading to reductions of government employment in peripheral regions, also would result in a cut-down of welfare services, gained previously through regional policy efforts (Grønlie, 1998).

The reason why the counter-arguments from the 1950's and 1960's did not appear in the 1980's and 1990's may be that there had simply been a change of policy. Paradoxically, this new policy may seem to have manifested itself through a lack of political attention to these questions.

On the basis of a White Paper from 1991-1992 the Storting stated the position, that the main rule should be that administrative bodies that were part of the central government (directorates etc.) should run government activities. The process of corporatization, which at that time had already been going on for several years, is evidently not in accordance with this position stated by the Storting. As mentioned, this process had come into being as a result of the government bodies' own desire for more autonomy, assisted by the international 'management-winds' which had made their impact throughout this period. Limited attention has apparently been paid to possible social and geographic inequalities, which might arise as a result of this process.

Great challenges

That the process of corporatization which has been implemented so far, could be reversed in the foreseeable future, may not be very realistic. This implies that one will have to live with the consequences that may appear. Some of these consequences may be increasing geographical and social inequalities throughout the country.

Such a political position is of course unacceptable. The rhetorical arguments for corporatization included more efficient strategic political direction and more local autonomy. Making this political direction more explicit and concrete is a political challenge today. It is important that the new autonomous government bodies observe built-in societal and social considerations. The point is how to ensure continued democratic control of a part of the public administration that has now obtained more autonomy in relation to political direction (Lægreid and Roness, 1998).

A further challenge is to develop methods that can give a better basis for calculating the costs of observing the societal and social considerations in question. An example can again be chosen from the mail service. Previously, the costs of offering a minimum acceptable service level in parts of the postal market that are unprofitable on strict commercial terms, would be covered by cross-subsidization. According to the new 'management'-dogmas, such cross-subsidization should no longer take place. Costs related to taking societal considerations should now be made visible, and they should subsequently be covered by explicit grants over the state budget.

The question then arises: How can such costs be estimated? Grant estimates of this type were made for the mail service for 1998, which was the first year of this new practice. These estimates are, however, said to be subject to considerable uncertainty (St.prp.nr. 1 (1997-98) Samferdselsdepartementet). Practice so far also indicates that such grants are vulnerable to cuts, when the price of taking societal or social considerations becomes visible.

More research is needed

In Norway, little attention has so far been paid to the local and regional consequences of this restructuring of the public sector. Such consequences will, however, be of importance to anyone who wishes to study how central government authorities influence conditions for local and regional development. The State is an important regional policy actor! It should, however, be possible to formulate some hypotheses about such consequences, based on a general knowledge of the functioning of markets.

An institution that no longer has its income (or deficit) granted over government budgets, is supposed to fund its activities through selling its services in the market. There is little doubt that such an organization will be subject to pressure to improve its efficiency. This has been part of the objective of the restructuring. In order to be able to compete with private market participants, in cases where markets exist, it is important that the new autonomous bodies are granted the same conditions of competition as private market participants.

To the extent that societal or social considerations imply that 'unprofitable' parts of the activities should be subsidized by the government, such costs are according to the 'management'-dogmas supposed to be made explicitly visible, and explicitly granted over government budgets. Profitable parts of activities subject to competition should not pay for this subsidization. Income of parts of the activities that stem from monopolized markets could, however, be used partly to pay for unprofitable activities, as in the case with the postal services.

Theoretically, this looks plausible enough. The new autonomous state-owned bodies are supposed to gain an ordinary return on the capital employed, similarly to enterprises in the private sector. In accordance with ordinary market conditions, they are further supposed to ensure incomes that fund their operations, and to ensure a financial basis for further expansion.

Societal considerations and the logic of markets

However, when societal considerations are to be observed by autonomous state-owned bodies that are supposed to operate under market conditions, several dilemmas naturally arise.

In markets where the new autonomous bodies meet competition, for instance in the telephone market, an ordinary competition strategy will imply that the competition is met first and foremost in market segments and in geographical parts of the market where the competition is keenest. A natural consequence of this is to lower prices in central parts of the markets where the competition is keen, whereas prices are maintained in peripheral regions where there is less competition. There are examples, for instance in the petrol market, that show that prices are kept high in parts of the market with little competition, to compensate for the losses inflicted by price wars waged in central parts of the country.

To the extent that new autonomous state-owned bodies are not directed to observe defined societal or social considerations, it should be expected that they will act according to a corresponding 'market logic' (as the state-owned oil company Statoil already does).

Another matter is that they as state-owned enterprises will often have a strong market position as monopolies. To the extent that this market position is actively or passively used to further the commercial ends of the enterprise, creating a super-profit, the question of misuse of market power may arise. The extent, to which this actually takes place, is an open question and should be an object of research. There are indications, however, that such a suspicion is not entirely hypothetical.

In examples known so far, there are indications that the restructuring of the public sector that has taken place, may have serious negative consequences especially for peripheral regions and peripheral local communities; consequences that have not been foreseen. It is a serious challenge for the political authorities to ensure necessary political direction through drawing up directions and conditions for concessions, in order to ensure that political goals are implemented and that essential societal considerations are observed.

Elucidating necessary knowledge through research, in order to focus on the consequences of this process, is a further challenge. This can contribute to more accurate political direction and action.

References

Christensen, T. and Lægreid, P. (1996), 'Administrative Policy in Norway: Towards New Public Management', *LOS-senter notat* 9647, Bergen.
Christensen, T. and Lægreid, P. (1998), *Den moderne forvaltning*, TANO Aschehoug.
Grønlie, T. (1998), 'Drømmen om en konkurransetilpasset stat, Ytre fristilling som styringspolitisk redskap 1945 – 1995', in T. Grønlie and P. Selle (eds), *Ein stat? Fristillingas fire ansikt*, Det Norske Samlaget.
Grønlie, T. and Selle P. (eds) (1998), *Ein stat? Fristillingas fire ansikt*, Det Norske Samlaget.

144

Lægreid, P. and Roness, P. G. (1998), 'Frå einskap til mangfald – Eit perspektiv på indre fristilling i statsforvaltninga', in T. Grønlie and P. Selle (eds), *Ein stat? Fristillingas fire ansikt*, Det Norske Samlaget.

OECD (1995), *Governance in Transition, Public Management Reforms in OECD Countries*, OECD.

St.meld. nr. 35 (1991-92), *Om statens forvaltnings- og personalpolitikk*.

St.prp. nr. 1 (1997-98), *Samferdselsdepartementet*, Programkategori 22.1 Post, page 138.

12 Consequences of regulation and deregulation in marginal and critical economies of the U.S. Pacific Northwest[1]

STEVEN KALE

Introduction

In the United States and other nations, deregulation has become an important topic for politicians, policy makers, academics, and others, especially during the last 20 years. The interest in deregulation has in part arisen due to perceived and real inefficiencies in existing social and economic regulations. Supporters of deregulation argue that eliminating or reforming regulations will reduce costs, improve profits, increase jobs, and result in lower prices to consumers. Deregulation is needed to 'get the government off the backs of the people' and reinvigorate the competitiveness of U.S. producers in the global economy.

Opponents counter by arguing that many businesses are so profit-oriented that they will overlook health, safety, and other concerns of the general public. Among the other concerns is the fear that deregulation will place marginal and critical regions at a disadvantage with more economically sophisticated and developed areas. With deregulation, safeguards and subsidised services are reduced or eliminated. At the same time, many marginal and critical regions have insufficient political and institutional savvy to figure out ways to replace or adjust to the elimination or reduction of safeguards or services. Moreover, marginal and critical regions often lack sufficient market size to entice deregulated businesses to provide services previously required by federal and state regulations

This paper addresses the consequences of governmental regulation and deregulation on the economies of the U.S. Pacific Northwest. The paper begins by identifying marginal and critical areas of the Pacific Northwest. It then discusses selected examples of governmental regulations that posi-

145

tively and negatively affect economies of marginal and critical areas. This is followed by a discussion of deregulation efforts, focusing primarily on economic deregulation for various modes of transportation. Lastly, the paper reviews beneficial and adverse impacts and summarizes ways to adjust to deregulation and other factors affecting economic and social change in marginal and critical regions.

Marginal and critical areas of the U.S. Pacific Northwest

The Pacific Northwest as defined in this paper includes all of the states of Idaho, Oregon, and Washington along with 17 counties in western Montana. The region is roughly synonymous with the U.S. portion of the Columbia River basin. This definition of the region is the same one used in a regional textbook of the area (Ashbaugh, 1997), as well as the definition used in a previous paper on transportation and economic development issues in marginal areas (Kale, 1996).

Of the region's 136 counties, 23 are metropolitan, generally defined as counties with a central city over 50,000 population along with contiguous counties with a relatively high percentage of persons commuting to work in the central county(ies). The remaining 116 counties are nonmetropolitan; these include 22 counties that are 'nonmetro adjacent' based on nearness and commuting to metropolitan counties (Butler, 1990).

The bulk (91) of the region's counties are nonmetropolitan and not adjacent to metropolitan areas (Figure 12.1). Most if not all of the region's 'marginal' and 'critical' economies are found in these 91 counties which range in population (1995) from less than 1,000 to about 100,000. Many of the counties historically have depended on natural resources (e.g., timber, fishing, mining) or agriculture for their economic livelihood (Kale, 1997). More recently, they have experienced diversification either through 1) declines in basic economic sectors without corresponding declines in nonbasic support sectors, or 2) growth in economic activities that previously were less important there.

Assessment of which of the 91 nonmetropolitan nonadjacent counties are 'marginal' or 'critical' depends on criteria selected for the analysis. According to criteria based on metropolitan integration and adjacency, all 91 counties qualify by definition. Based on other criteria, however, fewer counties qualify as marginal or critical. Moreover, social and economic conditions vary over time, suggesting that a relatively long time period is needed to arrive at meaningful assessments.

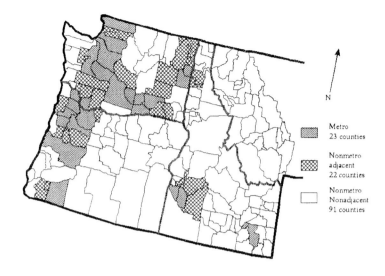

Figure 12.1   Metro and nonmetro counties

Table 12.1 shows information on population and employment in the 91 counties for selected time periods since 1970. The data was obtained from the U.S. Bureau of Economic Analysis' Regional Economic Information System, which can be found on the world-wide web at:

http://fisher.lib.virginia.edu/reis/.

In general, the table shows that over the 25 years from 1970 to 1995, most counties grew in population and employment, with slightly more growing in employment than in population. Counties fared better in the 1970s and 1990s than in the 1980s during the early part of which the Pacific Northwest experienced an economic recession, as did much of the rest of the United States.

In terms of income per person, the picture is somewhat different. Fewer than 10 nonmetro nonadjacent counties had a per capita income equal to or above the U.S. average. This, however, was similar to the pattern for Pacific Northwest metro counties where only the Seattle and Portland metropolitan areas had per capita incomes above the U.S. average. In 1970, only three counties had per capita incomes below 75% of state average per capita income. By 1995, 25 counties had per capita incomes below 75% of state average per capita income. Low incomes in the Pacific

Table 12.1   Nonmetro nonadjacent counties in the Pacific Northwest, number increasing and decreasing, 1970-1995

	Population	Employment
No. of Counties Increasing		
1970-1980	82	82
1980-1990	50	69
1990-1995	81	78
1970-1995	81	84
Number of Counties Decreasing		
1970-1980	9	9
1980-1990	41	22
1990-1995	10	3
1970-1995	10	7

Northwest's nonmetro areas tend to be ameliorated by lower costs of living although this too varies substantially from one location to another within the region.

In summary, of the counties doing worst in population and employment, most are wheat-growing counties less than 3,000 population or mining counties where mines closed. Of the counties doing worst in income per person, most are labour-intensive counties, declining timber harvest counties, or sparsely populated ranching counties. Most but not all are sparsely populated and remote from large population centres and scenic amenities.

Regulations

Analysts often distinguish between economic regulations and social regulations. Examples of economic regulations include those associated with international trade, telecommunications, agriculture price supports, transportation, and utilities. Examples of social regulations include those associated with environmental protection, safety, and equal opportunity. Table 12.2 (Hird and Hird, 1991) summarizes some of the types of economic and social regulations.

While all these regulations affect the Pacific Northwest, some are perceived to be especially important in the region's more remote areas. Numerous observers, for example, believe environmental regulations of varying types adversely affect remote areas more than more urbanized areas. The Endangered Species Act is often cited as having adverse effects on the production of natural resources. Listing of the Northern Spotted Owl and several salmon species as threatened or endangered has caused great concern among producers of timber and agricultural commodities. Regulations addressing leaking commercial fuel tanks have contributed to closure of gasoline stations in rural communities, in some cases the only station in town. Water quality and clean air regulations are cited as hindering economic development in a number of communities such as those near existing or proposed mines or those in non-attainment for various types of air emissions.

Table 12.2   Examples of economic and social regulations

Sectors Affected by Economic Regulations	*Sectors Affected by Social Regulations*
Agricultural Price Supports	Consumer Product Safety
Airlines	Drugs
Barges	Environment
Cable TV	Equal Employment Opportunity
Credit	Highway Safety
Davis-Bacon Act	Nuclear Power
International Trade	Occupational Safety and Health
Natural Gas	
Ocean Shipping	
Oil	
Postal Rates	
Rail	
Telecommunications	
Trucking	

The net effect of these regulations on marginal or critical areas is difficult to measure. Producers of the resources and property rights advocates argue for wise-use and against excessive regulations on extraction of resources from public and private lands. Such groups are especially vocal in the Pacific Northwest with its high percentage of publicly owned lands, which are predominantly in marginal or critical areas.

Others argue large resource-based companies, sometimes referred to as the 'lords of yesterday' (Power, 1996), have exploited the region's historical economic base, which further exemplifies the need for regulations. According to some observers, economic vitality is best assured through strategies emphasizing environmental protection, conservation, and natural landscape preservation (Power *et al.*, 1995; Rasker, 1995).

Deregulation

Much of the effort to deregulate in the United States has focussed to date on economic deregulation. Beginning in the late 1970s with the Carter Administration, the pace to deregulate accelerated during the Reagan Presidency during the 1980s. Deregulation during the Reagan Administration in part occurred through reducing budgets of federal regulatory agencies, requiring detailed and intensive benefit-cost analysis of new federal regulations, and passing laws to dismantle the regulatory process (Tolchin and Tolchin, 1983).

Most of the legislation signed into law addressed economic deregulation, especially the transportation and utilities sectors. Examples include the Railroad Revitalization and Regulatory Reform Act, Air Cargo Deregulation Act, Airline Deregulation Act, Natural Gas Policy Act, Staggers Rail Act, Motor Carrier Act, Bus Regulatory Reform Act, and Shipping Act.

Efforts to reduce federal regulation continued into the Bush and Clinton administrations, especially during the mid-1990s when the Republican Party held a majority of seats in both houses of the U.S. Congress. In 1994, President Clinton, for example, signed into law the Federal Aviation Administration Act and the Trucking Industry Regulatory Reform Act, both of which further eased trucking regulations.

According to the Heritage Foundation, the regulatory agenda of the 104th Congress (1995-1996) was the boldest in the past 20 years and was more successful than the Reagan Administration in reducing regulatory burdens (Antonelli, 1996). President Clinton further enabled passage of regulatory reform legislation by pledging to stop handing down mandates and to cut red tape. Among the legislation signed into law was the Telecommunications Competition and Deregulation Act of 1996 and the Federal Agriculture Improvement and Reform Act of 1996.

President Clinton, however, vetoed other legislation that Congress passed to reform federal regulations (e.g., the Comprehensive Regulatory Reform Act and the Common Sense Liability Reform Act). Proponents of deregulation and regulatory reform argue that more should be done. Some argue that the Clinton Administration is not sufficiently committed to reform and 'goes about implementing new burdensome regulations about as fast as it can take old ones off the books' (Antonelli, 1996).

Impacts of Economic Deregulation

At the national level, many observers of economic deregulation argue it has been highly successful. Numerous studies have shown that fewer regulations and increased competition has led to lower costs. Positive impacts from deregulation have been reported widely in the transportation industry, especially in truck and air transportation.

Trucking deregulation

In the trucking industry, savings resulting from provisions in the Motor Carrier Act have been estimated at $10 billion annually (Allen *et al.*, 1990). Further trucking deregulation in the 1990s is estimated to have resulted in another $4-8 billion annually (Teske, Best, and Mintrom, 1997). While a number of studies have shown net benefits at the national level, research also reveals that not everyone has benefited. In the trucking industry, the disadvantaged groups include less-than-truckload (LTL) carriers, labour unions, rate bureaus, and single-commodity shippers. Concerns also have been expressed that 1) deregulation results in poorer service to small communities, and 2) safety worsens with more trucks on the road, reduced maintenance, extended working hours, and other factors. Others argue, however, that little evidence exists to show poorer service in small towns or that safety worsens (Moore, 1994).

Airline deregulation

In the airline industry, deregulation is estimated to have resulted in $10-18 billion annually in gains to passengers (Moore, 1995; Morrison and Winston, 1995). The U.S. General Accounting Office (1996) has reported that between 1979 and 1988, the average fare per passenger mile declined by 9% at small community airports, 10% at medium community airports, and 5% at large community airports. Although decreasing nationally at various sized airports, passenger fares increased in the Southeast and Appalachian regions of the U.S., while substantial decreases occurred in the West and Southwest (U.S. General Accounting Office, 1996). The geographic disparities are thought to have occurred due to intense competition in the West and Southwest and the dominance of high-maintenance carriers in the Southeast. Additionally, large communities experienced a greater increase in service than did small and medium-sized communities.

The results of the GAO study are consistent with earlier research showing increases in the number and convenience of flights for large, medium-sized, and small communities nationally (Oster, 1988). Nonetheless, 106 airports in small communities that had received service in 1978 no longer had service five years later. According to the researcher, economic recession was more likely than deregulation to have been the cause for loss of airline service in nearly all of the 106 communities; 75 of the 106 communities lost service because their commuter airline went bankrupt between 1978 and 1983. Somewhat easing the loss of air service was proximity to other airports. Over half of the communities losing service were within a one-hour drive to another airport and nearly all were within a two-hour drive.

Other research showed service quality declined for small and medium-sized communities, primarily because very small communities lost service altogether after deregulation (Brenner, 1988). The research also showed service declines for small and medium-sized communities with jet service before deregulation but turboprop service afterwards. Additionally, passenger fares in small communities served by one airline are often much higher than fares for flights of comparable distances originating in larger airports with numerous carriers.

The federal government continues to subsidize service in many small communities that likely would not have airline service in a deregulated market. In 1994, the Essential Air Services Program provided about $32 million for maintaining air service to small communities (Brown, 1996). The federal Airport Improvement Program, financed by airline ticket taxes, also provides funds for airport planning, construction, and rehabilitation. In recent years, the budgets for both programs have been cut, raising further concerns about the viability of air transportation services in small communities and the remote areas many of them serve.

Rail deregulation

Impacts of rail deregulation also are mixed. Railroad mileage has decreased substantially since its peak in 1916 and continued to decline after deregulation in 1980. Deregulation has made rail consolidation through mergers and acquisitions easier, with the promise of cheaper, faster, safer, and more efficient rail service (Brown, 1997). The plausibility of this argument has been seriously questioned in the wake of the Union Pacific Railroad's acquisition of the Southern Pacific Railroad and the resultant congestion and poor service in many of the areas served by the combined railroad.

Several factors have ameliorated the effects of decreasing rail competition, poor service, and sometimes-higher rates to captive shippers. Deregulation of the trucking industry has contributed to rail-truck competition; communities poorly served by rail may be better served by truck albeit often at higher prices. Shipping by truck, however, puts a greater burden on roadway pavements and bridges, which often are in poor condition in rural areas (U.S. Department of Agriculture, 1991).

Branch-line abandonments, made easier by deregulation, also have been of great concern to a number of communities, particularly those in remote areas. Concerns have been eased somewhat by Staggers Act provisions for the expansion and establishment of short-line railroads, many of which operate on branch lines that would have been abandoned or converted to trails. Support for short-line railroads have been further facilitated through loan and grant provisions in the recently enacted Transportation Equity Act for the 21st Century (TEA-21).

Bus deregulation

Loss of intercity bus service, facilitated by the Bus Regulatory Reform Act, has been a major problem in remote areas. According to data collected by Oster (1988), scheduled bus service was decreasing prior to passage of regulatory reform legislation in 1982. For the seven-year period prior to passage, the number of communities receiving scheduled service declined at a rate of 3.3% annually. In the first year after passage, the rate increased to 9.2%, and in the second year, to 11.6%. Between 1975 and 1984, the number of communities receiving service declined from 3,609 to 2,288 (36%). Most of the communities abandoned had fewer than 10,000 residents, and in the two years immediately following deregulation, 84% of the communities losing service had fewer than 2,500 residents.

The establishment of small regional intercity providers has somewhat compensated for the abandonment of service by larger carriers such as Greyhound. Some of these providers are assisted by funds from the Federal Transit Administration's Intercity Bus Program administered through state Departments of Transportation. This program provides funds as loans or grants, which are used to support the operations of public or private carriers providing intercity passenger transportation in rural and small urban areas.

Summary

Considerable research shows that deregulation of transportation has had positive economic impacts at the national level. The positive impacts have been greatest for larger communities, which benefit from a higher volumes of freight and people and from a greater competition associated with a variety of services and carriers. In small communities, the record is more mixed. Some have fared reasonably well, probably better than in a regulated marketplace. Others have fared less well, with some likely experiencing worse and higher-cost services after deregulation than with regulation.

A number of researchers have tried to sort through the evidence with no conclusive results to date showing widespread negative impacts. Part of the reason is because the federal government and to a lesser extent, state governments, continue to subsidize transportation services. The funding of these services, however, is subject to the political process. Subsidies come and go in number and amount of funding, depending in part on prevailing values in society and government or influential segments therein. This seems in part due to prevailing notions about equity and efficiency. Deregulation places high value on efficiency. Countering this are concerns about equity. The funding pendulum seems to swing back and forth between equity and efficiency, seldom staying on one side over long periods of time.

A recent example of this is federal transportation funding. In 1991, the U.S. Congress passed the Intermodal Surface Transportation Efficiency Act, also known as ISTEA. In 1997, the act expired before Congress could agree on reauthorization. In the ensuing debate, numerous replacement bills were introduced. The prevailing bill – the Transportation Equity Act for the 21st Century (TEA-21) – resolved numerous concerns about who gets how much for what. TEA-21 provides for considerably more transportation funding than did ISTEA. Moreover, every state is guaranteed a specified proportion of funding. Many states get more than they did under ISTEA; a few get less. By providing increased funding for a wide variety of lending and grant programs, TEA-21 also mitigates some of the concerns arising from various transportation deregulation acts previously enacted. The 'E' for efficiency in 1991 had changed to an 'E' for equity by 1998. This may be a sign of a swing in the pendulum of transportation regulation, deregulation, and funding.

Closing notes

Regulation and deregulation are two of many factors influencing the economic and social well being of marginal and critical regions. Regulations serve as safeguards but also inhibit certain activities, some of which affect economic and social well being positively, some of which have negative impacts. Environmental regulations are a good example because they are intended to enhance the well-being of current and future generations in general but may adversely affect groups of persons previously dependent on benefits derived from activities now regulated.

Inherent in regulation and deregulation is the notion of risk. Regulations reduce the amount of risk. The issue for many is: how much risk is acceptable and who bears its burden? With deregulation, the prevailing view seems to be that we all must accept a certain amount of risk, more than regulation allows. Time is one of a number of factors influencing how changes occur in the perceptions of risk and procedures for dealing with it. Serious inequities arising over time with deregulation may lead to re-regulation.

Communities in marginal and critical areas need to adjust to a wide variety of changes over time. Deregulation is one of these changes. Nothing stays the same. Communities most likely to be successful are those that work with their strengths, understand their weaknesses, and take action to adjust to change.

In the U.S. Pacific Northwest, a variety of strategies have been developed to help cope with economic change, some of which is associated with regulation and deregulation. In several states, efforts of state economic development departments have shifted from focussing on the more successful areas to helping rural areas that have been hardest hit by change. This has included relatively conventional strategies such as summer and fall tourism. Other efforts have included promoting scenic byways and attracting retirees, many of which have migrated to selected mountainous, coastal, and otherwise scenic parts of the region.

Less conventional strategies have become more acceptable in some areas. Nature-based tourism is a small but growing activity. Establishing Native American gaming centres (casinos) has become increasingly popular in the Northwest. The first in the region began operation in 1992; by 1998 there were over 25, about half of which are in nonmetro nonadjacent counties. As more casinos open, concern grows about the size of the potential market and the number of casinos needed to supply consumer demand for gaming activities.

Development of landfills, chemical waste-disposal sites, and prisons has helped diversify economies in a few remote areas. Some communities view these activities as undesirable; others welcome them. Landfills have opened in remote parts of the region to handle solid waste from metropolitan areas in the Northwest and California. Prisons, viewed as undesirable by many residents in metropolitan areas, have experienced less opposition in remote areas where the number is increasing, especially in the wake of mandatory sentencing referendums and legislation.

A potentially emerging trend is the movement of 'lone eagles' to remote areas (Beyers and Lindahl, 1996; Salant et al., 1996). Lone eagles are businesspersons living in locations where information technologies allow them to conduct business from their homes or small offices. To date the number of lone eagles is small but growing; over time they may help further diversify economies of remote areas, especially those with scenic amenities and the necessary technological infrastructure. State and federal governments have played an important role in supporting the further development of technological infrastructure in remote areas, for example, the Bonneville Power Administration's work with economic development officials to provide rural areas with fiber optic links associated with BPA transmission lines (BPA Journal, 1998).

Several environmental groups are attempting to help resolve problems associated with declines in resource-based industries. Their objectives include helping local residents develop activities based on restoring the environment, manufacturing or gathering 'niche' products previously overlooked or underdeveloped, and producing goods or services previously imported to local areas. Ecotrust, the Pacific Rivers Council, and The Wilderness Society are among the environmental groups previously or currently engaged in such activities (The Wilderness Society, 1992; Johnson, 1993; Bryant, 1997).

As deregulation continues, remote communities in marginal and critical areas will need to continue to develop strategies to cope with deregulation along with a variety of other changes. Among these other changes has been a reduction in welfare and other support programs intended to reduce social and economic hardship. Residents of communities unable to adjust will eventually move to other areas or be left behind. For many, being left behind likely will result in diminishing social and economic well-being until equity considerations resume in importance among federal and state lawmakers and society in general.

Note

1   The comments in this paper are the author's and not necessarily those of the Oregon Department of Transportation.

References

Allen, W. *et al.* (1990), *The impact of state economic regulation of motor carriage on intra-state and interstate commerce*, DOTT9012, U.S. Department of Transportation, Washington, D.C.

Antonelli, A. (1996), *How the 104th Congress cut red tape and returned common sense to regulation*, FYI No. 216, August 9, The Heritage Foundation, Washington, D.C.

Ashbaugh, J., (ed.) (1997), *The Pacific Northwest: Geographical perspectives*, Kendall Hunt Publishing, Dubuque, Iowa.

Beyers, W. and Lindahl, D. (1996), 'Lone eagles and high fliers in rural producer services', *Rural Development Perspectives*, vol. 11, no. 3, pp. 27-29.

BPA Journal (1998), *Fiber optics update*, Bonneville Power Administration, Portland, August.

Brenner, M. (1988), 'Airline deregulation: A case study in public policy failure', *Transportation Law Journal*, vol. 16, no. 2, pp. 179-227.

Brown, D. (1996), 'Rural America's transportation network: issues for the 1990s', *Rural Development Perspectives*, vol. 11, no. 2, pp. 10-17.

Brown, D. (1997), *Consolidation in the rail freight industry and rural America*, Paper presented at the 93rd annual meeting of the Association of American Geographers, Fort Worth, TX, April 1-5.

Bryant, R. (1997), 'Earth tones', *Planning*, vol. 63, no. 1, pp. 19-21.

Butler, M. (1990), *Rural-urban continuum codes for metro and nonmetro counties*, Staff report no. AGES 9028, U.S. Department of Agriculture, Economic Research Service, Washington, D.C.

Hahn, R. and Hird, J. (1991), 'The costs and benefits of regulation: Review and synthesis', *Yale Journal on Regulation*, vol. 8, pp. 223-278.

Johnson, K. (1993), 'Emerging lessons for reconciling community and environment', *The Changing Northwest*, vol. 5, no. 1, University of Washington, Northwest Policy Center, Seattle, pp. 4-5.

Kale, S. (1996), 'Transportation and economic development in marginal areas of the U.S. Pacific Northwest', *Development issues in marginal regions II: Policies and strategies. Proceedings, 1995 meeting of the International Geographical Union Study Group on development issues in marginal regions*, Universidad de Cuyo, Facultad de Filosofia y Letras, Mendoza, Argentina, pp. 283-300.

Kale, S. (1997), 'The economy', in J. Ashbaugh (ed.), *The Pacific Northwest: Geographical perspectives*, Kendall Hunt Publishing Company, Dubuque, Iowa, pp. 309-44.

Moore, C. (1994), 'Intrastate trucking: Stronghold of the regulators', *Policy Analysis*, no. 204, Cato Institute, Washington, D.C.

Moore, T. (1995), 'Clearing the track: The remaining transportation regulations', *Regulation*, vol. 18, no. 2.

Morrison, S. and Winston, C. (1995), *The evolution of the airline industry*, The Brookings Institution, Washington, D.C.

Oster, C. (1988), 'Is deregulation cutting small communities' transportation links?', *Rural Development Perspectives*, vol. 4, no. 3, pp. 13-16.

Power, T. (1996), *Lost landscapes and failed economies*, Island Press, Washington, D.C.

Power, T. *et al.* (1995), *Economic well-being and environmental protection in the Pacific Northwest*, A Consensus Report by Pacific Northwest Economists, University of Montana, Missoula.

Rasker, R. (1995), *A new home on the range: Economic realities in the Columbia River Basin*, The Wilderness Society, Washington, D.C.

Salant, P., Carley, L. and Dillman, D. (1996). *Estimating the contribution of lone eagles to metro and nonmetro in-migration*, Technical report no. 96-19, Washington State University, Social and Economic Sciences Research Center, Pullman.

Teske, P., Best, S. and Mintrom, M. (1997), *Deregulating freight transportation: Delivering the goods*, American Enterprise Institute for Public Policy Research, Washington, D.C.

The Wilderness Society (1992), *From dreams to realities: Diversifying rural economies in the Pacific Northwest*, Washington, D.C.

Tolchin, S. and Tolchin, J. (1983), *Dismantling America: The rush to deregulate*, Houghton Mifflin Company, Boston.

U.S. Department of Agriculture (1991), *Transportation in rural America: A policy backgrounder*, Washington, D.C.

U.S. General Accounting Office (1996), *Airline deregulation: Changes in airfares, service, and safety at small, medium-sized, and large communities*, GAO/RCED-96-79, Washington, D.C.

13 Deregulation and marginality: New public policies and new approaches to the planning of tourism

FRANCISCO LÓPEZ-PALOMEQUE

The role of public administration in the new economic framework of deregulation

In the last half century the State has played a key role in the fostering of economic activities, in the spatial distribution of the latter and in regional planning. Thus, when confronted by regional imbalances, social inequalities and social and territorial marginality (induced by the system itself), state policies have sought, among other objectives, to eradicate regional imbalances and reduce these inequalities. In particular, the fostering of tourism and its harnessing as a factor in development, for the benefit of the whole region as well as in seeking to revitalize marginal areas (mountain areas, interior zones, rural environments), has been one of the fundamental elements in regional and sectoral policies in southern European countries in the last two decades. The intervention of the bodies of public administration has been directed at the exploitation of the tourist potential of an area through the application of tourist policies and various regional planning and management tools.

In every period of history, a regional policy is undertaken within the general framework of the economy and the internal political context of each country. In this evolution of the economic, political and regional system, what was seen, in very simple terms, were successive periods of protectionism and liberalism, until the end of the 20th century when we find ourselves in a situation characterized by economic globalization and deregulation. The change of productive paradigm and the introduction of a new economic order have led to the building of a new stage, a new reality of regional marginality and a new interpretation of this reality, which is manifest in various forms and at a range of scales (Jussila, Leimgruber and Majoral (eds) 1998) on the other hand, the role of public administration has acquired new meaning in the productive system and regional organization. Finally, we should not overlook the parallel evolution undergone by the notion of development and the very concept of marginality as well as the drawing up of development policies (Leimgruber, 1996; Schmidt, 1998).

In this 'new economy', the fundamental paradigms of which are globalization and deregulation, what is observed *a priori* is that public administration is now less involved in the productive system and the political arena has less say in economic decision making. This is evident in many aspects, but the wisdom of this is not shared by all social, economic and political agents. This situation, which has been defined as the 'reduction of the State', in contrast with its traditional role, affects hypothetically the will and capacity for intervention of the public administration in the productive system, the regional dimension of its interventions and the interrelationship between the public and private sectors. These characteristics are shaped by the principles defining the 'new economy', the most significant of which are: economic concerns take precedence over the political; the market solves everything; the role of the State should be slowly eroded, and, finally, the emphasis is placed on deregulation, privatization and liberalization (Estefanía, 1996). The diagnosis is that the process of deregulation threatens the balance between the State, the economy and society.

Today in this 'era of flexibility', Europe is going through a period of 'gentle growth' in which the weight of political thought in economic decision making has been reduced. Among the effects thus induced is the tendency towards an undermining of solidarity and towards the collapse or reconsideration of the systems of subsidies and regional policy, which in the widest terms include the structural funds (FSE, FEOGA and FEDER), and other initiatives taken both by the European Union and state administrations. To this we need to add - at the continental scale - the new stage created by the process of European expansion, and its needs and impact on the policies of the EU. Without doubt, these new co-ordinates, which contrast with those, inspired the structural and regional policies of the past.

It is against this changing background that new focal points and tools of regional policy, in general, and tourist policy, in particular, have emerged. Specifically, in recent interventions in disadvantaged regions, whether organized through global programmes or specific tourist sector plans, a progressive complementation or substitution has been observed in the principles underlying traditional regional policies and planning, by other principles for intervention based on strategy and a reaction to the specific context of the area, and oriented primarily towards taking positive action. An analysis of the undertakings of the public administrations of the European Union, of Spain and of Catalonia, which here we can but briefly mention, serve to illustrate and verify the processes and changes we have described.

New principles and tools in regional and tourist policy and planning

In recent years tourism has become a key factor -at times the only possible factor- in the revitalization of underdeveloped regions and the marginal zones of European countries, mountain areas, interior zones, rural environments (Fernandes, and Delgado Cravidao, 1997; WTO, 1993 and 1998). It has been adopted by various agents (public and private) and applied through various mechanisms (development plans, programmes, urban planning, strategic planning, etc.), corresponding to the regional and sectoral policies drawn up for the development of these zones and the eradication of territorial marginality. The role assigned to tourism justifies, therefore, the attention, which we shall pay to tourist planning and policies as an illustration of the changes that are occurring in the role of public administration as regards regional interventions. The significance of tourism acquires, without doubt, a new dimension when confronted with the disappearance of the traditional productive function -the agrarian sector- from the rural areas (taking with it the condition of marginality in the context of the parameters of productivity and efficiency of production) (Cals *et al.* 1995); when confronted with the new social value placed on the rural world in a post-productive setting; when confronted with the new social value placed on unique areas of natural beauty, the rarity of which makes them attractive, a factor made more powerful by the sensitivity for the environment and conservation that characterizes society at the end of the century.

In the framework of globalization a new tourist stage has been built which has been interpreted as the Post-Fordist phase of tourism, marked by the flexible production of leisure (Vera; López-Palomeque *et al.*, 1997).

The characteristics of the new tourist paradigm are the globalization of the markets, a highly segmented demand, economies of scale in tourist activities, the new technologies that are now available, the demands of environmental and social sustainability of the initiatives, the challenge of competition through quality and efficiency and, finally, the ubiquity of tourism. Without doubt, this new setting for tourism requires fresh content and new forms of public management, a new tourist policy, but in no circumstances should this mean that the State stops being a participating agent given the particular significance of tourism (Fluvià and Mena, 1998). The new tourist policy -which is known as that of the 'third generation'- requires the joint co-ordinated action of the private, public and voluntary sector to facilitate the achievement of competition through quality and efficiency (Fayos-Solà, 1995).

The reasons why tourism has merited and still merits special attention from the State are:

- The nature of tourist resources, which in many cases are public goods or possess a similar condition;
- The added value brought by an activity that is open to use and not exempt from being utilized in the defence or promotion of given political postulates, a strategy which is based on the added value of its significance (social, communicative dimensions, or that of the media, etc.);
- The strategic value of tourism, which is manifest at various scales and in the economic, regional and political terrain; and
- The significance of place or space as a tourist product, and the fact that only the public administration perceives 'tourist places and destinations' as management units and operative areas for policy undertakings, a fact that ensures the attainment of quality and competitiveness of the destinations as tourist products.

Among the tools of tourist policy are varieties of planning types (regional planning of tourism or strategic planning of tourism), that are linked with the economic policy instrumentalized in turn by sector through the tourist policy. Regional and urban planning is, de facto, the physical expression of the style of economic development and, therefore, regional planning of tourism should be linked with the economic policy. It can be shown that the processes of regional planning aimed at the development of tourist and recreational activities are more efficient in economic terms if, in addition to regulating correctly the best uses of the land and the optimum location of services, they implement a sustainable valuation and management of resources, and facilitate the creation of specific recreational and tourist products that allow the space to acquire its own distinct character and make the development strategy competitive. Moreover, strategic regional planning has been one of the most frequently used tools by public administrations when responding efficiently to the challenges posed by the major economic, political, social and cultural transformations which are taking place at the end of the millennium, and even today strategic planning is acquiring greater priority and more importance than traditional planning (Rullán, 1995; Forn, and Pascual, 1995).

There are many definitions of strategic planning, but perhaps the most widely accepted is that which considers it to consist in creating a desirable future and establishing the actual means of attaining this. What distinguishes strategic planning from other types of planning is that it is a process aimed at action: traditional planning draws up expectations, while strategic planning organizes actions. In addition, in a period such as the present, strategic planning acquires the form of an integral, global, participatory project that has a vision of the desired future and a number of specific objectives. Strategic planning has to be understood as an integral project as it is common to all entities, companies and institutions with the most capacity to have an influence on an area and has to be founded on the development of Cupertino between public and private sectors; it has to be understood as a global project because it has to consider in a unitarian and interdependent manner the set of factors which determine economic development and the quality of life in the region. Finally, this planning has to be participatory because participation is a fundamental aspect of a strategic plan, and the key to attaining social consensus and a wide strategic culture, to ensure the involvement of all parties.

The European Union: Measures in regional tourism and development

Tourism is an activity to which the European Union has only recently begun to dedicate its attention in any global or explicit manner (CCE, 1995). Initially dealings with the sector were conducted indirectly, through the measures taken in other Union policies (international traffic and tax issues, transport, regional policy, agricultural policy and the environment, among others), precisely because it is an activity which is the synthesis of many others and which is affected in turn by each of these (Valdés, 1996). Undoubtedly, it is the multidisciplinary and transversal character of tourism, and its complementary nature with the different sectors of activity, which explains that many policies are related to tourism. From the perspective of its incidence in disadvantaged zones, the importance of certain emblematic policies of the Union needs recognizing. These include regional policy, which seeks the full development of all the regions of the EU and is fed by the European Structural Funds (Majoral *et al.*, 1996), the CAP and the new rural policy, as well as undertakings derived from the initiatives established in Leader I and II, in which approximately half the investments have been oriented towards projects involving rural tourism.

In the evolution of these policies - which clearly take their final expression at the state and regional levels, that is in our case Spain and Catalonia - what is observed more or less is a watering down of these policies for one of four reasons:

1. Budgetary restrictions in absolute and relative terms
2. The elimination of certain programmes
3. The introduction of the requirement that there should be joint-financing between public bodies (various levels and territorial areas) and between the public and private sectors
4. The substitution of structural lines and programmes of action by open, strategic and context-specific plans.

In relation to tourist policy as understood in its strictest sense, that is explicit in nature, we should highlight the drawing up in 1996-97 of the Union's long-term programme in favour of tourism. The programme, PHILOXENIA 1997-2000, was intended to ensure the continuity of work undertaken in the previous four years. However, the Counsel of Ministers of the EU, sitting on the 26 November 1997 did not accept this programme because of the initial block orchestrated by Germany and the United Kingdom. The failure of this initiative together with the crisis suffered by the General Direction XXIII and the renunciation by the Intergovernmental Conference to incorporate any reference to tourism in the reform of the 1997 Treaty of the Union, places many question marks over the future of Union policy in relation to tourism (Navinés, 1997). However, the failure of this initiative has also to be interpreted as a clear reflection of deregulation and the 'reduction of the State' which - paradoxically - the European Union is also experiencing. The Union must therefore wait before returning to the issue in 1999-2000, and meanwhile work continues through an annual programme (1998) that tackles most of the immediate needs.

Spain and Catalonia: Notes on the regional policy and the planning of tourism.

Tourism in Spain has an asymmetric spatial pattern, heavily concentrated along coastal areas - particularly along the Mediterranean and in the island provinces, as well in certain cities and emblematic places of the regions of the interior and the mountains (Vila Fradera, 1997). Until very recently the tourist function of the rural areas and the interior of Spain and Catalonia had not become widespread, and still is conducted with little intensity and in a rather diffuse manner. Undoubtedly the spread of tourism (the 'touristification of territory') is closely related with the new tourist paradigm and with the new trends in demand in the tourist sector (Lanfant, 1994; López-Palomeque, 1997 and 1998). This has meant the valuation by tourism of the rural and natural environment and, consequently, a revaluation through tourism of areas, which were disadvantaged until now.

In recent years special attention has been paid by the tourist policy of Spain and Catalonia to obtaining an effective tourist system, which had acquired a state of maturity and was showing symptoms of exhaustion. The clearest evidence of this is the passing in 1992 of the Framework Plan for the Competitiveness of Spanish Tourism or the Futures Plan (Secretaría General de Turismo, 1992; Zabia, 1998). But concern has also been shown for the implementation of new products, which on many occasions have been associated with new tourist destinations coinciding with areas of the interior and mountain regions, with their profile of rural zone in crisis or marginal zone. Moreover, the regional policy for the revitalization of disadvantaged areas has incorporated as a sectoral strategy the exploitation of resources of the natural and cultural heritage for the development of tourist activities and the generation of wealth (Majoral *et al.*, 1996; Sánchez-Aguilera *et al.* 1996; Feixa, 1997; Valenzuela, 1997).

The process of the 'touristification' of the territory in Spain and Catalonia is bringing with it the progressive loss of the condition of marginality of certain areas traditionally characterized as such. This process is what we believe will occur in the medium term, the results of which confirm the changes already recognized in relation to the new perception of marginality: from regional marginality to social and cultural marginality.

The reasons for the tourist development and economic revitalization of rural areas and those of the interior are: the stimuli received by a spontaneous demand for recreational and tourist products; the mimetic effect of the success of the tourist zones and, finally, the need to find alternatives to the traditional economic orientations of the rural environment, among others. In this context, the role of the bodies of public administration has been key, through the use of various tools of intervention (Miró, 1997; Cals *et al.*, 1997).

These events have brought about a growth in tourism and the frequency of use, as well as the creation of a state of opinion in favour of the advantages to be gained from attracting outsiders and the businesses thus created. Moreover, the concept of tourism as a factor of development has to be highlighted given that the strategic function of tourism has been assumed by:

* The local promoters and leaders and the socio-economic agents in general
* The political leaders at the local, regional, state and European Union levels.

In relation to this last point, we should underline the explicit recognition, at the end of the eighties, in the heart of the European Union of the social and economic function of the rural world at the end of the century, with global policies which substituted the earlier sectoral policies. Similarly, we should highlight the leading role reserved for rural tourism in this evaluation, which is seen as a development factor and as an essential factor for the future of these areas. The result has been the multiplication of the 'tourist promoters' and the formal and functional proliferation of the offers markets.

In Catalonia, in the nineties, we have witnessed a blooming of tourist plans, with a variety of aims, and natures and applied in a range of contexts. There are plans that correspond to the coastal axis (municipalities and tourist zones already developed or in the process of being developed), but also - and this should be emphasized - plans which emerge in municipalities and *comarcas* of inland and mountain regions. This last phenomenon should be seen as a symptom or reflection of the ubiquity of tourism (López-Palomeque, 1997), and all this being conducted along the following lines: traditional planning is being substituted by strategic plans (in which tourism is given a key role) or strategic tourist plans or inventories of resources drawn up to promote tourism, to exploit the tourist resources of these areas of the interior, which are drafted and carried out thanks to the initiative of public promoters and planners and, on occasions, that of private promoters (López-Palomeque and Cors, 1998). Examples of these include the strategic plans (with a global tourist nature or inventory of tourist resources) for Alt Urgell, Val d'Aran, Osona, Vallés Oriental, el Bages, la Terra Alta, el Pla d'Urgell and la Segarra, among others. A clear example of this change in the behaviour of the public administration is provided by the model of management for the Catalan mountain area. Specifically, in recent years a transition has occurred from intervention based on expectations based on plans for the mountain *comarcas*, to an intervention of strategic actions contained within the Strategic Plan for the Mountain *Comarcas*, of 1998. Both interventions constitute regional policy tools of the Generalitat de Cataluña (autonomous regional government).

One of the strategies and lines of promotion of the Catalan regional government has been based on the promotion and development of tourism in the interior and in mountain areas, with particular emphasis on rural tourism and agrotourism, in particular the promotion and support given to the network of farmhouse -*residencias-casa de pagés*- accommodation, as we have shown in a recent study (López-Palomeque, 1996). Rural tourism is also the main objective and mechanism (accounting for 50% of investment) of the LEADER programmes in Catalonia. In addition, there are projects or plans for the municipalities - and so the number of examples multiplies - or those aimed at exploiting a particular resource. Among these are the Recreational-Tourist Project for the recovery of Estany d'Ivars d'Urgell (Pla d'Urgell, in Lleida), the Tourist-Recreational Project of the Ciudad de Sal (salt mines), in Cardona (Bages, Barcelona) and the tourist promotion of the castles of Catalonia (López-Palomeque, and Gómez, 1998).

We should conclude this review of the regional policy and tourist planning in Catalonia and Spain by clarifying that the transition from a centralized state to an autonomous state has meant changes, but also the consolidation of certain aspects, particularly the role of public administration in tourism. This role, which is central, is even more so in the 'state' of autonomies. A change of scale has been brought about, and with this administrations and tourist places have been brought closer together; tourist destinations and the competition between them has multiplied and 'formalized' in the political-administrative setting (autonomous communities). Finally, all the autonomous administrations have taken up the strategic role of tourism in the development of their respective regions, manifest in a diverse range of regional tourist policies. This policy of the regional administrations has to be added to that of the central administration and the local government. Without doubt, the already unique status of tourist policy has acquired a high degree of complexity (Bote and Marchena, 1996).

Provisional conclusions

The process of deregulation, in the framework of a new economy (globalization), has opened the way to a new stage on which the principles and tools of regional and sectoral policies have been modified (tourism as a factor in development), designed to intervene in the under privileged zones. The following reflections can be made by way of conclusion:

1. The role of public administrations in the economic and regional system is losing weight, acquiring new meaning and adopting forms that are distinct to approaches that are more traditional. However, in certain cases - the public administration of tourism and the intervention in marginal areas - the loss of protagonism is more apparent than real; while what is new are the tools and forms of intervention. This apparent contradiction can be explained by the importance of tourism - as explained above - and by the limitations shown by the marginal areas in relation to endogenous development.

2. In the countries of southern Europe those areas that traditionally are least developed are being affected by new sectoral and spatial manifestations of the productive system (post-productivism) and the new scales of development of socio-economic phenomena. In this context, and from the perspective of tourism, marginal areas - and all the rural world - acquire or can acquire a new social and economic value: new opportunities for development in which tourism, second homes and leisure activities are demands that give - and will give in the future - economic meaning to the productive function, to the protection and to the management of the rural landscape. In particular, the conditions that define regional marginality can be those that form the basis for its economic interest and exploitation: inaccessibility and isolation and its uniqueness convert them into exceptional enclaves - objects of attention and attraction. The ubiquity of tourism carries with it a progressive loss of the condition of marginality that many of these areas have had to date.

3. In relation with these two points, the public management of the region - in particular the intervention in traditionally marginal areas - is changing, and in broad terms it can be claimed that structural and physical planning is losing interest and operativeness, and in contrast, strategic planning (adaptable, flexible, with a consensus of opinion, etc.) has been widely adopted.

These changes can be observed both in the new focus given to tourist planning (sectoral), formulated in marginal spaces, as well as in regional planning (globality of the territory), which contemplates and incorporates tourism as a basic strategy of development.

These new forms of public management, with the implementation of flexible, context-specific policies and strategic plans, are not free from risks. Given their importance, two such threats need to be recognized:

• The reduction or annulment of collective participation in decision making, through democratic representation in the bodies and entities of a political nature, by setting up mechanisms of intervention which misrepresent or distort decision making with regards economic and regional planning; and
• The subordination of the collective to private interests because of obligations derived from the need for agreement and the strategies of consensus oriented towards action, in which those agents with the capacity to intervene take a leading role (financial groups, large companies, etc.), guided by the logic of the market.

References

Bote, V. and Marchena, M. (1996), 'Política turística', in A. Pedreño and V. Montford (eds), *Introduccción a la economía del turismo en España*, Cívitas, Madrid, pp. 295-326.

Cals, J., Capellà, X. and Vaqué, E. (1995), *El turismo en el desarrollo rural de España*, Ministerio de Agricultura, Pesca y Alimentación, Madrid.

Cals, J., Capellà, X. and Vaqué, E. (1997), *Gestió pública del turisme*, Fundació Carles Pi i Sunyer, Barcelona.

Comision de las Comunidades Europeas (1995), *El papel de la Unión en materia de turismo*, *Libro Verde de la Comisión*, Com (95) 97, Bruselas.

Estefania, J. (1996), *La nueva economía. la globalización*, Edit. Debate, Madrid.

Fayos-Solà, E. (1996), 'La Nueva Política Turística', in *Aquitectura y turismo: planes y pro-yectos*, Univ. Politécnica de Catalunya. Barcelona, pp. 59-70.

Feixa, L. (1997), 'Balanç dels plans comarcals de muntanya 1991-1995', en *Notes d'Eeconomia*, num.58, Generalitat de Catalunya, Barcelona, pp. 32-49.

Fernandes, J.L. and Delgado Cravidao, F. (1997), 'Tourism and sustainability in marginal regions: the case of portugal', in G. Jones and A. Morris (eds), *Issues of environmental, economic and social stability in the development of marginal regions: practices and evaluation*, Universities of Strathclyde and Glasgow, pp. 198-204.

Fluvià, M. and Mena, F.X. (1998), 'Política turística: entre la sostenibilidad y el desarrollo económico', in *La competitividad turística del municipio. Estudios de gestión turística*, Barcelona, ESADE, pp. 34-41.

170

Forn, M. and Pascual, J.M. (1995), *La planificació estratègica territorial. aplicació als municipis*, Diputació de Barcelona, Barcelona.

Generalitat de Catalunya (1998), *Pla Estratègic de les Comarques de Muntanya*, DPTOP, Direcció General d'Actuacions Concertades, Arquitectura i Habitatge, Servei d'Acció Comarcal; Barcelona, p. 122.

Jussila, H., Leimgruber, W. and Majoral, R. (eds) (1998), *Perceptions of marginality: Theoretical issues and regional perceptions of marginality in geographical space*, Ashgate Publishing Ltd., Aldershot, UK.

Lanfant, M-F. (1994), 'Identité, mémoire, patrimoine et 'touristificaction' de nos sociétés', *Société* 46, pp. 233-239.

Leimgruber, W. (1996), 'Marginal regions: a challenge for politics. Local government efforts: native potential and people participation', in M.E. Furlani de Civit, C. Pedone, and N.D. Soria, (eds), *Development issues in marginal regions II: policies and strategies*, Universidad de Cuyo , Mendoza, pp. 143-160.

López-Palomeque, F. (1996), 'Rural tourism as a strategy in the development of marginal areas: the case of Catalonia (Spain)', in Furlani de M.E. Civit, C. Pedone, and N.D. Soria, (eds), *Development issues in marginal regions II: policies and strategies*, Universidad de Cuyo, Mendoza, pp. 49-62.

López-Palomeque, F. (1997), 'La generalización espacial del turismo en cataluña y la nueva dialéctica litoral-interior', in *Dinámica litoral-interior* (2 vols). A.G.E. and Universidad de Santiago de Compostela, pp. 409-418.

López-Palomeque, F. and Cors, M. (1998), 'Estrategias de diversificación de las explotaciones agrarias. Actividades de turismo alternativo en Sant Mateu de Bages (Cataluña)', in *Actas IX Coloquio de Geografía Rural*, AGE and Universidad del País Vasco.

López-Palomeque, F. and Gómez, B. (1998), 'Nuevos productos de turismo cultural: castillos y fortalezas de Cataluña', in *Ciudad y Turismo*, IV Coloquio de Geografía Urbana y VI Jornadas de Geografia de Turismo, Ocio y Recreación. A.G.E. and Univ. Las Palmas de Gran Canaria.

Majoral, R., Font, J. and Sánchez-Aguilera, D. (1996), 'Regional development and incentives in marginal areas of Catalonia', in M.E. Furlani de Civit, C. Pedone and N.D. Soria, (eds), *Development issues in marginal regions ii: policies and strategies*, Universidad de Cuyo, Mendoza, pp. 27-48.

Miró, D. (1997), *Informe sobre els fons, programes i iniciatives de la Unió Europea que afecten i poden ésser d'interés per al turisme a Catalunya*, Generalitat de Catalunya, Barcelona, p. 36

Navinés, F. (1998), 'El turismo en Cataluña', en *La actividad turística española en 1996*, AECIT y Grupo Nexo, Madrid, pp. 281-292.

Rullán, O. (1995), 'Técnicas instrumentales y planeamiento para los años noventa', in *Las ciudades españolas a finales del siglo xx*, AGE-Univ.de Castilla-La Mancha, pp. 179-198.

171

Sánchez-Aguilera, D., Majoral, R. and Font, J. (1997), 'Mobility of marginal areas in Catalonia: a case in the Pyrenees', in G. Jones and A. Morris (eds), *Issues of environmental, economic and social stability in the development of marginal regions: practices and evaluation*, Universities of Strathclyde and Glasgow, pp. 205-217.

Schmidt, M. H. (1998), 'An integrated systemic approach to marginal regions: from definition to development policies' in Jussila, H., Leimgruber, W. and Majoral, R. (eds), *Perceptions of marginality. Theoretical issues and regional perceptions of marginality in geographical space*, Ashgate Publishing Ltd., Aldershot, pp. 45-66.

Secretaria General de Turismo (1992), *Futures. Plan Marco de competitividad del turismo español*, SGT, Madrid, 1992.

Valdez Pérez, L. (1996): 'Actuaciones en materia de turismo en la Unión Europea', in *Turismo y promoción de destinos turísticos: implicaciones empresariales*, Universidad de Oviedo, Oviedo, pp. 317-336.

Valenzuela Rubio, M. (ed.) (1997), *Los turismos de interior. el retorno de la tradición viajera*, Col. Estudios, UAM Ediciones, Madrid.

Vera, F., López-Palomeque, F., Marchena, M. and Anton, S. (1997), *Análisis territorial del turismo*, Editorial Ariel, Barcelona.

Vila Fradera, J. (1997), *La gran aventura del turismo en España*, Editur, Barcelona.

WTO/OMT (1993), *Sustainable tourism development: guide for local planners*, OMT, Madrid.

WTO/OMT (1998), *Rural tourism: a solution for employment, local development and environment*, OMT, Madrid.

Zabia, M. (1998), 'Política turística de la administración central', in *La actividad turística española en 1996*, AECIT and Grupo Nexo, Madrid, pp. 139-146.

Acknowledgements

This paper has been prepared as part of the research project entitled *Delimitación y análisis de las áreas marginales en Cataluña*, funded by the Dirección General de Investigación Científica y Técnica (DGICYT) of the Ministerio de Educación y Cultura (Research Project: PB95-0905), and by an *Ajut de Suport a la Recerca dels Grups Consolidats del II Pla de Recerca de la Generalitat de Catalunya (Grup de Recerca d'Anàlisi Territorial i Desenvolupament Regional*, 1997SGR-00331).

Part 3 – From economic to social issues

14 From economic marginality to the problems of 'quality of life'

MARIA ANDREOLI, VINCENZINA COLOSIMO AND
HEIKKI JUSSILA

Introduction

During the last 3-4 decades the politics and research concern on the standard of living has increasingly shifted from economic to socio-economic features and further. This shift could be explained with two main, correlated, reasons:

- First of all, once that a minimum level of economic development has been reached and the income level of the population has reached a 'satisfactory' level, other parameters become increasingly important. Among them there are characteristics, like the quality of the environment, the possibility to fully develop one's personality, the kind of personal and public services that it is possible to attain, etc.;
- Secondly, the awareness that economic reasons are not the only ones to push human behaviour. Indeed, especially during the last 10-15 years, there has been a flow of population coming back to the 'so-called' rural areas, although they are deemed weaker from an economic viewpoint.

This new concern at political level influences national and regional laws. In Tuscany Region, e.g., besides a law on mountainous areas distributing financial resources on the base of the municipalities' per capita added value (Regione Toscana, 1996), there have been other laws, aiming to cope with the problems of 'social-uneasiness'. This is the case of Tuscany Region Law 3 Oct. 1997 n. 37, which is trying to provide a policy for integrated socio-sanitary services (Regione Toscana 1997; 1998).

The aspects involved in 'Quality of Life' are numerous (see, e.g. Zani, 1997; Gattullo, 1996) and vary from the quality of housing, to the availability of public and private services, to the conditions of women and so on. Clearly, it is not possible to analyze all the facets of quality of life in this paper. Thus, this contribution focuses on some of the phenomena of social distress that can be seen as hampering or reducing the quality of life in Tuscany. From this point of view, special concern is given to the problems of elderly and of families. This study of the quality of life in Tuscany Region has been promoted by the Observatory-Network on Tuscany Rural Society, which is interested in analyzing the correlation between the Urban/Rural dimension and that of the quality of life.

Theoretical starting points and methods used

The theoretical approach used in this paper stems from the realization that marginality is increasingly more fragmented and in spatial terms more dispersed than before (e.g., Persson, 1998; Sommers and Mehretu, 1998, Sommers *et al.*, 1998). Besides, very often there is a correlation between the Urban-Rural dimension and that of the quality of life (Gade, 1991). In many cases it has been said that the quality of life is better in rural or semi-urban areas while areas with a very urbanized structure would be suffering for a 'poorer' quality of life (see, e.g., Gouérec, 1995). However, this generalization might not be true in all regions and areas, and one of the aims of this paper is to elaborate and investigate this issue.

This article approaches the issue of the quality of life from both the traditional economic point of view (level of income per capita) and from the 'softer' angles of ageing phenomena, family issues and other measurements of social crisis (drop in birth rate, etc.). These are then confronted with the issue of the Urban-Rural dimension as to see if they are interrelated.

Methodologically the analysis of the level and spatial dispersion of the quality of life in Tuscany has been done with the help of multivariate analysis. The statistical methods chosen are Principal Component Analysis, and Simple Regression Analysis (Johnston 1980), due to their capability to combine different variable groups into dimensions that more clearly represent the issues to be mapped at Regional level.

As regards basic data, there were some technical and 'accuracy' problems regarding the available variables, due to the way these have been collected. Since it was not possible to obtain all economic data directly from national statistics at municipality level, two of the variables, namely per capita income and consumption, are a 'proxy' representation of the municipality level situation. These have been calculated by IRPET (Regional Institute of Economic Programming for Tuscany) by means of a mathematical model disaggregating provincial data (see, e.g., IRPET,

1994). However, for some indices the use of 'estimated' rather than 'directly surveyed' data is the only possible way to reach information at municipality level, a level that is vital for this work.

Mapping economic marginality associated to income levels

The first analysis of the Tuscany situation is based on an economic view of marginality, namely to that of low income levels. For measuring economic marginality a set of indices, rather than only one variable, was chosen; this aiming to reduce the risk of 'mistakes', as the available data present drawbacks. The four indices used for this analysis come from two different sources. The first two indices are referring to the municipality amount of taxable income resulting from 740 and 730 tax-forms[1] for the year 1993, which has been related both to the total amount of population (Var2 = taxable income per inhabitant) and to the amount of taxpayers (Var1 = taxable income per taxpayer). The level of per capita income at 1993 (Var3) and the level of per capita consumption at 1991 (Var4) as they have been estimated by IRPET represent the second set.

While the first two variables have the drawback of not taking into account tax evasion (that in Italy is quite high), the second pair of indices represents a disaggregation of provincial data performed by means of a mathematical model and not direct measurements. The correlation inside each pair of indices coming from the same source is quite high, while the correlation between indices from different sources is lower. This is apparent from the data of Table 14.1, which shows the correlation matrix between the four indices of the set and the correlation between them and the first unrotated factor resulting from Principal Component Analysis (PCA), accounting for 75.3% of the total variance.

Table 14.1   Correlation matrix and correlation variables – first and second factor for the set of variables on economic marginalization

	Var1	Var2	Var3	Var4	1 Factor	2 Factor
Var1	1.000				-0.857	-0.469
Var2	0.888	1.000			-0.906	-0.348
Var3	0.534	0.602	1.000		-0.845	0.438
Var4	0.542	0.642	0.810	1.000	-0.861	0.403

Although the correlation between variables coming from the two different sources is not very high, the first factor represents the level of economic marginalization; i.e., it correlates negatively with all four indices. The second factor describes the situation where the two sources give opposite information, since the correlation between the factor itself and the first two variables is negative, while the one with the last two is positive. Due to this reason the second factor has been excluded from the analysis.

Figure 14.1 shows the representation on Tuscany map of the data relating to the factor of economic marginalization (='EM'). In all figures of this article the best situations are shown by white and light grays, while dark grays and black represent the worst. The four municipalities with the lowest level of economic marginalization are Florence, Fiesole, Pisa and Siena. The 'dark grays' coincide with the mountainous areas and those in relative terms more distant from the 'prosperous' Arno valley and the coastline.

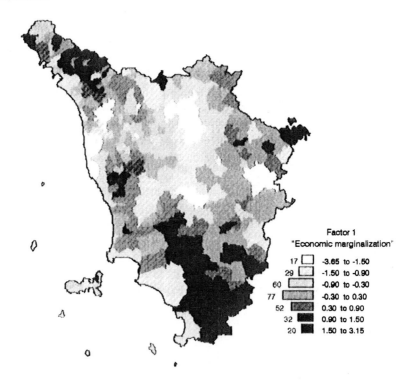

Figure 14.1   Economic marginalization due to low income levels, Tuscany, 1990s

The problems of elderly people

The first problem taken into account in the 'quality of life' approach is the one of elderly, since in Tuscany the share of population accounted by elderly and very old people is rapidly increasing.[2] Thus it is important to analyze the conditions in which elderly are currently living. This analysis has been performed by using the following variables:

Var1) Generation Substitution Index, 1996, (population <15 years - population >64 years)/population 15-64;

Var2) Share of population of age 85 and above, 1996;

Var3) Population/Families ratio in 1996 (a proxy of family dimension);

Var4) Share of population retired from his/her job, 1991;

Var5) Families with only one member living alone/total population 1991;

Var6) Couples without children, 1991;

Var7) Percentage of taxpayers declaring income under ten million ITL, 1993;

Var8) Number of widows/widowers for 100 married inhabitants, 1991.

These variables are not only linked to a high presence of elderly (index of generation substitution, population of age 85 years and above), but also to a condition of loneliness (families with only one member living alone; childless couples, widows/widowers) and to a low income level (share of taxpayers with income less than 10 million ITL). This set of variables has been used for performing a PCA. Table 14.2 shows the correlation matrix between variables and the correlation coefficients between the variables and the first unrotated factor, which is accounting for 57.9% of the total variance.

Table 14.2   Correlation matrix and correlation variables – first factor for the set of variables on ageing problems, 'AP'

	Var1	Var2	Var3	Var4	Var5	Var6	Var7	Var8	1 Factor
Var1	1.000								0.945
Var2	-0.802	1.000							-0.832
Var3	0.733	-0.572	1.000						0.825
Var4	-0.495	0.446	-0.244	1.000					-0.545
Var5	-0.779	0.640	-0.873	0.302	1.000				-0.886
Var6	-0.326	0.223	-0.003	0.259	-0.123	1.000			-0.175
Var7	-0.595	0.445	-0.430	0.381	0.523	0.206	1.000		-0.674
Var8	-0.826	0.720	-0.704	0.412	0.817	-0.037	0.505	1.000	-0.893

As Table 14.2 clearly shows, all variables in the set are strongly correlated with the 'AP-factor', with the exception of variable six (share of childless couples on the total amount of families) that is not necessarily linked to ageing phenomena, and with the partial exception of variable four (share of retired people). This last lack of correlation could be due to the fact that, especially in the past, women working regularly were a small share of population, and now they get only a social pension and are not included among the people retired from a job. Besides, there has been a quite recent period when it was easily possible to retire when aged only between 40 and 50.

Since the high share of variability accounted by the 'AP-factor' and the fact that it shows correlation which are consistent with the initial hypothesis of the analysis, this factor has been taken as a 'proxy' of the problem of the condition of elderly in Tuscany. The sign of correlation between 'AP-factor' and variables reveals that it is not directly linked to ageing phenomena, but to the opposite situation, and thus municipalities with ageing problems are those characterized by negative values, highest in absolute term. The factor scores of 'AP-factor' are mapped in Figure 14.2.

Figure 14.2 shows how the major problems for ageing phenomena are existing in the Apennines mountains and in the inland hilly and mountainous areas of Grosseto, Siena and Pisa provinces. A certain degree of ageing phenomena is present also in provincial capital cities like Florence and Siena, where – in any case – it is more likely that elderly have a family living close to hand, and it is easier to access social services or to have some help at home. The four municipalities with the lowest values for the ageing index are located around the municipality of Prato, the most recent provincial capital of Tuscany.

Family crisis in Tuscany Region

Many of the problems both of elderly alone and of young problematic children could be linked to their family environment. For this reason it could be interesting to analyse the situation of Tuscany families. The following set of variables has been used in this analysis:

Var1) Number of children borne yearly between 1991 and 1996 per 100 women, 15-49 years old (fertility rate);

Var2) Percentage of families with children and only one parent on total number of families, 1991;

Var3) Percentage of unmarried inhabitants older than 14 years, 1991;

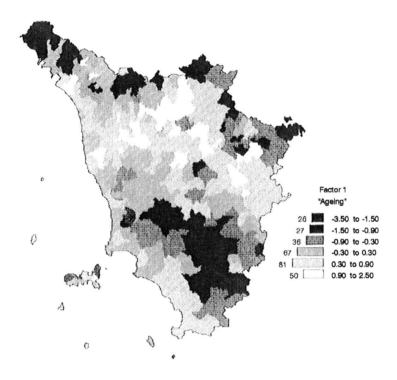

Figure 14.2   Ageing problems in Tuscany, 1990s (inverse polarity)

Var4) Divorced and separated inhabitants by every 100 married inhabitants, 1991;

Var5) Percentage of abortions on potential birth rate[3] in 1994.

Although a low birth rate and a low wedding rate do not necessarily imply a crisis of the 'family' institution, nevertheless it has been hypothesized that these two indices could be linked to a crisis of the 'traditional family values'. Moreover, in a better cultural and socio-economic context than the present, abortion could be substituted by family planning thus lowering the number of abortions. It is important to notice that in this analysis, since the data used refers to a single year, this index is not showing all its potential meaning. Families with only a single parent could be due to the loss of one of the partners, but more likely they are the result of divorces and of children of single mothers.

Table 14.3 shows the correlation between variables belonging to the 'family crisis' set and between these and the first two unrotated factors resulting from PCA. According to Table 14.3 these variables are very much less correlated than those used in the previous two sets. For this reason the first two factors account respectively only for 34.6% and 29.9% of the total variance.

Table 14.3   **Correlation matrix and correlation variables – first two factors for the set of variables on 'family crisis'**

	Var1	Var2	Var3	Var4	Var5	1 Factor	2 Factor
Var1	1.000					0.060	-0.742
Var2	0.079	1.000				-0.722	-0.332
Var3	0.042	0.443	1.000			-0.782	-0.239
Var4	-0.082	0.273	0.354	1.000		-0.743	0.295
Var5	-0.368	-0.096	-0.054	0.313	1.000	-0.197	0.831

As it is possible to see from the signs and from the strength of correlation between variables and factors, the first factor is linked to the absence of 'family crisis' ('FC') either real or potential, seen as a crisis in the relationship between partners. High levels of divorces, unmarried people and families with only one adult with children are consequently related to negative value of the first factor, highest in absolute value. The second factor is linked to the problem of low birth rate ('LBR') and high abortion rate and it shows a positive, although quite low, correlation with the incidence of divorced and separated people. Vice versa, the correlation with unmarried people and the incidence of family with only a single parent is negative, and again not very high in absolute value. Thus, municipalities with very high scores for the second factor are characterized by low birth rates, which already constitute a problem for Regions such as Tuscany and Liguria, where the natural balance tends to be negative.

Figures 14.3 and 14.4 show the maps of factor scores on first ('Family crisis') and second factor ('Low birth rate') for the municipalities of Tuscany Region. Since the 'FC-factor' has an 'inverse polarity', family crisis is linked to the negative pole and not to the positive one. The highest scores for the probability of the incidence of 'family crisis' can be found in Florence (-3.799),[4] but also Pisa, Livorno, Lucca, Pistoia, Siena, and Grosseto – that is to say, almost all provincial capital cities of Tuscany – have quite high scores ranging from -2.867 (Pisa) to -1.245 (Pistoia). According to Figure 14.3 the incidence of 'family crisis' is thus a more urban than rural phenomenon, since it does also prevail in the immediate adjacent 'urbanized transient rural areas' of the major centres.

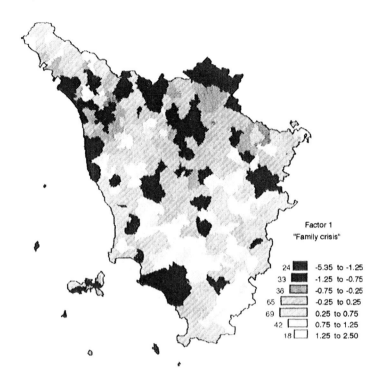

Figure 14.3 **'Family crisis' due to couple problems, Tuscany, 1990s (inverse polarity)**

The more positive situation can be found, despite the high negative value of Siena municipality, in the more mountainous areas of Siena province and in the province of Arezzo. The value of the city of Arezzo itself is slightly negative (-0.550), but the municipalities immediately adjacent to Arezzo have relatively high positive values, for instance Civitella val di Chiana has a value of +0.373. The most positive value of all is that of Montieri (2.477) in Grosseto province. This factor seems to confirm the hypothesis that – at least in general – rural areas suffer in a lower degree than other areas for problems related to 'family crisis'. This aspect will be analyzed again later by means of a Regression Analysis between the Urban-Rural dimension factor and the factor of 'family crisis'.

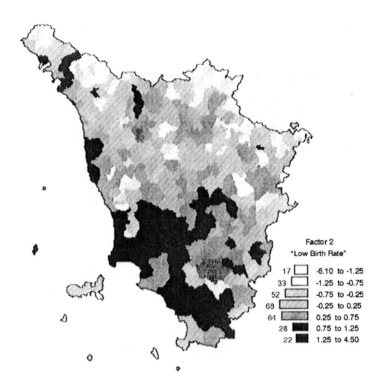

Figure 14.4   'Low birth rate' problems, Tuscany, 1990s

While Figure 14.3 is giving a picture of the areas where some social problems could be high due to an 'unsatisfactory' family fabric, Figure 14.4 is showing which are the areas that risk in having major problems of ageing and population decrease in the future due to the insufficient birth rate. However, it is possible that the 'Low birth rate' factor ('LBR-factor') includes more diversified information and consequently, in this case one should consider also the structure of the society, as a whole.

The problem of low birth rate in Italy is a relatively 'big' problem, since the number of children born per fertile woman has been decreasing and currently is very low. There are many reasons for this but surely the economic issues, longer times in education and the increased participation of women in work force have contributed to this phenomenon. At the same time the social structure has not been changing in the manner that it would take into account this change and consequently in Italy there are not enough services especially directed for families where both parents are working.

In this respect at first, the low birth rate is due to the fact that more women go through a longer education, during which a child birth is usually postponed to an economically more affluent situation. This in turn leads to a higher age of the mother when the first child is born. Currently in Italy the average age of mother having her first child is increasing. This in turn usually means that the amount of children per family is also reducing. Secondly, there are other economic reasons that in Italy have a negative effect on the birth rate, since for instance, the current tax reductions that a family might have because of children are quite low (from € 48.31 to € 97.13, 1997). Last but not least, children are often seen as hampering the activities (both at professional and leisure level) of the parents, especially of mothers, and they are considered to require too much time, care and attention. Moreover when a couple decide to have children, very often they prefer to have only one because they think that they would not be able to insure a sufficient level of attention to more than one child.

These economic and social reasons have undoubtedly had an effect on the level of birth rate. Accordingly to the situation at 1994, the abortions, which are a part of the factor, influence quite a lot the birth rate since they lower the number of children borne by about 25%. This situation should be analyzed more in detail, taking into account a period longer than one year for having more reliable information, especially when small municipalities are involved. Moreover they should take into account how many of these abortions are due to major diseases or problems of the foetus (or of the mother).

The Urban-Rural dimension and quality of life

The debate on the role and evolution of rural regions in the European Union is quite vivid; consequently it is important to analyze the correlation between the previously examined aspects of quality of life and the Urban-Rural dimension. A factor describing the Urban-Rural dimension in Tuscany Region, which has been proposed in chapter nine of this same book (Andreoli, Di Iacovo, Jussila and Tellarini), has been used for checking if there is a correlation between it and the phenomena which are object of this paper. Table 14.4 shows the statistical data relating to the correlation between the Urban-Rural dimension (x) versus the other phenomena (y) resulting from a single regression.

Table 14.4   Correlation between the Urban-Rural dimension and some aspects of quality of life

Aspects of quality of life	R	R^2	P
1st factor 'Economic Marginalization' ('EM')	-0.722	0.522	0.0001
1st factor 'Ageing (inverse polarity) ('AP')	+0.466	0.217	0.0001
1st factor 'Family crisis' (inverse polarity) ('FC')	-0.452	0.204	0.0001
2nd factor 'Low Birth Rate' ('LBR')	+0.141	0.020	0.0017

The negative correlation between the Urban-Rural dimension and the level of 'economic marginalization' is quite significant, as it is apparent from the data presented in Table 14.4. In other words, rural areas are still suffering for a weaker situation from the point of view of the level of income and consumption. The R^2-value between these two factors is 0.522.

It has to be noted that the only strictly economic variable of the set relating to the Urban-Rural dimension, namely the value per square metre of real estate in 1996, is above all correlated with the level of per capita consumption 1991 (0.578). The correlation between the real estate value and the other variables used for calculating the 'economic marginalization' factor are much less strong: 0.385, 0.321 and 0.185 respectively for the per capita income level, the taxable income per inhabitant, and the taxable income per taxpayer.

As regards the correlation between the Urban-Rural dimension and the problems of ageing, it is significant (P=0.0001) and quite strong (0.466), although not as strong as that of 'economic marginalization' (see Table 14.4). From this point of view the strong flows of outmigration of young people from countryside to the cities during the 1950s and 1960s have resulted in a problematic situation for the parents who have been left behind (Di Iacovo and Tellarini, 1999). In fact, when becoming elderly and in need of care, they have had to choose if staying in their home place alone or if moving to a city and an environment that it is probably felt by them as unusual if not even hostile. In this case, although cities usually provide more and better social services than the countryside, the situation of elderly in urban environment could be not better than in a rural context. On the other hand, since the presence of elderly is often associated to low per capita income (at least at territorial level, if not at personal level), this could imply that it is difficult for elderly people to pay for the help they would need for being able to stay at home. For adult children, too, to have old parents living far away could create problems and the need either to hospitalize them (in the case that it is not possible to guest them in their own home) or to find somebody taking care of them. In any case this usually means that the children who cannot take home their elderly parents and want to see them regularly, need to commute.

Since the 'family crisis' factor has an inverse polarity, its negative correlation with the Urban-Rural dimension means that family crisis tends to be more frequent in urban environment rather then in rural environment. Besides, this negative correlation is quite high (-0.452; see Table 14.4). Thus it seems that the countryside still retains a different kind of culture[5] where family values are in some way stronger than in urban environment. This higher importance of family values in the countryside could be a positive factor, thus the Tuscany Region has proposed an integrated plan for sanitary and social policies, where families, voluntary organizations and private firms all should have a role, together with public institutions, in preventing social distress.

If the correlation between rural environment and 'traditional family values' still holds, the correlation between rural environment and higher birth rates seems to have disappeared. This is apparent from the examination of data shown in Table 14.4, since the correlation between the two factors is only 0.141 (R^2=0.020), although it seems to be significant for P=0.0171. In this respect the ideas put forward about the changes in 'values' in different regions, can explain why there is such a low, although significant correlation between the Urban-Rural dimension and the Low Birth rate. It is possible to hypothesize that as the urban values are entering to the rural space also the ways people try to solve 'problems' become more similar. However, as said earlier, part of the information is tied to a one year and consequently more research is needed to confirm the above results.

Implication for policies

The connection between the Urban-Rural dimension and some of the aspects of quality of life could have some important implication for policies. Indeed, many Regions, since the increasing costs of sanitary and social policies and the problem of taking into account 'human aspects' besides medical ones, are promoting the role of family while trying to alleviate the pressure of the rising costs for the society. Consequently, there is the wish to promote the role of families in taking care of elderly and children every time that the situation is such that hospitalization is not necessary. On the other hand, families need economic and 'technical' help for being able to perform such a task. Voluntary and privates institution providing social and sanitary service have to be integrated, too, in order to achieve the highest possible effectiveness and efficiency in this sector. Last but not least, neighbours and local community could participate in creating a social 'protection network' for people in need. From this point of view and from the previous analysis it seems to emerge a picture of rural environment where families and – likely – local communities have still an important role.

On the other hand, although a 'rural culture' could be a positive factor in this task of service provision, it is often thought that it is more expensive and difficult to provide services in sparsely populated areas. This, especially in the past few years, has brought about tendencies to concentrate services, especially sanitary ones. Although up to a certain point, it is possible to achieve economies of scale, it is also true that large structures are often difficult to manage, as some of the recent scandals in Italy have clearly demonstrated. Besides, the concentration of all the services compels people to commute, sometimes for long distances – at least in time – in order to have services that could be provided also by a small and basic structure.

In many 'rural' areas of Tuscany, there is a flow of population coming back (return migration) in order to achieve better condition in housing, quality of the environment, chance of having open space for children, a higher level of 'community protection' than in the city (see Gouérec, 1995). Nevertheless, this happens only provided that some socio-economic problems could be overcome (e.g., by commuting or by having sufficient services, such as schools, postal services, etc.). Consequently if this phenomenon is seen as a positive one, it could be important to try to promote it by providing a minimum level of services.

This phenomenon of positive balance-sheet between immigration and out-migration is especially strong for those areas, which show intermediate features in terms of the Urban-Rural dimension. Very likely these are the areas where quality of life is higher since the municipalities are 'urban' enough to have a satisfactory access to services, but 'rural' enough to have a different culture and style of living.

In this respect, a further step of policy integration should be to integrate the old vision of 'economic development' with the new one of 'quality of life', trying to promote a more balanced distribution of inhabitants on the territory and consequently a more harmonious development.

Conclusion

This paper has tried to analyze a 'softer' dimension of the concept of marginality in order to see how it could be related and linked to the question of Urban-Rural dimension. The reason for this is the realization that marginality is a complex phenomenon and thus its manifestation could be found also within other groups or dimensions other than that of Urban-Rural. This in turn gives possibilities for creating integrated policies for alleviating marginality and diminishing problems existing on the spatial level.

The variables that have been chosen for the analysis all measure different aspects of the phenomenon of 'quality of life'. The first set of variables used in this analysis looks at the economic situation and it aims to measure the level of the 'quality of life' via the economic welfare aspect. In this respect the image of 'economic marginalization', presented in Figure 14.1, identifies those areas in Tuscany that currently can be viewed as 'economically marginalized', i.e., 'less well-off'.

The second set of variables looks at the ageing problem in Tuscany that in the future is most certainly going to be a major problem, as the levels of young people in the more spatially peripheral municipalities are already now quite low. In future this, incorporated with the current plans to increase 'cost effectiveness' of social services by concentration, may, in peripheral municipalities, lead to more costly situation than today. The reason for this is that 'distance problems' and the lack of close-by family support may increase the need for 'institutional' care, e.g., 'nurseries for the elderly' close to the centres, where services have been concentrated.

The third variable set measures the level of 'family crisis' in Tuscany. These variables concentrate on the issue of the family unit and its composition. The analysis of these variables reveals that family problems are now 'more evenly' distributed, although there still does exist a positive correlation with a 'better' family situation in the rural areas than in the urban ones, as can be seen from Figure 14.4.

One of the main aims of the paper was to look at the possible relationships between the three sets of variables and the Urban-Rural dimension. The analyses provide evidence that there is a correlation; the clearest case being that of the economic marginalization, which clearly shows a negative correlation, lower incomes and per capita levels of consumption in rural areas than in urban areas, and thus confirms the general picture about the economic marginalization. The dimensions of 'ageing' and 'family crisis' (inverse polarity) equally concur with the Urban-Rural dimension. The fourth dimension of 'low birth rate', however, gives a mixed picture that is more difficult to interpret. It most likely is 'signifying' the change in values that has taken place in Italy. When being partly only one-year representation, it is difficult to judge, if this is the case or not. The connection to the spatial dimension is, however, quite weak and without a trend analysis it is not possible to say if the small but significant correlation is a 'sign' of the change or not.

This analysis has provided probably more questions than it has been able to answer.

One of the most fundamental questions is:

* Is the observed correlation's part of a trend or not?

Secondly it is possible to put forward other questions such as:

* Does this type of approach provide enough evidence for policy purposes?
* How it is possible to improve the analysis?
* What other variables could be used to measure the 'quality of life'?

These questions form the basis for future research. It is imperative to try to confirm the correlation between the Urban-Rural dimension with a set of variables that also takes into account time factors, as much as possible. Secondly the question of low birth rate and its connection to the spatial dimensions needs to be clarified further.

This paper opens up many questions in the sphere of policy, in respect to the Urban-Rural dimension. One of the most apparent conclusions that can be drawn is that of the need for more integration of policies at territorial level. The question of concentrating services, for instance, is an issue that gets a completely new dimension, when put in the context of space and time as well as of cost to produce the service. It is – at least tentatively – apparent from this work that while investing more on the 'centres' for social and sanitary services, one at the same time increases the need for 'regional policy type intervention' in more peripheral areas. This due to the fact that people no longer have access to the services on daily basis and thus there is the need for more costly arrangements for service provision, e.g., in the form of longer hospitalization due to distance.

The other problems arise from the aspect of land management and general service provision when the population base is getting 'too' low. In this respect, too, there is a need to combine different policies, that in turn would lead to a 'cost saving' effect of the overall budget on regional level. This, however, would require that some, if not all, of the barriers between different sectors providing services to people both in the urban and in the rural areas would be 'abolished' or at least significantly reduced.

Notes

1. 740 and 730 are the tax forms to be filled by natural people. These forms did not include pensioners and workers whose income did not exceed amount 8,538,000 ITL in 1993, or

who did not have certain income sources (e.g., incomes deriving from freelance activities, shares, etc.). The amount of non-taxable income (8,538,000 ITL) was increased by about 400,000 ITL for every dependent child in the case of non-dependant spouse, while this was increased by 3,441,000 ITL in the case of dependant spouse with no children. In the case of presence both dependent children and spouse the increase of non-taxable income (3,441,000) was additionally increased by a minimum of 265,000 ITL (4th child) to a maximum of 796,000 ITL (first child) until the eighth child.

2. In 1996 the population of age 65 years and above was estimated as being approximately 21%: from this amount 12.1% were people between age 65 and 74 years, 6.5% were people aged between 75 and 84 while 2.4%. were of 85 years and above.

3. Potential natality is calculated as the sum of the number of children born in 1994 and the number of voluntary abortions in 1994.

4. The municipality of Capraia Isola (-5.349) due to its special nature - had a large prison - has not been taken into account in the analysis.

5. It could be argued that the lower importance of family crisis in rural areas than in urban areas could be also due to a lower level of income, which makes divorces and families with mothers living alone with children less frequent. Nevertheless the correlation between the family crisis and the economic marginalization factors, although present, is lower (R=0.381 and R^2=0.145) than the one existing with the Urban-Rural factor (R=-0.452 and R^2=0.204), making the hypothesis of cultural aspects more likely.

References

Di Iacovo, F. and Tellarini, V. (1999), *I bisogni degli anziani nel mondo rurale toscano, primi risultati di un'indagine*, http://www.osservatorio.arsia.toscana.it/sismon/sersoc/relazione.doc.

Gade, O. (1991), 'Dealing with disparities in regional development - The intermediate socio-economic region', in O. Gade V.P. Miller and L.M. Sommers (eds), *Planning Issues in Marginal Areas*, Volume 3, Occasional papers in Geography and Planning, Dept. of Geography and Planning, Appalachian State University, Boone, North Caroline, pp. 19-30.

Gattullo, M. (1996), 'La percezione della qualità della vita nella città di Corato attraverso un'indagine diretta', in *Atti della XVII Conferenza Italiana di Scienze Regionali*, Sondrio, 16-18 October, vol. 1.

Gouérec, N. (1995), 'La Comunità Montana della Garfagnana ovvero il fascino discreto della marginalità', unpublished research report.

IRPET (1994), 'Il reddito disponibile nei comuni di Toscana, Umbria e Marche Anni 1986/91. Metodologia e risultati', *Economia Toscana Note di congiuntura, Rivista mensile della Cassa di Risparmio di Firenze*, Anno 9, n. 3.

Johnston, R.J. (1980), *Multivariate statistical analysis in geography. A primer on the general linear model*, Longman, New York.

192

Persson, L. (1998), 'Cluster of marginal microregions', in H. Jussila, W. Leimgruber and R. Majoral (eds), *Perceptions of Marginality - Theoretical issues and regional perceptions of marginality in geographical space*, Ashgate, Aldershot, pp. 81-100.

Regione Toscana (1996), *Disciplina degli interventi per lo sviluppo della montagna*, Legge Regionale 19 Dicembre 1996, n. 95, B.U.R.T. n. 58, 30.12.96.

Regione Toscana (1997), *Organizzazione e promozione di un sistema di diritti di cittadinanza e di pari opportunità: riordino dei servizi socio-assistenziali e socio-sanitari integrati*, Legge Regionale 3 Ottobre 1997, n. 72, B.U.R.T. n. 37, 13.10.97.

Regione Toscana (1998), *Piano Integrato Sociale Regionale*, Legge Regionale 3.10.97 n. 72', unpublished working document.

Sommers, L.M. and Mehretu, A. (1998), 'International perspectives on socio-spatial marginality', in H. Jussila, W. Leimgruber and R. Majoral (eds), *Perceptions of Marginality - Theoretical issues and regional perceptions of marginality in geographical space*, Ashgate, Aldershot, pp. 135-146.

Sommers, L.M., Mehretu, A. and B.W. Pigozzi (1999), 'Towards typologies of socio-economic marginality: North/South comparisons', in H. Jussila, R. Majoral, and C. Mutambirwa (eds), *Marginality in Space - Past, Present and Future*, Ashgate, Aldershot, pp. 7-24.

Zani, S. (ed.) (1996), *Misure della qualità della vita. Un'analisi per i comuni dell'Emilia Romagna*, FrancoAngeli, Milano.

Sources of statistical data:
ISTAT (Italian National Institute of Statistics), various sources.
ANCITEL, data bank at 1997.

INTERNET Sources, http addresses:
http://www.regione.toscana.it/ita/cif/pubblica/indpubb.htm#cen.
http://cidoc.iuav.unive.it/sintesi/.
http://www.osservatorio.arsia.toscana.it/sismon/sersoc/relazione.doc.

Acknowledgements

This research has been funded from the University of Pisa under the following researches: 'Fattori di sviluppo in aree rurali svantaggiate' and 'L'intervento a favore delle aree rurali e gli strumenti di conoscenza del territorio' and by the Tuscany Observatory of Rural Society.

15 The 'old' and 'new' forms of inequality:
The case of Portugal

SANDRA MARQUES AND FERNANDA DELGADO CRAVIDÃO

Introduction

Reference to concepts of *mondialization* and globalization is indispensable to understanding the entirety of international, national and regional dynamics that characterize Portugal, the better to identify marginal spaces or regions, in the context of these very recent phenomena.

These concepts are applicable to all the dependent factors, on which the life-styles of peoples throughout the world, from economy to politics, from social aspects to culture, rely. Yet, it is not possible to study these two major phenomena in isolation from the process of modernization that is so closely linked with them.

The term *mondialization* may be defined as a complex phenomenon of many dimensions, combining the development of countries that were 'formerly' poor, the deregulation of market and the lowering of growth rates, with those countries that are more developed (Leimgruber, 1993).

Globalization of the economy multiplies uncertainties and threatens to lead to a more non-egalitarian society. The law of the markets and the opening up of the world dilute each country in an indistinguishable group in which no national society can be master of its own destiny. The crisis of the individual is redoubled by *mondialization*, contributing still further to render obscure the points of reference that are left to us.

Three phases have been attributed to *mondialization*, that is to say, to identifying the events that underlie it, or hasten the process. These eras are as follows:

- with the disappearance of the 30 years of glory model the so-called *mondialization* explosion began;

- the expansion of capital markets, supported by advances in information technology and the inversion of American monetary policy in 79 characterize this second *mondialization,* now based on the abolition of frontiers;
- What is termed the third *mondialization* was made possible from the beginning of the 90s, thanks to the opening of the ex-communist bloc and liberalizing pressures of the developed world.

Globalization has created difficulties that have accentuated the tendency to social and economic inequity that is a feature in many countries today, including Portugal. In this context, Portugal is confronted by, on the one side, areas where development is the order of the day, and, on the other, by territories that continue to be 'marginal' vis-à-vis the on-going process of development.

Despite the relativity of the concept of marginality, there is nonetheless a set of characteristics associated with the population in marginal areas, and these are important references. These include the existence of low population growth; fewer employment opportunities; less activity related to commerce, services, and a considerable degree of demographic ageing. However, marginality may be associated normally with areas of low population density, as well as marked migration. Furthermore, it may coincide with rural areas, but it is also present in urban areas, both in social exclusion, and in the different guises that poverty assumes.

Territorial marginality is of particular interest to geographers because of its spatial component. Nevertheless, it is an ambiguous concept, because of the relativity of the concept of marginality itself. It may characterize a territory remote from the centre in physical terms, just as it may be associated with a relative remoteness, in the ambit of determined human indicators (economic, social, political and others). This distancing implies a lack of availability of decision-making powers, located in the foci of development and at the service of them.

Marginal territories are usually characterized by a poorer quality of life and by scarcity and inadequate utilization of resources. These are territories where there is an increasing amount of social conflict, which sets these areas apart from the general system of 'normal standards' of life in the society. This fact brings about the perception of social exclusion as being a result of territorial marginality, since it is usual to associate marginal populations with marginal territories. Thus, one can be the cause of the other. However, territorial marginality may not find an explanation in territorial exclusion, that is to say, it might not be directly related with the social exclusion accompanied by a sparse population, and one that is age-ing.

Pessimism, dissatisfaction of the population, limited opportunities, the lack of development dynamics and remoteness relative to the principal structuring flows of territorial development characterize a 'problematic' space, territories that are isolated and neglected by the centres of power.

Other characterizing aspects of these spaces are bound up with the lack of productive structures and infrastructures, and enfeebled support services for the community.

The intention of this text is to show how Portugal, although integrated in the developed bloc that is the European Union, nevertheless displays economic, social and cultural indicators that are territorially well-defined in such a way that they could be regarded as marginal areas.

Economic inequalities: From the 'traditional' to the new inequalities

Portugal has been experiencing a visible evolution, in terms of both development and economic, social, political and cultural expansion. Portugal's membership of the European Economic Community (EEC), now know as the European Union (EU) has played a large part in making such expansion possible. The integration of the country into this economic group has become the chief orienting factor of policies and led to the opening-up of the Portuguese economy (Hadjimichalis, 1994).

This international incorporation of Portugal seems to accentuate economic inequalities, which implies unequal development. Indeed, along with all the advances that have been made, we find different disparities that are emerging due, not only to social transformation, but also to the absence of development models for the Portuguese territory. Portugal is not alone in having such a model. Other countries are also adding to their repertoire of inequalities in various domains (Cravidão, 1993).

Thus, to the structural (macroeconomic) asymmetries we may now add new ones, the so-called dynamic or microeconomic inequalities. However, regarding the 'traditional' inequalities that define the hierarchy of income among social categories, there are now new forms that concern, for instance, various situations relative to unemployment, within one particular category. When these inequalities intensify and persist to an increasing extent, a transformation takes place in the structure of society and in the representations that individuals make about it.

The inequalities are structural in the sense that, heirs to a long past, they have been partially assimilated into the society, which is not the same as saying that they are legitimate inasmuch as the degree of these inequalities vary from country to country.

The differentiated evolution of the system therefore overlays a 'traditional' structural inequality with a second one — dynamic inequality. This new type of inequality is, on the one hand, a reflection of the heterogeneity of the economic agents' situations, since individuals are not, even within the same category, confronted with the same situations, and, on the other, a product of the evolution of the system, of its own dynamic, given that the economy is in a constant state of mutation and restructuring. This means that there are some activities in expansion and others in decline, and, at the same time, there are cases of exclusion. The growth of inequalities may be a consequence of three things:

1. Weakness of the principles of equality;
2. Increase in structural inequalities, thereby widening the scope of inequalities;
3. The emergence of new inequalities.

These new asymmetries are going to have an impact on the populations and the new territorial structuring (Dunford, 1995). The so-called geographical inequalities comprise one of the most important dimensions of the modern matrix of inequalities. The less well-equipped localities are often those that serve as a place of refuge for persons in precarious situations.

There are, too, the social provisions produced by the complex between the individual and the Welfare State, and they too may be considered as inequalities. Starting from decentralization, we can see today a movement involving the overlapping of the national Welfare State by small local or private 'welfares'.

Other kinds of inequality arise from the economic, social, political and cultural evolution that has spread a little on every side, particularly in European countries, which includes Portugal, and this concerns the inequalities of access to the financial system. Inequalities of access to personal credit and investment have greatly increased and some (the poorest) will be excluded from it and will therefore not have the determination to improve their lot. The process thus generates cumulative inequalities that widen the gap between the individuals: imprisoned by their initial conditions, some cannot get away from them.

To these inequalities there may be added those that concern everyday life: inequalities vis-à-vis health; inequalities in housing; inequalities of access to public amenities; inequalities in the face of various forms of rudeness; inequalities with respect to matters of transport, aggravated by the social transformation of the territory, which serve to underscore the contrast between the social composition of the centre and that of the periphery, etc.

The list of inequalities is almost endless. This multitude constitutes the problem, as well as the likelihood of them accumulating with certain populations. Loss of employment often means, therefore, that the individual has to move house, leaving one place for another that is more polluted, less well served by public transport, enjoying less in terms of public amenities, all of which makes it more difficult to find another job.

These inequalities are precisely symptomatic of the social transformation and of a modification in the relations between one individual and another. Social disintegration conceals the points of reference, fragments social groups, creating differences among those who were formerly alike.

The issue at stake in this process is a breach of equality anticipated as being even more intolerable because it is without basis. The principles of equality, essential for social cohesion, are called into question by the multiplication of complex inequalities. In this context, it would be necessary to go back to the principal of equality, with the aim of remedying the excessive inequalities. The whole idea of equality consists in attenuating or compensating for the burden of the past to make conditions in the future less unequal.

At the back of the suffering engendered by the growth of inequalities a lurks a confusion: society wishes to rediscover points of reference where the craftsman, for instance, assumes forms of identification, criteria of equality, that allow him to better affirm his cohesion, while at the same time letting him better express his claims.

Re-establishing the conditions of equal opportunity, giving credit back to upward social mobility, is shown to be an essential issue: the fight against unemployment must become a credible one; the policy of public investment, urban renewal, education must be given the means to act in favour of equality of opportunity and, finally, the system of social welfare must pay more heed to biographical course of the individual.

Regional asymmetries — a scenario that remains

The recent evolution of some indicators that enable us to discern forms of marginality in Portugal leads us to the conclusion, albeit in an abbreviated form, that between 1991 and 1996 (Tables 15.1 and 15.2) the asymmetries that characterized Portugal for many years are still in place (Barreto, 1996).

Table 15.1   Concentration of regions with higher and lower values relative to various indicators, for 1991

Demographic Indicators	Regions with > value	Regions with < value
Resident Population	Greater Lisbon Greater Porto	Pinhal Interior South Serra da Estrela
Ageing Index	Pinhal Interior South Beira Interior South	Ave Cávado Tâmega
Overall Mortality Rate	Pinhal Interior South	Entre Douro e Vouga Ave
Infant Mortality Rate	Tâmega	Beira Interior South Pinhal Interior South
Illiteracy Rate	Pinhal Interior South Alentejo Litoral	Greater Lisbon Greater Porto
Percentage in Primary Sector	Alto Trás Montes	Greater Lisbon Greater Porto
Unemployment Rate	Baixo Alentejo Setúbal Peninsula	Entre Douro e Vouga
Housing Conditions: Mains Water	Greater Lisbon Setúbal Peninsula	Tâmega Dão Lafões
Electricity	Greater Lisbon Greater Porto	Alentejo Litoral
Drains	Greater Porto Greater Lisbon	Tâmega

Source: INE (1996), Recenseamento Geral da População and Estimativas da População.

Table 15.2   Concentration of regions with higher and lower values relative to various indicators, for 1996

Demographic Indicators	Regions with > value	Regions with < value
Resident Population	Greater Lisbon Greater Porto	Pinhal Interior South Serra da Estrela
Ageing Index	Beira Interior South Pinhal Interior South	Tâmega Ave Cávado
Overall Mortality Rate	Pinhal Interior South	Cávado Minho-Lima
Infant Mortality Rate	____	____
Illiteracy Rate	____	____
Percentage in Primary Sector	Centre	North
Unemployment Rate	Alentejo	Centre
Housing Conditions: Mains Water	____	____
Electricity	____	____
Drains	____	____

Source: INE (1996), Recenseamento Geral da População and Estimativas da População.

Analysis of the tables shows the two principal central areas: greater Lisbon and greater Porto. These are, effectively, the two metropolitan areas with the greatest levels of centrality, since they have organized economic structures, wider decision-making powers and capability to respond to external and internal factors, and they are the places where the concentration of activities and individuals is frankly greater.

This analysis will extend a little further than what is contained in the Table, nevertheless, we should reach the same conclusions by confirming that the situation found there, in the light of the demographic indicators, is one of the most favourable, in the context of centrality, in stark contrast to peripheralism (Ferrao, 1996).

The region of Pinhal Interior South may be regarded as a peripheral or, marginal, area, using the criteria under study. In both 1991 and 1996, a smaller number of the resident population was concentrated there, overall mortality is higher there, as is the illiteracy rate. No other region concentrates these characteristics, and this could lead to the conclusion that it is a relatively marginal region (Reis, 1993).

In fact, the existence of central areas presupposes the existence of peripheral areas, which usually depend on them for survival. Thus, defining centres implies the definition of peripheries and, emphasizing the role of the centre as a locality of growing innovation, the periphery is implicitly defined as space that is unfavourable to innovation. But there are still areas considered to be intermediate, neither central nor peripheral, occupying an intermediate place in terms of development and a position that is simultaneously one of subordination and autonomy. This characteristic is more applicable at international level, identifying the situation of each country relative to the rest. However, the classification of areas as central, semi-peripheral and peripheral is acceptable at regional level.

There now remains the pretension[1] of defining, on the Table, the areas that may be regarded as intermediate. Thus we have the Serra da Estrela, the Beira Interior South region, Alto Trás-os-Montes, the Alentejo Litoral and the Baixo Alentejo that are closer to peripheralism than to centrality, as their circumstances are not particularly advantageous, in terms of the indicators used. The regions of Ave, Cávado, Tâmega and Entre Douro e Vouga could already be regarded as being nearer to centrality than the preceding ones. They have better characteristics: lower ageing index; overall, mortality rate with low values, they have lower unemployment figures and good standards of housing.

Demographic ageing is one indicator that is hard to analyze. It represents development, if we are looking at a high index, bearing in mind that where high rates of ageing are attributed, then there are also high levels of development and growth. At the same time, however, these elevated indices might be related to marginal areas, which, because of that condition, have seen their young people and labour force leave the area. Therefore, the definition of marginal areas is a difficult task because of the complexity of factors and intervening agents, as well as the very difficulty of finding the criteria most appropriate to do it.

As with ageing, other indicators may not necessarily signify either marginality or centrality. For instance, the percentage in the primary sector: for some statistics this sector is under-valued, that is, part-time farming is not taken into consideration, and it still exists to a large extent in many areas. So the analysis of this indicator as instructor on territorial marginality is also very relative (Fernandes, 1996).

Indeed, what can be found are areas with different marginalities; in other words, areas that might be held to marginal according to some indicators, while they are not, if other ones are used. For example the region already identified as marginal, Pinhal Interior South, in spite of containing various unfavourable conditions when all the indicators under study are put together, with respect to the infant mortality rate, the percentage in the primary sector and the unemployment rate, the values found for that area were not the least favourable. In this respect, Tâmega (with the highest rate of infant mortality), Alto Trás-os-Montes (highest number in the primary sector) and the Baixo Alentejo and Setúbal Peninsula (high rates of unemployment) would earn the designation of marginal.

What has been said for the ageing index also applies to the unemployment rate. Usually it is the more developed areas that have a higher number of unemployed, or at least a higher rate of unemployment. Other areas exist, less developed, which, because of this status, do not concentrate desirable activities attractive to the labour force, nor do they have the viable employment structures that are needed. This means that the population looks for work in other areas, usually more developed ones. And so we come full circle: the population that is looking for work in the developed areas continually increases, and so there comes a time when there are not enough jobs for everyone, and the unemployment rate rises.

It has to be said that the case of the Islands has to be looked at separately, because of their localization. By themselves, they are considered to be isolated territories, where the centres (taking a geometric view) usually coincide with economic peripheries, since the coast is, in effect, the best locality for agreements, foreign relations, decision-making and, furthermore, for the sphere of transportation.

Given the existence of a whole series of circumstances militating against the realization of a truly solid and credible analysis that would lead to the definition of marginal areas, the aim proposed at the outset, it has only been possible to characterize regions as relatively marginal, in some aspects, or in others, or, on the contrary, central areas, not being entirely definitive or objective. It was, however, the only analysis possible just now, given the breadth of this work, on one side or another, due to the very recent nature of these phenomena, which makes them still ambiguous.

After the analysis of various indicators, paying heed to their evolution in the period 1960-1991/96, by districts for 60 and by NUTS III/NUTS II for 91 and 96, it may be acknowledged that there is a genuine and striking heterogeneity in Portugal.

The asymmetries that characterized Portugal for some time, especially between north/South and Coast/Interior, with particular focus on the coastalization of the country, now appear diminished, bearing in mind that heterogeneity among the various Portuguese territories is today greater and also more differentiated.

In addition, as regards defining the marginality of a region, we have found such heterogeneity to the point that it is not now possible to identify large areas as being peripheral, or to designate them as marginal territories, as the Interior of the country to some extent was once regarded. In fact, nowadays, an area does not need to be particularly large to contain a wide diversity of situations, permitting the coexistence of marginal regions and completely innovative areas.

Conclusion

In Portuguese society, opened to the world through emigration, mass communications, European integration and the globalization of markets, all expectations are allowed. Nevertheless, as a peripheral country, which it is still considered to be, Portugal is inferior in many aspects in comparison with western countries as whole. Despite having the same problems as other western countries, there is a disproportion between economic capacities and expectations, frequently leading to frustrations that are difficult to remedy.

It is in this fact of being the most peripheral of the countries of the centre that we find the special problem the Portuguese have in facing up to the social evolution of this decade and those to come.

At regional level, mondialization and globalization have been creating new difficulties, promoting the centrality of certain areas to the detriment of others regarded as territorially marginal. There is a strong coincidence between the 'modernization', partial disintegration of traditional rural spaces and 'urbanization' of Portuguese society, leading the marginal or central areas to exclusion or integration.

Although the North/South and Coastal/Interior dichotomies still persist, they are not as striking now as they once were; other, more markedly regional ones have been added to them, and these today need more care paid to them than do the differences between North and South, and the Coast and the Interior.

The chief tendencies that generally characterize Portuguese society today concern the rapid ageing of the population, the growing number of people engaged in the tertiary sector to the detriment of the primary sector, a considerable decline in infant mortality and a dramatic increase in the rate of unemployment. This global tendency is frequently broken when analyzed on a regional scale; in other words there are distinct local and regional differences that are the origin or consequence of the territorial centrality or marginality to which they are appointed.

Portugal is, effectively, a heterogeneous country where the economy plays an important part. Nevertheless, within this heterogeneity, there coexist fragilities and potentialities and, in this context, the country needs to know how to take advantage from what is positive and reduce the negative aspects, which is a hard task. Territories should, therefore make their mark through difference, searching for what is traditional to their chief potential relative to the surrounding spaces.

Note

1 The word 'pretension' is used since this is not an absolute definition, on the one hand because the terms of centrality, semi-peripheralism and peripheralism, given their actuality, find themselves having a major problem of definition, on the other, due to the fact that only some indicators perceptive of these characteristics are being considered.

References

Bailly, A., Jensen-Butler, C. and Leontidou, L. (1996), 'Changing cities: restructuring, marginality and policies in urban Europe', *European Urban and Regional Studies*, vol. 3:2, pp. 161-176.

Barreto, A. (1996), 'Três décadas de mudança Social', in António Barreto (ed.), *A situação social em Portugal, 1960 - 1995*, Instituto de Ciências Sociais, Universidade de Lisboa, pp. 35-60.

Barreto, A. and Preto, C. (1996), 'Indicadores da evolução Social', in António Barreto (ed.), *A situação social em Portugal, 1960 - 1995*, Instituto de Ciências Sociais, Universidade de Lisboa, pp. 63-162.

Copus, A. K (1997), 'Does Peripherality matter any more?', in G. Jones and A. Morris (eds), *Issues of Environmental, Economic and Social Stability in the Development of Marginal Regions: Practices and Evaluation*, Universities of Strathclyde and Glasgow, Glasgow, pp. 8-23.

Cravidão, F. Delgado (1994), 'Portugal: a Marginal Country in the European Community, or a European Country with Marginal Regions?', in Chang-Yi D. Chang *et al.* (eds), *Marginality and development issues in marginal regions*, National Taiwan University, Taipei, Taiwan, pp. 179-194.

Dunford, M. (1995), 'Winners and losers: the map of economic inequality in the European union', *European Urban and Regional Studies*, vol. 2:2, pp. 95-114.

204

Fernandes, J. L. (1996), *O Homem, o Espaço e o Tempo no Maciço Calcário Estremenho-o olhar de um geógrafo*, Master's Dissertation in Human Geography, Universidade de Coimbra, pp. 89-91.

Ferrão, J. (1996), 'Três décadas de consolidação do Portugal demográfico moderno', in António Barreto (ed.), *A situação social em Portugal, 1960 - 1995*, Instituto de Ciências Sociais, Universidade de Lisboa, pp. 165-190.

Fitoussi, J. P. and Rosanvallon, P. (1997), *A Nova Era das Desigualdades*, Celta Editora, Oeiras, pp. 41-99.

Forrester, V. (1997), *O Horror Económico*, Terramar Editora.

Hadjimichalis, C. (1994), 'The fringes of Europe and EU integration: a view from the South, in *European Urban and Regional Studies*, vol.1:1, pp. 19-29.

Leandro, M. E. (1994), 'Inter-confluências. Idoso-modernidade', in *Cadernos do Noroeste*, vol.7:2, pp. 55-67.

Leimgruber, W. (1993), 'Marginality and Marginal Regions: Problems of Definition', in Chang-Yi D. Chang et al. (eds), *Marginality and development issues in marginal regions*, National Taiwan University, Taipei, Taiwan, pp. 1-15.

Lonsdale, R. and J. Clark Archer (1997), 'Demographic factors in characterising and delimiting marginal lands, in H. Jussila, R. Majoral and C. Mutambirwa (eds), *Marginality in Space - Past, Present and Future*, Ashgate, Aldershot, pp. 135-149.

Nazareth, J. M. (1988), *Unidade e diversidade da demografia portuguesa no final do século XX*, Lisboa, Fundação Calouste Gulbenkian.

Reis, J. (1993), 'Portugal: Heterogeneidade de uma Economia Semiperiférica', in Santos Boaventura de Sousa (ed.), *Portugal Singular*, Centro de Estudos Sociais, Edições Afrontamento, Porto, pp. 131-161.

Rodrigues, T. (1995), 'A população portuguesa nos séculos XIX e XX. O acentuar das assimetrias de crescimento regional', in *População e Sociedade*, Centro de Estudos da População e Família, nº 1, pp. 57-86.

Rosa, M. J. Valente (1996), 'O envelhecimento e as dinâmicas demográficas da população portuguesa a partir de 1960 - dos dados ao dilema', in António Barreto (ed.), *A situação social em Portugal, 1960 - 1995*, Instituto de Ciências Sociais, Universidade de Lisboa, pp. 191-214.

16 Mill town without its mills: Preliminary assessment of the consequences of industrial abandonment

WILLIAM R. STANLEY

Introduction

South Carolina, in the south-eastern United States, has a score of communities derived from the location of a textile mill and provision for worker housing. Recently, failure to modernize coupled with severe competition from abroad has resulted in numerous plant closings. Unlike communities with industrial diversification, the traditional mill town frequently has only this one industry. Once its textile mills close, the town can be subjected to extraordinary economic and social trauma. Great Falls, South Carolina, is one such place. Located approximately 80 km north of the capital city of Columbia, astride the Fall Zone of the Catawba River, the town's three mills closed in rapid succession ending in 1985. Third, fourth and even fifth-generation mill workers found themselves out of work. Lost wages and reduced purchasing power in turn led to a decline in urban services. Redundant workers, especially those seeking meaningful employment, were obliged to go farther afield for jobs. In some instances, the choice was to work locally in poorly paid or at best minimum wage jobs or, as often the case, the need to leave the area and resettle elsewhere. Footloose replacement companies enticed to Great Falls proved to be unreliable neighbours. This type of company often seeks to take advantage of financial subsidies provided to depressed areas. The long-term objectives of some of these replacement companies seem less to produce products at competitive prices while offering stable employment opportunities and more to stay in place only so long as the financial subsidies continue.

If mill closings were not sufficient pain to this once thriving textile manufacturing town, then the fact that the Interstate Highway connecting Charlotte, North Carolina to Columbia was built 16 km to the west of Great

Falls proved to be a severe handicap to the town's prospects for economic recovery. Orientation of this particular highway made it difficult for the leadership of Great Falls to consider tourism as an alternative source of employment.

Critical issues

Workers, their labour unions, politicians and local leaders to varying degree voice concern for job retention and concomitant community vitality in an era of ever increasing employment insecurity. There is increasing out sourcing of jobs, downsizing of the work force, greater emphasis on off-shore manufacturing and ever increasing complexity in a sometimes confusing new world order. A situation has emerged in which opportunities for employment in information technology are seemingly unlimited whereas older, more established industries including some once considered the core of industrial societies are in serious decline. The number of jobs in these older industries is shrinking. It is not enough to say that worker re-tooling is the golden elixir and the solution to the post-industrial society faced with plentiful and well paid information technology jobs on the one hand and minimum paying service employment on the other hand. This is not a recipe for national stability.

Textile manufacturing has dominated the Southern Piedmont's industrial base for all of this century. Nevertheless, its relative position in manufacturing and regional employment is in decline and plant closings are increasing. Often only of passing interest to outsiders, the loss of a textile mill is always painful to the workers and constitutes a serious blow to the economic health of the local community. This paper examines some of the impact of a series of mill closures in a small South Carolina community.

Globalization – winners and losers

The consequences of the globalization of manufacturing are best viewed from the particular perspectives of the critical players namely, the locality or political entity gaining a new manufacturing plant and, in some cases, the locality losing one. The first of these by most accounts is the perceived winner. Leaders and the impacted population in a country, region or rural-urban setting mired in poverty or in economic backwardness of long standing are usually thrilled to attract the attention of a manufacturer, especially one whose name has international recognition. It is anticipated that such an acquisition will provide numerous opportunities for employment. Knowing that these workers will be paid at an enhanced local wage scale only adds to the attractiveness of this new neighbour. Indeed, many countries and regional entities have offices whose sole purpose is to attract new industry, firms previously located or still operating in the more affluent areas of the world. The companies for their part may be seeking expansion sites or, as is all too frequent, replacement sites for existing manufacturing facilities.

Once the suitor finishes extolling the beauty or overall attractiveness of the local environment and the positive work habits of prospective employees, the company representatives usually will shift the conversation to wages, work standards, environmental constraints and to the need for the corporate entity to insure that its labour and other manufacturing costs will be competitive in a global economy. Being competitive does not necessarily refer to wages and other expenditures in the country being abandoned but to labour, social services and environmental costs in more or less similar, industry-seeking developing countries. The additional perks of low taxes or lengthy tax-free holidays also are considered. It is an added benefit if the local education system produces a literate work force (even more of advantage if the language of instruction is English). Depending upon how eager is the suitor to attract new firms and the employment to be generated once the company is in operation or begins to construct the physical plant, the first newcomers may be offered exceptionally enticing financial incentives to relocate. These are offered on the assumption that, once in place, new arrivals may help to stimulate still more industrial relocation and the enhanced economic linkages certain to evolve.

Intra-regional manufacturing relocation within a technologically sophisticated country such as the United States often hinges on intangibles, all else being more or less equal. For example, decision-makers for companies considering expanding to South Carolina (or in similar settings) usually pay particular attention to the location of cultural and educational opportunities. Managers and senior staff want quality education for their children and some measure of exposure to the better things in life. In practice, it means that locations with nearby universities or other special attractions are more attractive than the less culturally endowed rural settings.

Unfortunately, these latter usually are the very places most in need of economic development through new manufacturing. Agglomeration of employment opportunities effectively negates efforts to shift manufacturing induced economic growth to the most needy areas. By comparison, the company considering the building a new manufacturing plant offshore in a Third World country may rank labour costs as the most important factor in any expansion. This could be attributed to the small number of key staff being positioned overseas and to the likelihood that they will live in an urban rather than a rural setting. Admittedly, there are many factors and not all companies share the same priorities.

In way of contrast, the situation in the locality soon to be vacated by the company undertaking seemingly wise overseas economic expansion or relocation is less promising. Moreover, the future is viewed with concern for both the short term and long term economic and social consequences. No matter how well planned and economically rationalized and notwithstanding goodwill on the part of the company, the fact remains that a significant corporate member of the local economic hierarchy is preparing to depart. Indeed, some of these departures have been singularly acrimonious and conspicuously lacking in goodwill. Notice to depart (or abandon) stimulates varied responses. If the town or region is otherwise economically well diversified, then the negative economic impact is softened by alternative employment opportunities. Alternatively, were the locality to be unusually dependent upon the departing company for jobs (the classic mill town model), then the situation can be disastrous.

This potential outcome is recognized as such by the participants. A company poorly positioned in its particular industry for whatever reason, or one that chose to enhance its dividend payments instead of allocating profits toward the modernization of its plant(s) in order to meet competitive challenges may envision real, immediate and substantial economic advantages in moving to another country. Low wages, lack of union activity and anticipated improvements in labour efficiency are powerful inducements for financially strong and growth oriented international companies. Consider how much more attractive are these same factors to corporations poorly positioned competitively in their sectors, or in declining and outmoded industries? There surely is a powerful attraction to at least contemplate a move offshore. If nothing else, such action represents something close to a corporate stay of execution and is an opportunity to at least enhance short-term profits.

Restructuring in the global economy

Evidence for an interconnected world economic system appears daily. If it is not the domino-like effect of stock exchanges (bourse) appearing to move in tandem with economic news, then it is the residual socio-economic consequences of companies taking their manufacturing offshore in order to reduce labour costs. World-wide, geographic specialization can be the death knell for certain low technology industries in technologically sophisticated countries. This is especially the situation for the workers, their families and the communities dependent upon the declining industry for sustenance. Moreover, loss of a manufacturing facility negatively impacts a variety of people and geographic settings. Textile manufacturing is a case in point. It once brought prosperity to places as distant in time and geography as Medieval Flanders and late 19th Century South Carolina. A year from the Millennium, the focal point for this industry has shifted to Asia and to Latin America, especially to countries with aggressive economic development aspirations. Only the most modernized, capital intensive components of this industry are assured of retaining a long term presence in what was once the important southern textile belt of the United States. These survivors are nimble, innovative and quick to adopt the newest technology or to seek the latest market niche. No longer, however, can such companies be considered labour intensive. The region's remaining textile companies are world leaders and able to compete with anyone.

Textiles, of course, are but one of several industries undergoing painful downsizing and restructuring. Ask anyone connected with the steel industry in Western Europe or in North America about restructuring and the discussion inevitably will shift to the negative impact of low cost imports from places as diverse as Korea, South Africa or Brazil. Those adversely impacted by low-priced imports produced in countries with relatively low labour costs often seek political protection in the form of higher tariffs. Industry specific protective tariffs are not without cost and governments in wealthy countries are faced with a dilemma. Constructs of the dilemma may encompass these and other possible options. For example, it is widely accepted that prosperity in the technologically sophisticated countries is best sustained and enhanced for the long term by maintaining qualitative and quantitative superiority in the information-technology sectors and not with traditional labour intensive industries. The reasons are not difficult to discern.

Trading partners among the emerging economic giants of tomorrow must have a substantial portion of low cost products in their export mix.

Otherwise, these countries will not be able to generate the requisite foreign exchange necessary to buy high tech imports. What may seem logical in theory, however, is viewed differently in practice. This is especially the case when you, your family or friends are among those left behind by industrial restructuring. This paper deals with a town in South Carolina whose early growth and economic prosperity were coincidental with textile manufacturing and whose present, near comatose situation is in large measure due to the closure of its mills.

Study site

Great Falls is a typical southern mill town (in the northern United States, a mill town generally denotes steel manufacturing. In the South, however, this term most often is applied to textile manufacturing, either of the basic fabrics from cotton and artificial thread or apparel from these fabrics) situated astride the Fall Zone of the Catawba River, roughly midway between Columbia, South Carolina's capital, and Charlotte, North Carolina's largest metropolitan area and one of the country's emerging banking centres. Prior to Duke Power Company's construction of the first of a series of hydroelectric dams and power plants on the Catawba River in 1905, the name Great Falls better described the swirling white water flowing over rocks on this meeting point between the easily eroded sedimentary stratum of the Coastal Plain and harder material comprising the Piedmont. There had been an earlier and relatively small textile mill in the vicinity that was used by the Confederacy during the American Civil War but this facility was no longer in operation. Duke Power, presently one of the leading players in the American energy sector and a corporation with its roots in this particular location, was at the time in the business of generating electricity. It eventually sought out an established textile company to take over operation of mills that Duke was then operating. It was by this succession that Republic Mills became an early user of these facilities and it was through this company and with time that the JP Stevens and Company was to come onto the scene, to remain until its final departure in 1985.

The first textile mill was built in 1910. Two additional mills were constructed in 1916 and 1925. Coincidental with mill construction was the provision for worker housing in the immediate vicinity of each of the three mills; this housing is one of the important spatial manifestations of Great Falls and, in its time, was a major inducement for attracting labour. Not only was this community to emerge as a typical southern mill town, its internal urban morphology was built around three mills each with its separate housing scheme. This provided it with a special appearance. There are numerous rock outcroppings at the site of Great Falls and one marvels at the regularity of building lots and the layout of streets guaranteed to afford workers easy walking distance to their particular mill. Many homes have one or more large boulders on the grounds and the neatly manicured lawns so common to the American scene are the exception in this mill town.

Provision for housing must surely have been a significant capital expense during the early evolution of the mill town. Mill owners at the outset considered it necessary in order to attract and maintain labour. In time, however, the cost incurred in maintaining the homes and in providing utilities at minimal rents to the occupant was viewed by some in management as an unwise use of capital. The view was that this resource might better be employed in mill operation, plant modernization or expansion. In time, this led to the privatization of housing. As long as the mills were operating, privatization of housing had little effect on the internal morphology and social dynamics of the town. Worker occupants were given first option to buy and reasonably favourable financial terms were made available. Indeed, it was a difficult transition for the corporate entity and the long-standing ethos of corporate paternalism was to be maintained almost to the last. For example, middle aged residents of Great Falls recount with considerable nostalgia how JP Stevens provided the children at the Great Falls schools with a Christmas bag containing fruit, candy and a 50 cent coin. When asked about children who did not have family or relatives employed in the mills, the response was that all of the children received bags! This suggests the level of interconnection between town and mill. Once mill closures started and unemployment increased, the housing environment became cause for concern.

All three sub-communities formerly shared a relatively small, nearby shopping district centred on a company owned and operated general store and a somewhat larger, more distant alternative business area less directly controlled by JP Stevens and Company. This dichotomy is not unique to Great Falls but certainly helped to characterize the 'them' and 'us' spatial differentiation of the model mill town.

This is not to suggest that worker-management relations were strained in the typical mill town. They were unusually harmonious, especially when compared to other industries or to other regions of the country. Aside from a short, bloody and intense period of strife in the 1930s when unions were trying to organize southern mill workers, the picture of tranquillity best describes the situation. Through World War 2 and continuing into the period of civil rights legislation of the 1960s, southern mill workers were best described as white, Protestant, of limited formal education and likely to have a number of relatives as fellow workers. Housing, while somewhat plain in appearance, was functional and obtained for relatively low rent. Not only were workers housed within walking distance of their place of employment, their housing in the mill town often was of better quality than what had been left behind in the rural, agricultural South. If nothing else, mill housing had running water. Rents were deducted from wages, as were debit accounts at the company owned store. Furthermore, it was the rare mill town that lacked playing fields or a quality indoors recreational facility. Mill towns were well known for the excellent quality of their athletic teams (baseball) and work schedules at the mills and throughout the town frequently were arranged around home games

JP Stevens and Company once had 48 textile mills scattered throughout the Southern Piedmont; parent companies of more recent corporate buyouts of portions of JP Stevens remain major players in textile manufacturing, particularly of speciality apparel. Indeed, it was the higher margins possible from apparel manufacturing that led in the final analysis to the closing of the Great Falls mills. The two oldest mills produced basic fabrics from raw cotton and synthetics and it is these operations that in recent years have consistently generated the lowest profit margins. They also are manufacturing processes readily shifted overseas due to the lower technical innovations when compared to apparel and other finished products such as furniture covering.

There was a time when this single company purchased 5% of the total cotton production in the United States. Participating in an industry-wide trend of the early 1960s, JP Stevens sealed heretofore-open windows of its three Great Falls plants in order to prepare the buildings for central air conditioning. This financial expenditure would enhance mill production and add to worker comfort. The timing is important. It seems clear in hindsight that neither the JP Stevens Company nor the American textile industry at large was sufficiently perceptive at the time to comprehend the forthcoming economic and political impact of foreign textile production and its marketing in the United States. Nor was the industry at the time alert to the willingness of succeeding American administrations in Washington to gradually increase import quotas for foreign textiles and fabrics. Were this not the case, then one must question whether locally expensive improvements such as air conditioning would have been undertaken in buildings and in a town destined to be abandoned in less than twenty years.

The impact of plant closures has a statistical face to its human dimensions. Making use of census reports and estimates provided by the South Carolina Department of Commerce, it is possible to define with reasonable precision the critical years of abandonment. In 1980 for instance, manufacturing employment in Great Falls amounted to 2045 jobs and of these, 1549 were in the three plants of JP Stevens and Company. Local emphasis on this one sector is better appreciated by the fact that 387 of the 497 employment slots not accounted for by JP Stevens were also in textile related employment. By 1984 and closure of two of the three main mills, total manufacturing employment in Great Falls had fallen to 1389 jobs. Only 761 manufacturing jobs remained in Great Falls at the time of the 1990 Census. Loss of nearly two-thirds of its jobs in a decade, more precisely in the first half of the decade, surely had serious geographic multiplier ramifications for this relatively small and socially compact community. No less ominous was the fact that little would be accomplished in alleviating the negative impact of so many lost jobs. There were efforts to do so.

Conclusions

Measuring the human impact of so many lost jobs is complicated. It is not only the individual or his or her household, but the larger community and its role that are subject to change. Many mill workers found that they owned their home but lacked the financial means to maintain it and, in some cases, even to keep up with mortgage payments. This has led to speculation on the part of some with financial resources, both local and from out of town, to buy several homes and to rent them wherever possible. One individual owns as many as 100 dwellings. Responsible behaviour of the typical home owner often is replaced by the less desirable but hardly uniform renter attitudes toward cleaning up of the premises and undertaking timely and often necessary maintenance. No longer able to call upon the maintenance team formerly maintained by JP Stevens, the latest generation of residents includes many who are not prepared to do for themselves that which formerly was provided gratis. Needless to say, pockets of decay within each of the three housing communities have appeared and it is the unusual street that lacks at least one eyesore. Community led redevelopment efforts have led to major renovations to several homes but are constrained because of a lack funds. These monies come largely from federally funded redevelopment programs.

Those unable to qualify for company pensions or Social Security (national mandatory insurance program) at the time of plant closing were faced with difficult decisions. One option was to stay put and to seek alternative employment. As previously noted, there was little opportunity for this in the Great Falls area. Local leaders and South Carolina State agencies endeavoured to attract new employers but these efforts were at best marginally successful. Indeed, the few companies that were attracted to Great Falls through the use of liberal financial incentives did not bring lasting benefit to the community. It is not difficult to understand.

There exists in every country or political subdivision individuals and firms looking forward to the prospects of tying into relocation subsidies as an objective in its own right. These people and the entities they control follow the financial inducement trail only for so long as the inducements remain. This represents at best only a partial and usually a short-term solution to unemployment problems in towns abandoned by their primary employer. Indeed, there is a growing constituency, which questions subsidies of this nature. That said, there seems little prospect of ending corporate relocation inducements however poorly they satisfy the long term job creating needs of impacted communities. It is widely accepted that Government has an obligation to try to resolve certain of the inequities inherent in the market. To do nothing entails political risk. The effect of this type of subsidy on the community and the spatial parameters of this town's internal cohesiveness during a long decade of economic distress and emotional pain are to be studied in the follow-up investigation.

17 Demographic factors contributing to regional imbalances in Spain

DOLORES SÁNCHEZ-AGUILERA AND ROSER MAJORAL

Introduction

During the second half of the present century, the Spanish territory has undergone a series of far-reaching demographic, economic and social changes culminating in a situation today which is characterized by the notable regional and local imbalances to which the territory is subject. These contrasting conditions are partly a result of the physical nature and the history of the country, but without question they are also heavily indebted to vital economic changes affecting the country.

Several official institutions have recently been simultaneously empowered by their relevant competent bodies – the EU, the state government, the autonomous communities and the local governments – to put an end to this situation of imbalance, the origins of which lie rooted in the past (Font, *et al.*, 1996). The firm establishment of the country's decentralized political organization and its admission to the EU constitute two major steps for the implementation of regional development policies. These policies have, nonetheless, proved to be insufficient to mitigate the marked contrasts between Spanish territories and between Spain itself and the EU. Thus, even though Spanish national income has progressively fallen into line with the average EU income – in 1981 Spanish national income amounted to only 71% of the average EU income, whereas in 1991 it amounted to 81% – and even though a similar trend has been recorded among the regions of Spain, the continuation of such imbalances may well be the sign of deeper territorial conflicts that suggest no immediate solution. In this light, the analysis of the delimitation of emerging marginal areas and their effects on the whole of the Spanish territory may be an interesting starting point from which to assess the effectiveness of the regional development policies mentioned above.

Obviously, the identification and exhaustive characterization of the marginal areas of Spain is a task, which far exceeds the scope of this paper. However, what we do aim to present are criteria, which will allow us to define and delimit marginality in Spain more accurately. In so doing we refer to a previous paper focusing on this same issue as it affects Catalonia, which this present study seeks to complement (Majoral, and Sánchez-Aguilera, 1998). Here we deal with the many demographic factors which, deriving from a long process of re-distribution of space, have given rise to geographical areas of low population density and with overall structural characteristics typical of marginal areas suffering economic decline (Lonsdale and Archer, 1998; Sánchez-Aguilera, 1996).

The main source of data for this study is the CERCA, a compilation of the most recent censuses conducted. Specifically, data have been used from the Agrarian Census of Spain (1989), the Population Census of Spain (1991) and the Census of Buildings (1990). This statistical compilation boasts two new features not previously seen in publications released by the National Institute of Statistics: first, it is published in computerized format with a tailor-made program for data transfer; second, it allows highly detailed spatial studies to be conducted, since the statistics provide a spatial breakdown of the data at the scale of the municipality, a feature rarely found in printed statistical data. It is precisely this second feature, the availability of data from the municipalities, that particularly recommends the data source for use in our study as it allows us to rigorously delimit territorial areas.

In spite of these advantages afforded by the data source, we should perhaps also identify some of its limitations. Basically, there are two weaknesses to using the CERCA data: first, some of the statistics are relatively out-of-date; second, the number and detail of the cross-data are sometimes left wanting. Thus, in relation to the first point the most extreme case is that of the Agrarian Census conducted in 1989. The source is almost a decade old but no alternative is as yet available, since the next Agrarian Census will not be conducted until next year and new data will not see the light of day for yet a few more years. In the case of population, the data are more recent, being drawn from the 1996 Census, although we have chosen to use data from 1991 as they correspond more closely to that of the Agrarian data. As for the number of variables contained in the CERCA, these are fewer than in the printed provincial data and at times they are insufficient, e.g. the lack of detailed cross-data (for example a detailed classification of the branches of economic activities or complex cross-data such as marriage status according to age and sex).

Regional imbalances and economic change in Spain

The evolution of the Spanish economy and, in particular, the effects on it following the establishment of a certain model of territorial organization became especially relevant after 1959, when a notable shift occurred in economic policies with the initiation of the Stabilization Plan. This brought to an end a previous stage of imposed economic self-sufficiency and ushered in a new period, which proved to be that with the greatest economic growth in the recent history of Spain. The modernization and mechanization of agricultural activities, the new investments made by foreign capital in the country and the resulting increase in industrial and tourist activities were some of the signs of an emerging economy. However, the transition did not keep an even pace. Thus, after a number of years of vibrant growth in the 60s and the early 70s, there came the effects of the 1973 economic crisis. The period of economic decline started in Spain towards the end of the 70s as a consequence of the delayed implementation of counteractive economic measures and the peculiar Spanish political situation in the mid 70s – the end of Franco's dictatorship and restoration of Spain to democracy. The period's most salient characteristics were a rise in inflation, a decrease in the rate of investment, a deficit in the balance of payments and an alarming unemployment growth rate. This stage of economic decline, spanning from 1979 to 1985, would later be superseded by one of moderate economic renewal, which, with some ups and downs, takes us up to the present day.

Parallel to these changes in the Spanish economic structure, other changes in the then territorial organization of the country were being brought about. Up to the end of the 70s, the country had been largely characterized by the continuing fragmentation of the territory in terms of the concentration of population and economic activities, which favoured certain areas at the expense of others. This spatial distribution was clearly the result of other trends. First, vast rural areas had been deserted and this out-migration led to a considerable fall in the agricultural working population. Second, the economic expansion during the 60s and early 70s had come to strengthen the privileged position of the existing industrial areas of Catalonia, the Basque Country, and that of Madrid (Majoral, Andreoli and Cravidao, 1997), which was emerging as a generator of economic activity, though already boasting a considerable power. Third, new industrial areas (Valencia, Asturias) had rapidly established themselves. These, thanks to the implementation of certain political measures, such as the so-called Polos de Desarrollo (Development Focuses) of Valladolid, Zaragoza,

Sevilla, Vigo among others, had given rise to new economically active areas, though to a somewhat lesser extent than the traditional areas described above (Bosque and Méndez, coord., 1995; Méndez and Raquin, 1997). And last, the intense growth of tourism in coastal areas, particularly on the Mediterranean coast, and on the Balearic and the Canary Islands, demarcated these zones as territories of high economic activity.

The duality of the Spanish territory economically active versus economically stagnant areas – which undoubtedly contributed greatly to the establishment and strengthening of regional imbalances, was first called into question in the early 80s. The severe economic crisis affecting most industrial areas of Spain – especially the Atlantic coast and, to a lesser extent, Catalonia – together with the emergence of new economically dynamic territories – expansion south of the densely-populated Madrid industrial area to include both Guadalajara and Toledo, consolidation of a new axis along the river Ebro joining Zaragoza and Navarra – marked a turning point in the territorial organization. However, the powerful effects of the major trends leading up to the 70s, which had contributed to the regional imbalances, were difficult to erase by the simple implementation of regional balancing policies. Thus, regrettably, the efforts made to reduce the inequalities between Spanish territories have been insufficient, and many of the imbalances originating in the trends prevailing in this second half of the century are still very much evident.

Spatial redistribution of the population

The changes in the Spanish territorial organization during the second half of this century are better understood if seen in the light of trends in population redistribution and demographic evolution (Puyol (ed.) 1997).

Population density in Spain is quite low if compared with other European countries. However, the mean population density (80 inhab./km^2) is the result of combining extremely low densities (below 10) and extremely high figures (those corresponding to major cities such as Madrid, Barcelona and Cádiz). These sharp contrasts reflect a long-standing trend amongst the population to concentrate in very specific areas, as well as an equally significant trend: that of the rapid relocation of the population to coastal areas (Figure 17.1). The latter is not new and is perhaps the unfailing characteristic of the 20th century. Earlier efforts during the decades of economic over-development laid the foundations, which account for the biased

219

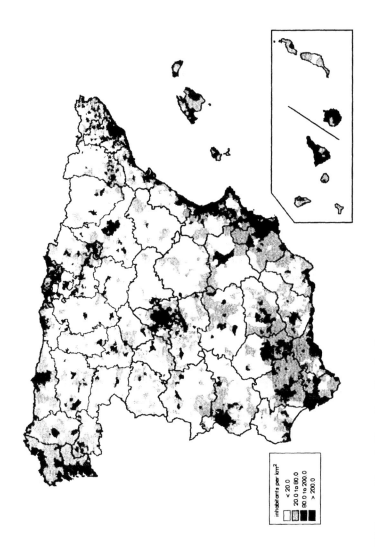

Figure 17.1   Population density, Spain

Source: INE: Censo de la Población de España, 1991.

population distribution and which resulted in the apparent duality: over-populated on the coast and under-populated inland. This pattern of population redistribution, albeit oversimplified, is complemented by the north-south pattern of population relocation, particularly apparent in the plateau area rising in the heart of the country.

However, to have an entirely plausible picture of the country's population distribution demands attention be paid to additional evidence, which is not completely at, odds with the patterns described above. First, there is the disruption of the 'demographic desert' spreading over the central plateau caused by the presence of the city of Madrid. The fact that Madrid was chosen as the capital of the state is critical in accounting for this otherwise unusual site for a large city, although a further factor, essentially economic, also had a considerable role to play in the expansion of the city throughout the 20th century. Around the periphery of Madrid an industrial belt has grown up. A similar expansion, however minor, affected the other capitals on the plateau, including Segovia, Ávila, Valladolid, Salamanca, Toledo and Burgos, all of which record high population densities because of their essentially urban nature.

Another issue worth analyzing for a complete understanding of population distribution in Spain is the existence of a number of densely populated areas which do not fit into the patterns described above: remarkable in this respect are the areas along the rivers Guadalquivir and Ebro. These are more densely populated than would normally have been expected given their physical characteristics, which favour agriculture and the establishment of large population settlements, though not on the scale to which it has actually occurred. Finally mention should be made of the mountain areas, such as the Pyrenees, the Iberian System and the Central System, which unlike the above, are characterized by low population densities.

The relocation and redistribution of the population has obviously affected the demographic evolution of Spanish villages, towns and cities. If one examines the cumulative rate of yearly demographic variation between 1971 and 1991 (Figure 17.2), it is quite apparent that the areas of lowest population density correspond well with those showing a steep demographic fall. Thus, much of the plateau, particularly the northern section, suffered a stark demographic recession with a mean yearly loss of 2% of its population during this 20-year period. The southern section of the plateau and part of Andalusia were also affected by the same process, if not quite so severely. Indeed, a large proportion of the Spanish territory suffered

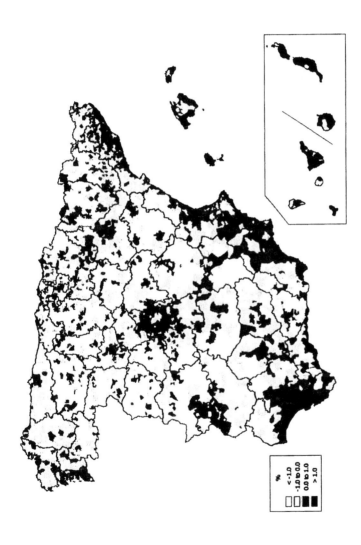

Figure 17.2   Annual population change rate (%), Spain

Source: INE: Censo de la Población de España, 1970 - 1991.

demographic decline during these two decades. In the early 70s, this decline was still the result of population fleeing rural areas to either urban – Madrid, Barcelona – or more economically active areas – Mediterranean coast, Catalonia, Basque Country – (García-Coll et al., 1995). From 1980 onwards, the continuing demographic decline can no longer be explained in terms of migratory movements but rather as the result of a negative balance of natural demographic growth. Rural areas, badly affected by the emigration of most young adults, have been unable to recover: deaths clearly outnumber births leading to demographic recession.

This picture is not complete without considering briefly the distribution of population by age. Today, the most outstanding characteristic is the ever-growing mean age of the population (Abellán, dir., 1996). A map showing areas with the highest relative proportion of population over 65 years not unsurprisingly overlaps with a map showing those areas most affected by the trends described above, since both are in effect the opposite sides of the same coin. Again the north-south pattern is visible here, complementing that of the core-periphery (López-Jiménez, 1991). First, the population in the southern half is, on the whole, younger than that in the north. This duality in part reflects the different paces of demographic evolution experienced in the north and south: southern Spain was not exposed to demographic changes until only recently, having until now presented high birth and fecundity rates, which significantly contributed to the preservation of a somewhat younger mean population age. In the north of Spain, on the contrary, the already low fecundity rate was aggravated by the age-selective out-migration (young adults moving out). The combination of these two factors yielded a further propensity for the mean age of population to increase.

Second, and as described earlier, the north-south pattern of population redistribution coexists with an additional core-periphery pattern of population relocation. Indeed, coastal areas tend to show lower percentages of population over 65 years than are shown by inland areas. The reason for this is to be found in inland migratory movements. By the same token, the areas with the lowest mean population ages, even inland, tend to correspond with areas receiving immigration. Likewise, migratory movements provide the key to account for the high relative proportion of population over 65 in certain mountainous areas (Figure 17.3). These traditionally under-populated territories were exposed to severe demographic decline, which, in many cases, led to their disappearance because of the non-existence of younger generations to supersede the older generations (García-Coll and Sánchez-Aguilera, 1997).

223

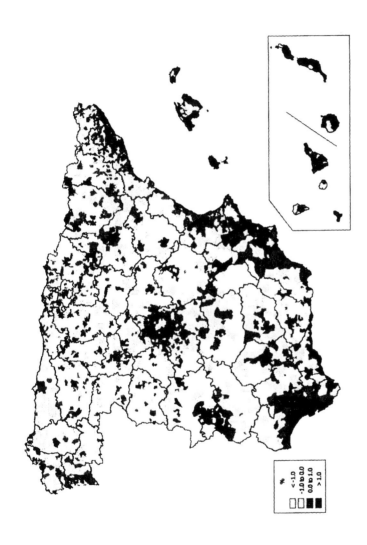

Figure 17.3   Population over 65 (%), Spain

Source: INE: Censo de la Población de España, 1991.

This can also be seen if we examine the relation between those receiving a pension and the active population. While not all pensions are retirement pensions, they are usually the main determining element of this group, in certain areas of the country they have gained considerable relative importance. Thus, while in Spain as a whole there were 36.7 pensioners for every 100 active members of the population in 1991, in about 1,000 municipalities (approximately 12.4% of the total number), the number of pensioners is greater than the number of active members of the population. In general, the highest figures are to be found in areas suffering the effects of an ageing demographic process usually coinciding with mountainous areas whose demographic structure has been ravaged.

Consequences for the agricultural population: An ageing population unlikely to be replaced

The demographic predicament of the Spanish population is considerably aggravated if we analyze only those areas living off agricultural production, which in the 50s still represented 50% of the Spanish working population, and in 1970, almost 30%. Although by 1991 such figures had decreased to almost 10% (two and a half million jobs in agriculture were lost in 20 years), the geographical distribution of these workers of the land is of great interest: indeed, in certain territories, such as the Basque Country, Catalonia, Balearic Islands or Madrid, the percentage is below 3.5%, whereas in Galicia or Extremadura it is still over 25%, and in certain provinces, such as Lugo (Galicia), it surpasses 30%.

One of the major effects of migratory movements on the rural population is a remarkable asymmetry in the remaining population as regards age and sex. Indeed, the mean age of the farming population has grown constantly, and by 1989, 43% were over 55 years, and 20% were over 65. Age-selective out-migration (young adults moving out) makes it impossible for younger generations to replace their elders in the exploitation of the land (Figure 17.4). For the whole of Spain, the ratio between the number of farmers retiring in the forthcoming years (over 65 years) and the number of those who have joined agricultural activities in the last 10 years (below 25 years) is only 0.337. In other words, only one third of present farm workers is certain to be replaced (Majoral, 1997). As regards sex asymmetries, they vary in importance according to the area and the type of agriculture.

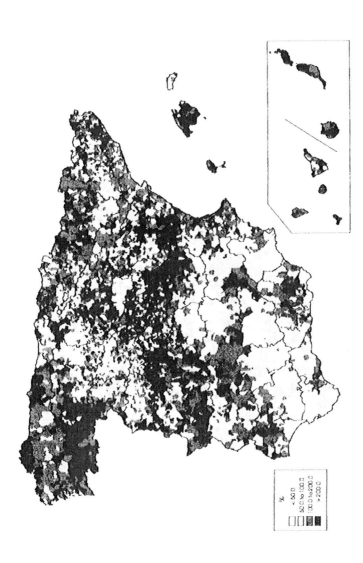

Figure 17.4   Replacement rate in agriculture labour force, Spain

Source: INE: Censo Agrario de España, 1989.

In some areas, both age and sex asymmetries are severe, so that population under 25, or even 35, is practically non-existent. Thus, in the Balearic Islands, from an overall 3.3% of farming population, only 3% are under 25 years, while 25% exceed 65; Galicia, although exhibiting a somewhat higher percentage of young farmers (7%), has nevertheless the highest percentage of population over 65 (29%). In other areas, however, the replacement of the old by the young does not seem to be under such great a threat: in Andalusia, the farming population under 25 years is 11% compared with 14% of farmers over 65; Castilla-La Mancha shows 10% and 19% respectively. Additionally, there appears to be, generally speaking, a correlation between mean age of the farming population and average yard size (or economic profits from the poor to support their workers tend to coincide with areas with the highest mean ages, from which it might be assumed that the meagerness or the barrenness of the land is often the cause of emigration.

There seems to be a further correlation between age and the part-time exploitation of the land: areas with moderately high proportions of young farmers tend to coincide with areas in which farming is increasingly becoming a part-time activity, particularly amongst the young, who look for an extra source of income. This, unfortunately, casts some doubt on the above assertion that, in some areas, the replacement of the old by the young is not under threat: it is not at all clear that young people who are currently working part-time on the family land and who have a second job will as a matter of course opt to enter the farming business.

Synthesis and conclusion

Of all the variables discussed, the five most significant (population changes between 1970-1991, population density, mean age of overall population, mean age of farming population, and degree of difficulty for younger farming generations to replace the older ones) have been used to draw a map which shows the areas of maximum demographic decline in Spain, that is, the areas where most of these variables overlap (Figure 17.5).

The claims made in the preceding pages are unambiguously demonstrated here. First, there is a stark contrast between the northern and southern halves of the country, the south presenting on the whole lower mean ages of the overall population, which in turn correlate with lower overall mean ages of the farming population, thus enhancing the possibility

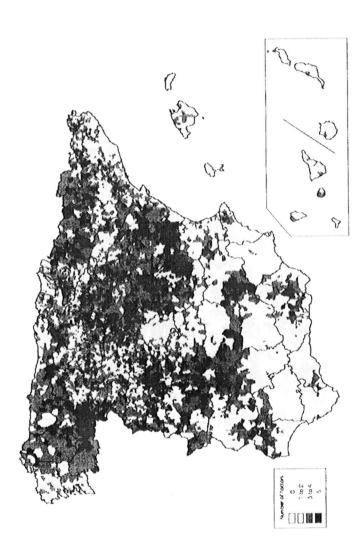

Figure 17.5   **The marginal Spain according to demographic factors**

Source: INE: Censo de Población de España, 1991 & Censo Agrario de España, 1989.

that younger farming generations will replace the older ones. This, however, does not preclude high rates of emigration in this half (in fact, this is the only variable apparently operating in some areas). Second, coastal areas, particularly along the Mediterranean, appear to have been clearly favoured by the immigration of young adults due to the flourishing of tourist and industrial sectors. Third, the overlapping of the five variables in certain mountainous areas is obvious, marking the limits of the Iberian System, the northern part of Madrid and certain isolated mountain territories. In contrast to this are the valleys of major rivers, where the exploitation of irrigated lands reflects on the demography of the zone. Finally, the emergence is clearly visible of other areas spreading out from and around developing settlements, both major and minor, well-established and those, which are still embryonic. Amongst these are Madrid and its industrial belt, Barcelona along with a good part of the Catalan territory, the Basque Country, and some other minor cities and nearby villages.

The vastness of the territory shaded in dark colours on the map confirms the scope of the phenomenon discussed: large areas where emigration has left the remaining farming population bereft of the possibility that it might ever have had of being replaced by younger generations. These areas constitute what might be termed marginal Spain, where demographic decline - certain to bring, sooner or later, the disappearance of the settlement altogether - contributes to the grim socio-economic prospects of the territories, plunged in a crisis from which there seems no escape.

References

Abellán, A. dir. (1996), *Envejecer en España. Manual estadístico sobre el envejecimiento de la población*, Fundación Caja de Madrid, Madrid.

Bosque, J. and Mendez, R. coord. (1995), *Cambio industrial y desarrollo regional en España*, Oikos Tau, Barcelona.

Font, J., Majoral, R. and Sánchez-Aguilera, D. (1996), 'Regional development policies and incentives in Marginal areas of Catalonia', in M. E. Furlani *et al.*, *Development issues in marginal regions II: Policies and Strategies*, Universidad Nacional de Cuyo, Mendoza, Argentina, pp. 27-48.

Garcia-Coll, A., Pujadas, I. and Puga, D. (1995), 'Migraciones interiores en España. Tendencias recientes y perspectivas de futuro (1971-2001)', *Revista de Geografía*, vol. XXIX, núm 3.

Garcia Coll, A. and Sánchez-Aguilera, D. (1997), 'Tamaño demográfico municipal y población: posibilidades de análisis a partir del censo de 1991', *Estudios Geográficos*, n° 45.

Lonsdale, R. and Archer, J.C. (1998), 'Demographic factors in characterizing and delimiting marginal lands', in H. Jussila, R. Majoral and C, Mutambirwa (eds), *Marginality in Space - Past, Present and Future*, Ashgate Publishing, Aldershot, UK, pp. 129-143.

López Jiménez, J.J. (1991), 'Envejecimiento, tamaño demográfico y sector de actividad en los municipios españoles', *Estudios Geográficos*, n° 36, pp. 163-182.

Majoral, R. (1997), 'Socioestructuras agrarias en España. Un análisis regional', in Bretón *et al.* (eds.), *La agricultura familiar en España. Estrategias adaptativas y políticas agropecuarias*, Ediciones Universidad de Lleida, Lleida, pp. 45-82.

Majoral, R., Andreoli, M. and Cravidão, F. (1997), 'Regional perceptions of marginality. A view from Southern Europe', in H. Jussila, W. Leimgruber and R. Majoral, (eds), *Perceptions of Marginality – Theoretical and regional perceptions of marginality in geographical space*, Ashgate Publishing, Aldershot, UK, pp. 147-165.

Majoral, R and Sánchez-Aguilera, D. (1999), 'Remaining Marginal areas in Catalunya', in H. Jussila, R. Majoral and C. Mutambirwa (eds), *Marginality in Space - Past, Present and Future*, Ashgate Publishing, Aldershot, UK.

Mendez, R. and Raquin, J. (1997), 'Nouvelles tendances de la localisation industrielle en Espagne', *Méditerranée*, n°. 3-4, pp. 55-62.

Puyol, R. (ed.) (1997), *Dinámica de la población en España. Cambios demográficos en el último cuarto del siglo XX*, Síntesis, Madrid.

Sanchez-Aguilera, D. (1996), 'Evaluating marginality through demographic indicators', in R.B. Singh and R. Majoral (eds), *Development issues in Marginal Regions: Processes, Technological development and Societal Reorganizations*, Oxford & IBH Publishing Co. Pvt. Ltd., Delhi, India, pp. 133-148.

Acknowledgements

This paper has been prepared as part of the research project entitled *Delimitación y análisis de las áreas marginales en Cataluña*, funded by the Dirección General de Investigación Científica y Técnica (DGICYT) of the Ministerio de Educación y Cultura (Research Project: PB95-0905), and by an *Ajut de Suport a la Recerca dels Grups Consolidats del II Pla de Recerca de la Generalitat de Catalunya (Grup de Recerca d'Anàlisi Territorial i Desenvolupament Regional*, 1997SGR-00331).

18 Social neighbourhoods in peripheries:
A Finnish-Swedish comparison

JARMO RUSANEN, TOIVO MUILU, ALFRED COLPAERT AND
ARVO NAUKKARINEN

Introduction

The principal method employed to identify areas entitled to support from
EU structural funds is to calculate a metric on the basis of surface area and
population, i.e. the number of inhabitants per square kilometre. This is easy
to do and in practice represents the relation between the population of an
administrative unit, e.g. a local government district, and its surface area
(e.g. Malinen *et al.* 1994). In Finland and Sweden, the two northernmost
EU countries, and also in Norway, a non-EU country, local government
districts vary greatly in size, so that calculations of population density may
run into the ecological fallacy (Martin 1991, pp. 57-58), i.e. that the situation described by the regional average does not exist in any actual area or is
rare. We endeavour in this paper to approach the problem, and preferably to
eliminate it altogether, by means of georeferenced data, which will remove
from the analysis any bias caused by uninhabited areas and concentrate attention on inhabited ones.

The article is part of a programme of research undertaken by the
authors to provide a more profound picture of the structure of rural settlement, one more specific aim of which is to visualize internal differences
within rural areas and regional differences between them. Although the
countryside is often perceived or experienced as a homogeneous entity,
there are in effect many types (e.g. Muilu *et al.* 1997). The aim is to ensure
that people perceive the differences between rural areas and particularly
between sparsely populated areas.

The present article analyzes by means of georeferenced data the questions of population density, distance from one's nearest neighbour, applying
the focal sum method, and the proportion of persons living a long distance
from the local centre.

Marginal areas are usually regarded as comprising a) sparsely populated areas, b) areas (grids cells) lacking any immediate neighbours, and c) areas lying more than 20 km away from any local centre.

Aims

The purposes of this paper are:

1) To compare the picture provided by the population density criterion traditionally used to identify remote and marginal areas with that gained from georeferenced data
2) To present a GIS-based visualization of the measurement of socio-spatial distance and of regional variations in this
3) To analyze and visualize the influence of distance on the population structure of a local government district, and
4) To continue the comparison of regional structures in Finland and Sweden.

The content of this work and the questions discussed in it were influenced by a paper given by Walter Leimgruber entitled 'Marginality and Marginal Regions: Problems of Definition' in the IGU Study Group on Development Issues in Marginal Regions, Taipei, Taiwan, in 1993. Geographical dictionaries such as that of Johnston *et al.* (1994) were also used as an aid. The problems considered were also affected by the authors earlier comparative research into demography in Finland and Sweden (Rusanen *et al.* 1997) and their numerous other investigations.

Material and methods

The material consisted of georeferenced data for 1 x 1-kilometre grid cells produced by the statistical offices of Finland and Sweden:

1) population in 1995
2) age structure of the population in classes 0-6, 7-15, 16-44, 45-64 and 65 years and above
3) sex ratio
4) location of the grid cells to an accuracy of 1 x 1 -kilometre
5) distance from local government centre.

The data on Finland used in some of the analyses include material from 1970 and 1980.

Maps can be regarded as perhaps the best indicators of peripheral status. Our group has previously published maps of settlement structure in Finland and Sweden (e.g. Rusanen *et al.* 1997), of which many copies have already been ordered. Feedback indicates that they have been used for a variety of purposes, such as indicating peripheral status, outlining areas of low population density or diffuse settlement, visualizing the pattern of long distances from local centres and describing the relations between inhabited and uninhabited areas. The results discussed in the present article are also largely based on visualization of local and regional phenomena by means of the GIS system. The related maps invariably employ a quartile classification. As some of the maps of Finland drawn up for the present purpose have already been published elsewhere (e.g. Rusanen *et al.* 1993), they will be referred to here only in the text. Most of the examples given concern Sweden.

Conventional population density vs. grid cell based population density

As stated above, population density is calculated here as inhabitants/square kilometre. A conventional population density map for the local government districts (communes) of Sweden is shown in Figure 18.1a, and alongside it, in Figure 18.1b, one based on georeferenced data, i.e. grid cells of size 1 x 1 kilometre. The latter excludes from the analysis all uninhabited areas, so that it includes only the inhabited areas, whereas calculations based on the traditional map would also take into consideration uninhabited areas. At first glance, the two maps appear identical. It can be stated by way of generalization that the densest population zone starts out from north of Stockholm and extends south-westwards to Gothenburg, whereas western and northern Sweden are the most sparsely populated areas.

More detailed scrutiny nevertheless points to fairly small differences. Firstly, the georeferenced data distinguish many communes in southern Sweden that represent the most sparsely populated quartile. Secondly, many communes in the north, particularly those on the Gulf of Bothnia coast, no longer fall into the most sparsely populated quartile but into the next class, i.e. their settlement structure is denser and more centralized than that of other communes with a low population density.

Measured in both the above ways, most communes with a low population density are located in northern Sweden, excluding most of the coastal districts. Assuming that low population density is an indicator of marginality, the approximately 40 communes which fall into the lowest quartile on both maps (Figures 18.1a and 18.1b) can represent the most marginal areas and local government districts in Sweden.

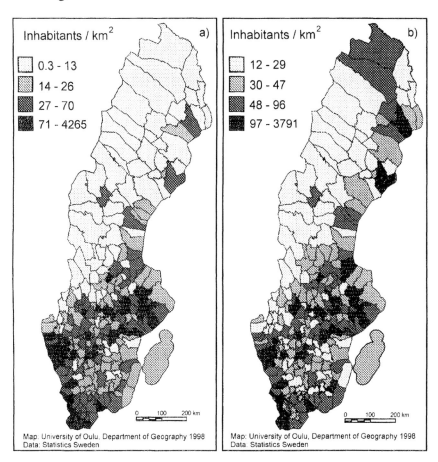

Figure 18.1   Population density by communes in Sweden in 1995. Conventional model (a) and grid cell model (b)

The situation in Finland is not as straightforward. Measured in the traditional manner, population density is low in the east and north (cf. Rusanen *et al.* 1993), whereas the analysis based on grid cells of size 1 x 1 kilometre shows the most sparsely populated areas to be located in Central Finland, while the north has an average population density.

Comparison of the pairs of population density maps for Sweden and Finland indicates that there are more than 40 local government districts in Sweden that represent the lowest population density quartile on both, whereas there are great differences between the two sets of results in Finland and the areas with a low population density differ greatly in their spatial distribution.

A summary of the proportions of the total population accounted for by the quartiles in the traditional and grid cell models is presented in Table 18.1. The figures produced using the two metrics differ in both countries. The lowest population density category contains a fairly small proportion of the total population in both countries, approximately 10% or less. The most notable difference can be observed in the most densely populated quartile, which contains a markedly greater proportion of all the communes in Finland. This may be mainly attributable to the considerably larger number of communes in Finland (455) than in Sweden (288).

Table 18.1   Proportions of total population in population density quartiles determined by the conventional and grid cell-based metrics

	Finland		Sweden	
	conventional model	grid cell model	conventional model	grid cell model
Quartile	%	%	%	%
1 (sparsest)	8.7	6.5	10.4	8.1
2	9.7	9.3	15.0	15.5
3	14.1	15.4	22.9	21.8
4 (densest)	67.5	68.7	51.7	54.6
Total	100.0	100.0	100.0	100.0

Sources: Statistics Finland and Statistics Sweden.

The number of inhabited 1 x 1 kilometre grid cells and the surface area data for the communes also enable another marginality metric to be calculated, i.e. the inhabited area as a proportion of total area. The resulting map can also be interpreted in the reverse manner by calculating the uninhabited area as a proportion of the total. The examples drawn up for both countries (Figures 18.2a and 18.2b) suggest that Sweden can be divided into two

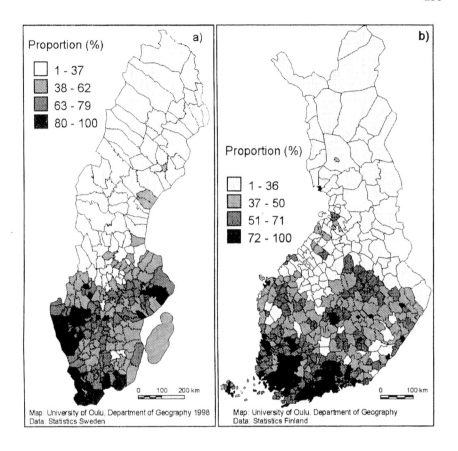

Figure 18.2   **Proportion (%) on inhabited areas by communes in Sweden (a) and in Finland (b) in 1995**

parts more distinctly than in the previous examples or the previous population density maps, and an evident dichotomy between the southern and northern parts of the country can also be observed in Finland. In both countries the minimum proportion of inhabited areas grid squares may only be slightly over 1%, the three extreme cases in Sweden being Kiruna, Jokkmokk and Arjeplog, and in Finland Enontekiö, Savukoski and Inari, all of which are located in the northernmost province of their country.

As regards the more densely populated southern parts, it may be noted that there are 21 communes in Sweden, which completely lack uninhabited areas, and 24 in Finland. This category includes the capital in both cases.

Socio-spatial distance in Finland and Sweden

An attempt was made above to provide a picture of the location of marginal areas in Sweden and partly also in Finland by means of three metrics. We now endeavour to fill out this macro-level regional structure by means of georeferenced data, which are completely independent of administrative divisions.

Socio-spatial distance here denotes the number of neighbouring grid cells around inhabited cells. Neighbours have been analyzed by using the hermit macro programmed by the authors (see also ESRI 1997), setting the height and width of the rectangle at 3 km (Figure 18.3a). The value one (1) was assigned to each inhabited cell regardless of the number of inhabitants in it (Figure 18.3b). The theoretical minimum indicated in Figure 18.3c is 1 which in practise means that there are no inhabited cells immediately adjacent to a given cell. Cases of this type are called hermits. Correspondingly, the theoretical maximum, including the cell to be analyzed, is nine (9); i.e. all the cells bordering on it are inhabited. It should be noted, however, that such cases occur only in built-up areas.

The purpose of the method is to provide an impression of the extent to which Finland and Sweden contain settlements of the most marginal type, i.e. isolated settlements. It also provides information on opportunities for meeting other people, for example. It should be noted that this is the first time that the term socio-spatial has been employed in this sense, so that it should be regarded for the time being only as a preliminary term.

The trend for Finland in 1970-1995 is quite clear. The proportion of areas, which by using the hermit macro analysis gave values of one or two, has increased most notably in relative terms (Table 18.2). This means in practice an increase in the number of instances of the sparsest level of population, presumably as a result of the thinning of conventional rural settlements. This conclusion is also backed up by the developmental features attached to sparse population in earlier research. Table 18.2 also points to a dichotomy in which the proportion of grid cells with a value 5 or less has increased whereas that with values exceeding 5 has decreased, except for the densest settlement of all.

The comparison between Finland and Sweden in Table 18.1 indicates that on this basis the countries differ in settlement structure in two ways. The most interesting phenomena from the point of view of socio-spatial distance are hermits, the grid cells that received the value 1 in the analysis;

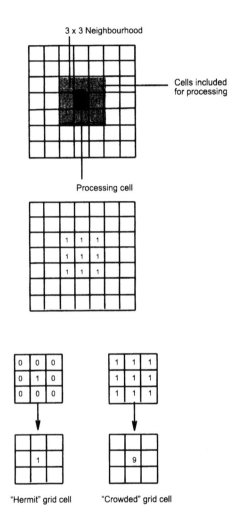

Figure 18.3   The hermit macro method

Table 18.2   **Grid cells by number of neighbours (% distribution) in Finland in 1970, 1980 and 1995 and in Sweden in 1995, using the hermit macro method with 3 x 3-kilometre neighbourhoods**

Number of neighbour grid cells	Finland 1970 %	Finland 1980 %	Finland 1995 %	Trend 1970-95	Sweden* 1995 %
0	1.8	2.1	2.0	+	2.9
1	4.0	4.4	4.6	+	4.4
2	7.3	7.8	8.0	+	6.7
3	10.7	11.1	11.4	+	9.7
4	14.3	14.8	14.6	+	12.7
5	16.6	16.5	16.3	-	15.3
6	17.4	16.8	16.5	-	16.2
7	16.0	15.1	14.6	-	16.3
8	11.9	11.4	12.0	+	15.8
Total (%)	100.0	100.0	100.0		100.0
Number of grid cells	110,477	104,540	103,037		117,905

* Data for 1970 and 1980 are not available for Sweden

Sources: Statistics Finland and Statistics Sweden.

i.e. they had no inhabited neighbours. Although these make up a surprisingly small proportion of all cells, there are almost 50% more of these in Sweden than in Finland, 2.9% vs. 2.0%. Such grid cells can occur almost anywhere in both countries, although they are far more common in the northern parts. On the other hand, the proportion of grid cells with a value of 2 or 3 is markedly smaller than in Finland. Another interesting finding is that the figures for Sweden exceed those for Finland by a wide margin as far as the extremes of settlement structure are concerned. This can be taken to indicate that the settlements in Sweden are more centralized and compact than those in Finland.

The comparison between Finland and Sweden in Table 18.1 indicates that on this basis the countries differ in settlement structure in two ways. The most interesting phenomena from the point of view of socio-spatial distance are hermits, the grid cells that received the value 1 in the analysis; i.e. they had no inhabited neighbours. Although these make up a surprisingly small proportion of all cells, there are almost 50% more of these in

Sweden than in Finland, 2.9% vs. 2.0%. Such grid cells can occur almost anywhere in both countries, although they are far more common in the northern parts. On the other hand, the proportion of grid cells with a value of 2 or 3 is markedly smaller than in Finland. Another interesting finding is that the figures for Sweden exceed those for Finland by a wide margin as far as the extremes of settlement structure are concerned. This can be taken to indicate that the settlements in Sweden are more centralized and compact than those in Finland.

Distinct conclusions can be drawn regarding the spatial distributions in Sweden (Figures 18.4a and 18.4b). The south and south-west coasts and the zone which extends from Stockholm and its surroundings to Gothenburg constitute a compact settlement core in Sweden, while the area located inside this together with the inland areas of northern Sweden are the most peripheral ones in terms of their socio-spatial properties.

The core settlement area in Finland comprises the Helsinki-Tampere-Turku triangle in the southern and south-west (Figures 18.5a and 18.5b). Socio-spatially peripheral areas are most numerous in the northern and eastern parts of the country, though they are also frequent in the south and west.

In theoretical terms, the sparsest settlement class can either increase or decrease in size. The present hermit macro method shows its proportion in Finland to have increased. Socio-spatially, this is a sign of a detrimental trend, a greater proportion of isolated settlements, since it is the most marginal settlements that are in the greatest danger of disappearing entirely with time (cf. Naukkarinen *et al.* 1991).

The measured socio-spatial distance may also influence relative distances. One could assume that a long distance between neighbours detracts from the number of occupational contacts among farmers, for example, and thus from occupational solidarity.

The method was also applied to the extremes in the age structure, i.e. the groups aged 0-15 years and over 64 years. The purpose was to find out the number of persons of the same age in the immediate surroundings, with the aim of examining the extent to which such people have access to potential companions.

It can be stated for both Finland and Sweden that the age-specific distributions differ greatly from those defined for the population as a whole. As far as marginalization is concerned, the large number of hermits in the above age categories is striking in both countries (Table 18.3). Many children in the Finnish countryside in particular completely lack friends of the same age in the neighbourhood.

240

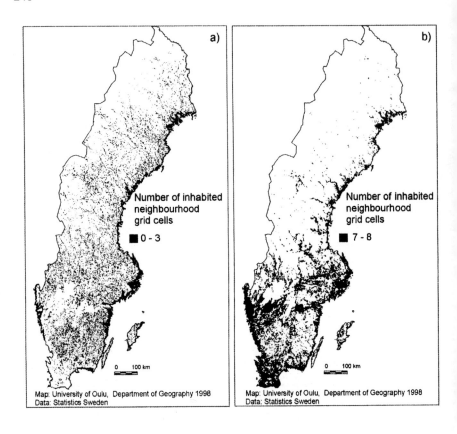

Figure 18.4 Spatial distribution of grid cells values 0-3 (a) and 7-8 (b) in Sweden in 1995

The number of inhabited grid cells for a given age group will naturally be below the figure recorded for the population as a whole, although the discrepancy is not so marked in Sweden as in Finland, indicated by the fact that where 56.2% of all grid cells in Finland contained persons aged under 16 years, the figure in Sweden was 63.2%, the corresponding figures for persons aged over 64 years being 67.7% and 72.0%, respectively. It has been stated in earlier research (Rusanen *et al.* 1997) that the age structure in the rural areas of Sweden is more balanced overall than that in Finland and it seems that this situation also holds good regarding spatial coverage. Since the regional distributions obtained resembled those for the whole population of each country, they will not be discussed in detail here.

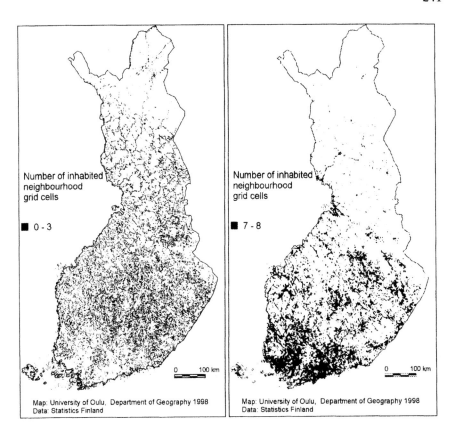

Figure 18.5   Spatial distribution of grid cells values 0-3 (a) and 7-8 (b) in Finland in 1995

Age structure as a function of distance

Georeferenced data enable the distance between each cell and a given point to be calculated. In practice this means indicating the distance as a bee line, so that the calculations employed here do not take into consideration water areas or other physical obstacles. In accordance with centre-periphery theory, the analyses below calculate the distance of each grid cell from the relevant local population centre (commune centre), i.e. the cell with the

Table 18.3   Grid cells by number of neighbours (% distribution) in the age groups 0-15 years and 64 years and over in Finland and Sweden in 1995, using the hermit macro method with 3 x 3 kilometre neighbourhoods

Number of neighbour grid cells	Finland 0-15 years	Finland Over 64 years	Sweden 0-15 years	Sweden Over 64 years
0	6.5	4.6	4.7	4.7
1	11.0	9.7	7.6	7.6
2	14.1	13.6	10.9	11.4
3	15.3	16.4	13.9	14.7
4	15.5	17.3	15.8	16.5
5	13.2	14.9	16.0	16.2
6	10.4	11.3	13.9	13.3
7	8.2	7.7	10.7	9.9
8	5.7	4.5	6.5	5.7
Total (%)	100.0	100.0	100.0	100.0
Number of grid cells	57,884	69,797	74,546	84,920

Sources: Statistics Finland and Statistics Sweden.

largest population. The resulting distance will be used as a means of examining in the light of a few examples the frequency of living in a remote area far away from a centre of population. It should be noted that the resulting definition of remoteness and thus the table for Sweden used as an example (Table 18.4), does not rest on any theoretical foundation. Persons living more than 20 km away from their commune centre are assumed to be remote as regards the daily services available in the centre.

More than 500,000 Swedes lived more than 20 km away from their commune centre in 1995 (Table 18.4a), the proportion varying in terms of sex in that women were more likely to live in dense settlements and men at a distance exceeding 20 km. The selectiveness of migration, which means that young women move away from rural areas more commonly than men, is thus well reflected in the figures in Table 18.4a.

The above conclusion is confirmed when the situation is examined in terms of age and sex. Tables 18.4b and 18.4c indicate that where the proportion of persons aged under 16 years is still more or less uniform in all distance zones, that of women aged 16-44 years living in or close to centres already exceeds the average. This imbalance in regional structure is greatest among persons aged over 65 years.

Table 18.4 **(a) Population of Sweden in 1995 by distance from a commune centre (densest populated grid cell), (b) female population, and (c) male population**

a)

Distance (km)	Population N	%	Total Female N	%	Male N	%
0-5	5,251,272	59.8	2,701,172	60.7	2,550100	58.8
6-20	3,031,107	34.5	1,501,145	33.8	1,529962	35.2
21-	503,621	5.7	244,081	5.5	259,540	6.0
Total	8,786,000	100.0	4,446,398	100.0	4,339,602	100.0

b)

Distance (km)	Female age groups, (%) 0-15	16-44	45-64	> 64	Total Female (%)
0-5	55.2	62.2	60.0	64.4	60.7
6-20	38.9	33.2	34.4	29.0	33.8
21-	5.9	4.6	5.6	6.6	5.5
Total (%)	100.0	100.0	100.0	100.0	100.0
N	857,009	1,672,468	1,036,702	880,219	4,446,398

c)

Distance (km)	Male age groups, (%) 0-15	16-44	45-64	> 64	Total Male (%)
0-5	55.0	61.6	57.4	58.4	58.8
6-20	39.1	33.3	36.4	33.3	35.2
21-	5.8	5.1	6.2	8.3	6.0
Total (%)	100.0	100.0	100.0	100.0	100.0
N	903,038	1,745,565	1,042,010	648,998	4,339,602

Source: Statistics Sweden.

The distance at the local level is examined with respect to two medium-sized communes in Central Sweden, Ljusdal and Hudiksvall (Table 18.5). The distance classification employed in the analysis of the entire country was applied as such to the local level. Ljusdal has an area of some 5300 km^2 and Hudiksvall 2500 km^2, the traditional population density figures being 4 and 16 inhabitants per square kilometre, respectively.

Table 18.5   Distribution of the population in Ljusdal and Hudiksvall in 1995 by distance from a commune centre

LJUSDAL

Distance km	Total population		Number of grid cells		Inh./km^2 Conventional model	Inh./km^2 Grid cell model
	N	%	N	%		
0-5	8 056	38.4	57	7.7	?	141
6-20	9 638	46.0	375	51.0	?	26
21-	3 261	15.6	304	41.3	?	10
Total Average	20 955	100.0	736	100.0	4	28

HUDIKSVALL

Distance km	Total population		Number of grid cells		Inh./km^2 Conventional model	Inh./km^2 Grid cell model
	N	%	N	%		
0-5	16 801	43.3	61	7.5	?	275
6-20	12 876	33.2	357	43.7	?	36
21-	9 088	23.4	399	48.8	?	23
Total Average	38 765	100.0	817	100.0	16	47

Source: Statistics Sweden.

It could be expected when examining the traditional population density that Ljusdal would be more peripheral and marginal in terms of its settlement structure, for even the georeferenced data suggest that it has a lower population density in all distance zones than does Hudiksvall. Yet more than 23% of the inhabitants of Hudiksvall live more than 20 km away from the centre but less than 16% of Ljusdal. Hudiksvall would thus seem to be more problematic in terms of marginality.

The use of georeferenced information also offers another advantage, as indicated in Table 18.5, in that it enables population density to be calculated for each distance zone separately, which would of course be impossible when using commune-specific averages.

The final example of the effect of distance on age structure is based on the distance classifications employed earlier. Persons living over 20 km away from the centre are indicated in Figures 18.6a and 18.6b for each commune separately as a proportion of all persons of the same age. Again persons under 16 years and over 64 years are considered. The resulting maps are almost mirror images in spatial terms. There are a number of rural communes in northern Sweden where most children live in the built-up areas and the number living more than 20 km from a centre is very small, whereas the number of children living far away from the centres is well above the average in many districts in southern Sweden. The situation is the opposite among old people, with some communes in a large area around Stockholm in particular, which do not contain a single old person living over 20 km from the centre or where the proportion of such persons is small.

The above results suggest that the ability of the local authorities to organize services tends to vary. In the Nordic model of the welfare state the organizing of services for children and old people living far away from municipal centres entails considerable costs to local councils when compared with a situation in which most of the settlement is located in built-up areas and their surroundings. If one could develop a distance-based metric capable of describing the situation with a commune, this would undoubtedly bring to the fore the major discrepancies in spatial structure between them, which are of immediate relevance to the organizing of welfare service.

Summary and conclusions

The above analysis is part of a programme of basic methodological research into the use of GIS being conducted by the working group. The aim is to find applications to regions where considerable areas of territory possess a sparsely distributed population that plays no more than a marginal demographic role. Borne in mind of course that the smaller the number of inhabitants in an area, the more impact it will have on the situation locally.

Georeferenced data can be used to give exact data on the frequency of peripheral location and other aspects of remoteness which can certainly be of use in planning and decision-making within regional organizations of different types. The areas can also be visualized where necessary, yielding maps, which are the best means available for illustrating peripheral location. The problem in the case of Finland and Sweden is finding a way to define marginality caused by distance from a centre, for example. There may not be any theory for defining a suitable distance; it is very easy to manipulate the results by altering the class boundaries. A specific aim could be to compare the population density, socio-spatial and distance maps

246

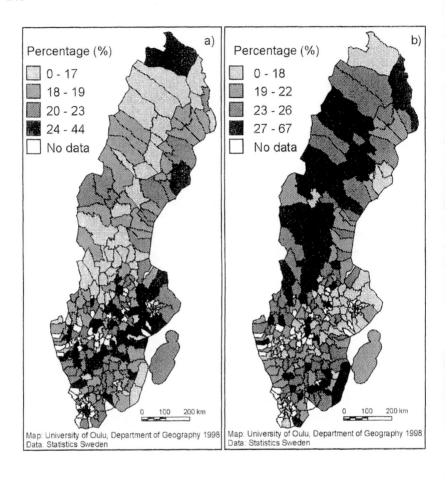

Figure 18.6   **Percentages of the population aged 0-15 (a) and over 64 years of age (b) living over 20 km from their commune centre in Sweden in 1995**

generated from georeferenced data with the area classifications drawn up for defining EU objective areas entitled to support from the structural funds. Discrepancies would almost certainly be found.

It is obvious that GIS, and above all positionally accurate georeferenced data, would enable marginal areas to be identified statistically. This is above all a matter of being able to phrase the theoretical questions regarding marginality correctly. Even this, however, will only result in a statistical truth. A subjectively thinking and acting individual living far

away from the centre does not necessarily regard himself as belonging to the
category that he is classified into statistically.

References

ESRI (1997), *Arc/Info online-manual*, version 7.01.

Goodall, Brian (1997), *The Penquin Dictionary of Human Geography*.

Johnston R.J., Gregory, Derek and Smith, David M. (eds) (1994), *The Dictionary of Human
Geography*, Blackwell publishers, Ltd., p. 724.

Leimgruber, Walter (1993), *Marginality and Marginal Regions: Problems of Definition.*
Paper presented at IGU Study Group on Development Issues in Marginal Regions,
Taipei, Taiwan, R.O.C.

Malinen, Pentti, Keränen, Reijo and Keränen, Heikki (1994), 'Rural area typology in Finland - a tool for rural policy', *University of Oulu, Research Institute of Northern Finland,
Research reports: 123*, p. 78.

Martin, David (1991), *Geographic information systems and their socioeconomic applications*, Routledge, London and New York, p. 182.

Muilu, Toivo, Rusanen, Jarmo and Naukkarinen, Arvo (1997), 'Huoltosuhde ja aluekehitys:
kuka elättää tulevaisuuden maaseudun?', *Maaseudun uusi aika 2/97, Maaseutututkimuk-
sen ja -politiikan aikakauslehti*, pp. 130-137.

Naukkarinen, Arvo, Rusanen, Jarmo and Colpaert, Alfred (1991), 'Maaseutu karttaruututie-
tojen perusteella 1980-luvun ensimmäisellä puoliskolla, (English summary: The Finnish
countryside in the early 1980's on the basis of map grid data)', *Terra 103:3*, pp.184-199.

Rusanen, Jarmo, Naukkarinen, Arvo and Colpaert, Alfred (1993), 'Square Kilometre Grid
System: An Efficient Database in Rural Studies', *Geography Research Forum*, Vol. 13,
pp. 129-138.

Rusanen, Jarmo, Naukkarinen, Arvo, Colpert, Alfred and Muilu, Toivo (1997), 'Differences
in the Spatial Structure of the Population between Finland and Sweden in 1995 - A GIS
viewpoint', *Statistics Finland, Research Reports: 221*, p. 46.

Tomlin, Dana C. (1990), *Geographical Information Systems and Cartographic Modelling*,
Prentice Hall, Englewood Cliffs, New Jersey.

19 People who were not there but are now!

Aboriginality in Tasmania

PETER SCOTT

Introduction

'Aboriginality in the island state is not an issue of colour; it is an issue of culture. Nowhere in Australia have people who feel themselves to be Aborigines been taken closer to the physical fact of extinction nor to the edge of the ultimate cultural abyss: being told they do not exist' (The Age, Melbourne, 30 April 1988). These words poignantly encapsulate the tragedy of the Aboriginal community in Tasmania. In 1961 the State's total of persons of Aboriginal and Torres Strait Islander descent was officially 38 (Borrie, 1975, p. 2, p. 458), and as recently as 1983 counsel for the Tasmanian Government in a case before the High Court of Australia claimed that the Tasmanian Aborigines had been a distinct race but were now extinct (The Sydney Morning Herald, 9 June 1983). Yet the 1996 Australian census returned the indigenous population of Tasmania made up mainly of persons of mixed descent as 13,870.

This seemingly sudden appearance of a large Aboriginal community in the State stems from a national referendum in 1967, which empowered the Federal Government to assume responsibility for Aboriginal affairs, resulting almost immediately in Aborigines being granted citizenship rights and included in the census. Hitherto Aboriginal affairs had been well-nigh exclusively a State responsibility, full-blood Aborigines had been excluded from the census, and Aboriginal Tasmanians had suffered not only deprivation and discrimination but also alienation from the dominant society. Recent Aboriginal writings reveal that while the authors had always proudly acknowledged their indigenous heritage many white Aborigines, who had felt they belonged neither to the indigenous community nor to the wider society, had hidden their Aboriginality to avoid unpleasantness and possible violence (West, 1984; Friend, 1992; tunapi, 1992). Since the late

248

1960s, numerous government programs have been provided for Aborigines, the attitudes of white people toward Aborigines have on the whole ameliorated, and Tasmanian Aboriginal activists have waged remarkably successful campaigns to redress a few of the wrongs perpetrated against their people. Accordingly an increasing number of persons of indigenous origin have declared their identity in the census.

Indigenous people remain however the most marginalized community in Tasmania, where over the past fifteen years national economic reform has in general impacted adversely (Scott, 1994; 1999). Throughout the 1990s the downsizing and closure of factories, offices, and the government sector alike have led to the State's economy and population growing ever more slowly. By 1996-97, when Australia's economy was buoyant (GDP 2.6%), Tasmania was in recession. Its Gross State Product was -1.4%, its labour force growth rate -2%, its jobless rate lessened by outmigration was 11.6 compared with Australia's 8.3%, and its population growth rate -0.2%. This downward slide acutely affected the Aboriginal community, of whom some had prospered but most lived on very low incomes, nearly one-half of adults being dependent on social welfare.

This paper seeks to examine the involvement, dynamics, and disadvantage of Aboriginal Tasmanians in contemporary society. After outlining key features of Aboriginal evolution since the British first occupied the island nearly two centuries ago, the paper compares on selected cultural, demographic, economic, and social criteria the indigenous population of the State firstly with the indigenous population elsewhere in Australia and secondly with the non-indigenous population of Tasmania. Finally the paper discusses briefly the recent achievements of Tasmanian Aboriginal activists with special reference to the vexed question of land.

Tasmanian Aborigines since white settlement

In Tasmania, for almost a century following the death of the last full-blood Aboriginal in 1876, the Aborigines who had inhabited the island for at least 35,000 years (Jones *et al.*, 1983) were widely held to be extinct. In 1803, when the first British settlement was established at Risdon Cove near the present Hobart, Tasmanian Aborigines numbering at least several, perhaps many thousands were dispersed throughout the main island, absent only from the rugged western ranges (Ryan, 1996, p. 15); their distribution was in fact more widespread than that of today's white population, who are largely confined to an arcuate belt through the north and east. From 1803 to

1834 the Aborigines were progressively deprived of their lands by the British invaders (Scott, 1965), and from 1824 to 1831, as Reynolds (1995) contends, fought a highly effective guerilla campaign that ended not with military defeat but a negotiated settlement. Under the settlement terms, which included a guaranteed peace in return for a limited exile, more than 200 survivors were transferred in 1933 as a 'free people' to Wybalena Settlement on Flinders Island, where most eventually died, mainly from influenza and pneumonia (Plomley, 1987, 1989). In 1847 the remaining 46 Aborigines were moved to Oyster Cove south of Hobart, where they also died.

Yet part-Aborigines survived on the eastern Bass Strait Islands, where early in the nineteenth century European sealers cohabited with Aboriginal women (Plomley and Healey, 1990), in the Huon Valley south of Hobart (Friend, 1992), in 'isolated pockets' on the Australian mainland (Cameron, 1994, p. 66), and certainly within the wider Tasmanian society (Plomley and Healey, 1990, pp. 25-27). On the Bass Strait Islands they evolved as a highly distinctive community (Murray-Smith, 1979), many of whom later dispersing to urban centres and rural districts throughout Tasmania. There they retained elements of their evolving culture (Clark, 1986) and nurtured their Aboriginality, their pride in their Aboriginal heritage, and their sense of 'community belonging' (Cameron 1994, p. 66). Officially, however, until the late 1960s they were non-existent, and in so far as their existence was recognized, they were regarded as outcasts in a white society (Rowley, 1972; West, 1984). In 1937 Australia's adoption of an assimilation policy for Aborigines further discouraged part-Aborigines in Tasmania from declaring their origins. In 1954 and 1966 persons of Aboriginal and Torres Strait Islander descent were officially numbered 93 and 80 respectively (Borrie, 1975, p. 2, p. 458).

From 1966 to 1996, however, the number of Tasmanians recorded in the census as having indigenous origins increased rapidly. By the mid-1960s, Australia's postwar immigration policy had necessitated the repeal of all discriminatory domestic legislation, and highlighted the anomalous plight of the Aborigines, prompting the 1967 referendum. In 1971 the Federal Government financed the first Tasmanian part-Aboriginal Conference, which was held in Launceston and attracted some 200 participants (Ryan, 1996, pp. 251-3). Their discussions revealed the existence of nearly 2,000 of their people living in the State or on the Australian mainland. In the 1971 census the number of self-identifying Aboriginals was 671 and in 1976 it had risen to 2,942. Subsequent to the 1981 census, when the total fell to 2,688, the Australian Bureau of Statistics (ABS) undertook an awareness campaign in Tasmania to stress the importance of counting Aborigines accurately. Consequently the 1986 census gave the total of indigenous Tasmanians as 6,716. Further substantial increases were recorded in the 1990s, when the totals were 8,885 in 1991 and 13,873 in 1996. From 1966 to 1996 the proportion of the State's population classified as indigenous had soared from 0.2 to 3%, from being the lowest of the six Australian States to emerging as the highest.

Aboriginal Tasmanians in the 1990s

In 1996 the indigenous population of Tasmania, which the census indicated had grown by 56% since 1991 compared with the general population growth of one percent, comprised predominantly persons of mixed European and Tasmanian Aboriginal descent but also included full-blood Australian Aborigines, who are not differentiated in the census, and Torres Strait Islanders, who are Australian indigenous Melanesians. It seems highly probable that the multiplicity of government programs specifically for Aborigines – health, education, employment, housing, legal aid, inter alia – has boosted the total with what have been termed 'paper blacks' (The Examiner, Launceston, 21 April 1995). What defines a Tasmanian Aboriginal has in fact been the subject of a case before the Federal Court, which found that the onus rests with the Aboriginal community to establish who is Aboriginal (The Australian, 5 August 1997). The Tasmanian Aboriginal Centre (TAC) commented that the decision would increase the number of people claiming Aboriginality, thereby imposing additional demands on the scarce resources and limited services set aside for Aborigines (The Mercury, Hobart, 21 April 1998).

An indication as to the socioeconomic composition of the population identifying themselves in 1996 for the first time as Aboriginal may be gleaned by comparing the indigenous workforce in 1991 and 1996. In 1991 the indigenous unemployment rate was 26% but by 1996, when the indigenous labour force was 52% larger than in 1991 and the non-indigenous rate had risen from 8% in 1991 to 11, the indigenous rate had fallen to 20, implying that unemployment was low among the newly identified Aborigines. Among indigenous occupational groups the largest numerical increase (560) by a substantial margin (318) occurred among clerical, sales, and service workers and the largest relative increases among paraprofessionals (from 3.8 to 7.8% of the indigenous workforce) and professionals (from 4.6 to 8.1), though paraprofessionals, professionals, managers, and administrators together continue to be under-represented in the workforce by comparison with the non-indigenous (22 compared with 38%). The period 1991-96 was one of low inflation and small wage rises, and the number of Aboriginal persons receiving an individual annual income of A$20,000 or less increased by slightly less (45%) than the workforce increase while those receiving A$20,001-A$30,000 increased by slightly more (62%). Yet the number of indigenous employees receiving A$30,001-A$40,000 jumped by 145% and those receiving over A$40,000 by no less than 216%. Clearly indigenous people who before 1996 had been reluctant to declare their Aboriginality would appear to have included many of the more affluent and well established. Caution has therefore to be exercised in using the 1991 and 1996 censuses to estimate trends in indigenous disadvantage over this period.

In 1996 the distribution of indigenous people in Tasmania broadly corresponded with that of the State population but there were some striking differences (Table 19.1). An outstandingly high proportion of indigenous people resided in the southern countryside and throughout the north-west, while Launceston, which over the years received so many migrants from the Bass Strait Islands, had a remarkably low ratio, as to a lesser extent had the north-east generally. Yet the 1991 census showed that the indigenous population has a high level of mobility, only one-half residing at the same address as five years before, more than one-quarter living in a different Tasmanian locality, and nearly 5% living previously on the Australian mainland (ABS, 1996d, p. 85). In 1996 only two of 43 local statistical areas had ratios of indigenous to total population greater than 6%: the eastern Bass Strait Islands, where the ratio was 15.4% but numbers were small (population 924, Aborigines 146), and the Huon Valley with 9.5%, which was two-thirds of the southern rural indigenous total and one-third of all Aborigines in rural Tasmania.

A comparison of Tasmanian and Australian Aboriginal populations

In 1990 the Federal Government established the Aboriginal and Torres Strait Islander Commission (ATSIC) to give indigenous Australians (1996 total: 352,970) more power to make decisions for themselves and their future through 36 elected regional councils. In 1994, owing to the paucity of statistical data, the ABS conducted a National Aboriginal and Torres Strait Islander Survey (NATSIS), which involved trained indigenous interviewers collecting attitudinal and factual data from a random sample of over 15,000 people living in about 5,000 households across Australia. Among the resultant publications are the detailed findings (ABS, 1995), State reports (e.g. Tasmania, 1996a), a Social Atlas with 45 choropleth maps (ABS, 1997d), and a separate report on each ATSIC region, the Tasmanian report being designated Hobart (ABS, 1996b). These reports not only enable regional comparisons to be made but cover key topics not included in the census.

Table 19.1   Aboriginal and total population of Tasmania by urban and rural subregion, 1996

Subregion	Aboriginal		Total	
	No.	%	No.	%
Urban				
Greater Hobart	4,705	33.9	189,944	41.3
Greater Launceston	1,965	14.2	95,982	20.9
Burnie-Devonport	3,136	22.6	75,788	16.5
Rural				
South	1,930	13.9	33,293	7.2
North-east	794	5.7	33,782	7.4
North-west	1,036	7.5	23,902	5.2
Mining				
West	297	2.1	6,336	1.4
Offshore and migratory	10	0.1	632	0.1
Tasmania	13,873	100.0	459,659	100.0

Source: ABS, 1996, Indigenous Thematic Profile, Table 103.

Such topics furnished abundant evidence to show that in general the Tasmanian Aboriginal community is considerably more integrated in the wider society than are their counterparts elsewhere in Australia. Thus, for instance, among the ATSIC regions Tasmania had by far the lowest ratio of indigenous families with all members indigenous: 19% compared with eastern Victoria, the next lowest, with 32% and Australia 60. It follows that Aboriginal Tasmanians are unlikely to have a high level of involvement in Aboriginal cultural activities. The Survey revealed that on each of the four criteria listed in Table 19.2 Tasmania returned the lowest ratio of the ATSIC regions. Yet cultural bonds would appear to be strong, certainly regarding the importance attached to elders and at least significant regarding the three other criteria, particularly the recognition of homelands. The

NATSIS also gave the percentage of indigenous Tasmanians who spoke English at home as 99, a figure confirmed by the 1996 census. Incidentally they still use remnants of the Aboriginal Tasmanian languages (Cameron, 1994; Crowley, 1993). The 1996 census gave the number of indigenous people in Tasmania who spoke an Australian Aboriginal or Torres Strait Islander language as 28.

Table 19.2   Tasmanian and Australian indigenous populations: Culture

Persons aged 13 years and over	Tasmania %	Australia %
Identified with clan, tribal or language group	17.7	59.8
Recognized an area as homelands	39.9	75.2
See elders as important	66.4	84.4
Attended cultural activities over the past year	31.4	72.1

Source: ABS, 1996, Catalogue No 4196. 0.00.029.

It is scarcely surprising that in Tasmania, given the low ratio of Aboriginal families with all members indigenous, Aboriginal children are less likely to be removed from their families for social welfare reasons than Aboriginal children in almost all other States. The Human Rights and Equal Opportunity Commission found that on 30 June 1995 the rate per 1,000 indigenous children of those on care and protection orders was 10.4 in Tasmania, the second lowest among the States (average 14.7), the lowest being Western Australia with 7.6 (HREOC, 1997a, p. 447). Since the 1970s the TAC has provided legal representation in potential removal situations and succeeded in keeping many families together (HREOC, 1997b, p. 91 and p. 98). The personal loss incurred by removal is not confined to family but extends to a sense of culture and identity, as personal experience testifies (tunapi, 1992, pp. 8-15). The Commission described the continued removal of children from their families for reasons of 'neglect' rather than 'abuse' as evidence of entrenched disadvantage and dispossession.

Education, employment, income, and socioeconomic well-being are all closely interlinked. Although the overall school participation rate among Aboriginal persons aged 13 to 18 years in Tasmania was average with 81% (Australia 82%), since most children left school at 15, Tasmania ranked sixth among the ATSIC regions with 23% of persons aged 15 years and over having post-school qualifications (Australia 17%) and among the States shared 23% with Victoria and South Australia. Significantly Tasmania also ranked sixth in its employment rate of 72% of the labour force (Australia 62%) but higher rates were confined to remote regions of northern Australia where employment was boosted by the Federal Government's Community Development Employment Policy scheme (CDEP). Accordingly, of the ATSIC regions Tasmania had the highest percentage of persons whose main source of income was earned (41%; Australia 24%). While Tasmania's ratio of those dependent mainly on government allowances, pensions, and other payments ranked 29, the percentage was even higher than the earned income ratio (48%; Australia 55%). This finding alone highlights the poverty experienced by most indigenous Tasmanians, for a report prepared by the University of New South Wales Social Policy Research Centre for the Federal Government concludes that social security payments fail to provide an acceptable income for any type of family and fall far short of need (The Australian, 13 April 1998). It is nevertheless noteworthy that among the Tasmanian Aboriginal community home ownership was the highest of the ATSIC regions, more than double the Australian Aboriginal average (52%, Australia 25%) and markedly higher than for the second ranking region of central and south-western NSW (40%).

Yet notwithstanding a comparatively favourable economic status, the health status of the Tasmanian Aboriginal community, as the NATSIS reveals by self-reported information unverified medically, would seem to be remarkably poor. Nearly one-half the Tasmanian respondents had experienced an illness within two weeks of the survey (48%, Australia 41%), and almost as many reported having one or more illness conditions (asthma, heart problems etc) lasting more than six months (42%, Australia 35%). Among ATSIC regions Tasmania's response to these two questions ranked 8 and 7 respectively. Of persons aged 13 years and over, smokers numbered 46% (Australia 50%) but Tasmania had the lowest ratio of people who perceived alcohol to be a major local problem (26%, Australia 59%). An Expert Panel on Indigenous Health sponsored by the Australian Medical Association has reported to the Federal Government that Australia's performance in curbing indigenous community deaths and disease rates fell far behind the United States and New Zealand, where the life expectancy gap between US Indians and non-indigenous Americans was only three to four years and between Maoris and other New Zealanders five to six years (The Australian, 15 September 1997). In 1996 Australian life expectancy at birth was 75 years for males and 81 for females but only 57 years for indigenous males and 66 years for indigenous females (ABS, 1997a, p. 35; 1998b, p. 48). Thus Aboriginal males continue to die on average 17 years earlier and Aboriginal females 15 years earlier than their non-indigenous counterparts. Life tables are not available for indigenous Tasmanians and those for indigenous Australians are experimental.

On matters of law and justice the record of Aboriginal Tasmanians compares well with that of Aboriginal Australians generally. In 1986, for instance, Tasmania had the lowest level of Aboriginal over-representation in prison of any State, though the level was four times that of non-indigenous Tasmanians compared with Australia's tenfold over-representation (Cave, 1992). Tasmania's low level was attributed to cultural homogeneity both among Aboriginal Tasmanians and between them and wider society. In 1991 the Royal Commission into Aboriginal Deaths in Custody reported that while Australian Aborigines die in prison custody at a rate nearly 13 times that of non-Aboriginal people no Tasmanian Aboriginal death in prison custody was recorded over the study period 1980-89 and only one in police custody (RCADC, 1991b, p. 61 and pp. 105-6). Among the States Tasmania had the second lowest rate per 100,000 of indigenous children in juvenile detention on 30 June 1996, the rate being 301 compared with Victoria 132 and Australia 540 (HREOC, 1977b, p. 31). Similarly, the NATSIS found that the percentage of indigenous persons aged 13 years and over who said they were arrested in the previous five years was 12% (Australia 20%), Tasmania ranking 32 among the 36 regions, and of those who considered family violence to be a problem in the local area also 12% (Australia 45%), in this case the lowest percentage for any region. However, only 15% (Australia 22%) perceived relations with police to be better than five years previously, Tasmania's ranking among the ATSIC regions being 28.

In sum, by comparison with Australian Aborigines and Torres Strait Islanders, Tasmanian Aboriginal communities comprise predominantly families with indigenous and non-indigenous members, have much less cultural involvement, are generally better educated, have a higher proportion gainfully employed, are better remunerated, less dependent on government payments, have most families owning their own home, less crime and delinquency, but poorer health. They are also the least troubled by alcoholism and family violence. Yet the NATSIS reveals serious, multi-faceted disadvantage, which is examined further by comparing indigenous with non-indigenous communities in Tasmania.

A comparison of Tasmanian indigenous and non-indigenous populations

Demographically the indigenous and non-indigenous populations present a sharp contrast. Aboriginal people have a much higher fertility and a far shorter life expectancy than other Tasmanians. Proportionately they have almost twice the number of persons aged 0-14 (41% compared with 23%) but only one-sixth the number of persons aged 65 and over (2% compared with 12%). Consequently persons of working age make up only 57% of the indigenous population compared with 65% of the non-indigenous. Since the first census publication of Aboriginal age and sex data in 1981, the indigenous child/woman ratio, which measures the combined effects of fertility and mortality (by the number of children below the age of 5 per 1,000 women aged 15-44) has remained high (549 in 1981, 587 in 1991, 550 in 1996), though it declined 1991-96 with the addition of the newly identified Aboriginals. But the non-indigenous ratio has continued its long downward trend from the 1960s through 344 in 1981 to 319 in 1996. Indigenous fertility remains high not only in rural (591) but also urban (528) areas, so that the urban-rural differential is proportionately one-half that among the non-indigenous (urban ratio 306, rural 371). However, Aboriginal fertility seems to be belatedly falling. Thus in 1996 the indigenous percentages of women aged 55+ and 45-54 who had borne five or more children were 40% and 14% respectively and the non-indigenous 17% and 6% respectively.

Traditionally indigenous people have enjoyed strong family relationships within closely-knit communities but increasingly family life, as among the non-indigenous, is becoming more fragmented and complex. The 1994 NATSIS study ranked Tasmania 34 among the ATSIC regions in the ratio of families with only one parent, the percentage being 18.5, for Australia 28.5%, and the range for the regions 15.1% to 46.6%. The 1996 census returned a lower ratio for indigenous Tasmanians, the percentage being only slightly lower than for the non-indigenous population (Table 19.3). Yet Tasmanian indigenous and non-indigenous one-parent families present important differences, the most notable being the higher ratio of one-parent families with children among indigenous people and, because of their lower life expectancy, the considerably lower ratio of one-parent families without dependants. Both indigenous and non-indigenous populations display marked urban-rural differentials but again the differential is most pronounced in respect of indigenous families without dependants. Among both populations the incidence of one-parent families whether in urban or rural subregions tends to be related directly to the size of the urban centre but among indigenous people Launceston and the rural north-east exhibit remarkably high ratios, the rural families being resident mainly near Launceston. It should be added that in 1996 one-parent families dependent on social welfare payments were living in poverty, a one-parent family with two children, for instance, receiving only 70% of the minimum deemed necessary to meet barely acceptable standards (The Australian, 13 April 1998). Yet it is widely recognized that even though attempts have been made to estimate poverty among Australian Aborigines, its measurement requires more than data on family size and income (Saunders, 1998, p. 61).

Table 19.3   One-parent indigenous and non-indigenous families as a percentage of total families in Tasmania, 1996

Sub-region	Indigenous			Non-indigenous		
	with dependants	without	Total	with dependants	without	Total
Urban						
Greater Hobart	17.1	2.9	20.0	11.9	4.6	16.5
Greater Launceston	18.5	3.4	21.9	10.7	5.5	16.2
Burnie-Devonport	11.7	2.5	14.2	10.7	4.5	15.2
Total urban	15.6	2.8	18.4	11.4	4.5	15.9
Rural						
South	9.4	1.5	10.9	8.2	3.5	11.7
North-east	14.3	1.2	15.5	6.9	2.9	9.8
North-west	8.1	1.8	9.9	5.7	3.5	9.2
Total rural	10.1	1.5	11.6	7.1	3.2	10.3
Mining						
West	9.2	-	9.2	9.0	0.7	9.7
Tasmania	11.6	2.4	14.0	10.5	4.2	14.7

Source: ABS, 1996 Indigenous Thematic Profile, Table 119.

However, the single most important contributor to Australian poverty in the late 1990s is unemployment (Fincher and Nieuwenhuysen, 1998). Although the 1994 NATSIS showed Tasmania had the lowest indigenous unemployment rate not only of the States but aside from five remote areas with large CDEP programs also of the 36 ASTIC regions, unemployment in 1996 was nearly twice as high among indigenous Tasmanians as among the non-indigenous (Table 19.4). In the western mining zone it was well-nigh three times as high, in urban centres elsewhere twice as high, and in rural areas 50% higher. Aboriginal male workers are over-represented among labouring and related occupations, among production and transport workers, tradespersons, and clerical, sales, and service workers. The first three groups have borne the brunt of the recent downturn in mining and of restructuring and downsizing in manufacturing but have suffered less in agriculture where they are also over-represented. In each subregion other than the rural north-east, Aboriginal unemployment is higher among male than among female employees. Aboriginal women work chiefly in health and community services together with retailing, though also to a much lesser extent in manufacturing, services, and agriculture. Aboriginal unemployment is higher in urban than in rural areas for reasons cited above; this holds for the State and each of the three subregions (south, north-east, north-west), the only exception being female unemployment in the rural north-east which is marginally higher than Launceston. By contrast, the non-indigenous have higher rates in rural areas other than the north-west where the impact of national economic reform in the 1990s has been acute.

Table 19.4   Indigenous and non-indigenous unemployment rates (%), in Tasmania, 1996

Subregion	Indigenous			Non-Indigenous		
	Male	Female	Total	Male	Female	Total
Urban						
Greater Hobart	21.5	16.5	19.3	10.9	7.7	9.5
Greater Launceston	29.9	20.9	25.7	12.0	9.9	10.4
Burnie-Devonport	23.3	13.7	21.3	14.0	11.4	12.4
Total urban	23.8	16.4	21.2	11.8	8.8	10.5
Rural						
South	15.5	13.6	14.8	13.6	10.3	12.3
North-east	20.7	21.2	20.9	13.1	10.1	11.9
North-west	21.4	13.3	18.0	11.2	9.4	10.5
Total rural	18.2	15.0	16.9	12.7	10.0	11.1
Mining						
West	27.0	23.8	25.7	10.2	7.8	9.3
Tasmania	23.0	16.2	20.1	12.0	9.5	10.7

Source: ABS, 1996, Indigenous Thematic Profile, Table 112.

In sum, the numerous facets of disadvantage experienced by Aboriginal Tasmanians in contemporary society include, by comparison with the non-indigenous population, a much higher fertility albeit starting to decline, a proportionately smaller workforce, a persistently low life expectancy, a higher and growing ratio of one-parent families with dependent children, and much higher unemployment notably among males and youth. In addition, HREOC (1997b, p. 31) found that in Tasmania indigenous children were three times more likely to be removed from their families for social welfare reasons and eight times more likely for juvenile detention than non-indigenous children. Yet it is symptomatic of the State's marginality that among the States and Territories Tasmania had the highest rate (3.3 per 1,000 in 1995, Australia 2.5) of non-indigenous children on care and protection orders and the second highest rate (36.6 per 100,000; Australia 25.3) of non-indigenous children in juvenile detention.

Tasmanian Aboriginal issues and political achievement

Over recent decades Tasmanian Aboriginal politics have achieved marked success. Aboriginal skeletal remains, including those of the last full-blood Tasmanian Aboriginal, have been recovered from museums not only in Tasmania over the period 1978-84 and other Australian States but also in Europe and North America for cremation in accordance with Aboriginal custom. In the early 1980s the TAC participated effectively in the campaign to save the Franklin River in Tasmania's south-west wilderness on the grounds that the construction of a hydroelectric dam would have flooded two caves of outstanding archaeological and Aboriginal importance. By the mid-1980s these and other achievements had already given TAC leaders prominence not only in national but also international Aboriginal affairs, and among First Nation Aboriginal groups Aboriginal Tasmanians are now known as the Pallawah people. The success of TAC activists encouraged a high turnout of Aboriginal voters at the polls, and in the 1991 federal elections Tasmania, compared with other ATSIC regions, had the highest percentage (87%, lowest 40%, Australia 66%) of Aboriginal persons aged 18 years and over who cast their vote (ABS, 1997d, p. 70). A perspective on the TAC's initiative and early achievement is provided by the resolution of Federal and State Governments as recently as 1998 to return almost 20,000 Aboriginal sacred objects and skeletal remains stored in museums across Australia to their traditional owners (The Australian, 2 March 1998).

Yet the primary aim of TAC activists since the early 1970s has been to claim that Tasmanian Aborigines had not become extinct and that they were therefore entitled to land rights. Aboriginal Tasmanians have always maintained that while their forbears had fulfilled their part of the 1831 Agreement government had not; Aborigines had neither been allowed to return to their homelands nor given land in Bass Strait (Reynolds, 1995, pp. 125-137). In a petition to State Parliament in 1977, the Aboriginal community claimed land rights to all sacred sites, Wybalena Settlement, Oyster Cove, all muttonbird (shearwater) islands used traditionally for mutton-birding, Cape Barren Island, Cape Grim where Aborigines were massacred in 1830 and now of spiritual significance, compensation for land dispossession, and the return of Crown land not used by whites (Clark, 1986, p. 51). There followed a protracted, continuous campaign, which has been fully documented by Ryan (1996, p. 263-312).

In 1992 the issues were sharpened by the High Court Mabo judgement, which declared the concept of terra nullius inapplicable to Australia and native title applicable only to land with which Aborigines can claim unbroken links; on other land native title had been eliminated by British sovereignty. On this basis the Tasmanian Aboriginal community was widely regarded as having virtually no claim to land rights in the State. After further intensive negotiations, the Tasmanian Government announced in October 1995 that Tasmanian Aborigines would be given ownership of twelve sites on Crown land totalling 3,895 ha, or 0.06% of the State; 'it was the Government's first and final transfer of land to the Aborigines' (The Australian, 18 October 1995). The sites comprise five Bass Strait islands and part of a sixth (totalling 2,423 ha), three caves of Aboriginal spiritual significance and international archaeological importance located in the Tasmanian Wilderness World Heritage Area (867 ha), Mt Cameron West which has rock carvings, shell middens, and Aboriginal quarries (523 ha), Oyster Cove (11 ha), and the site of the first settlement and first European-Aboriginal conflict at Risdon Cove near Hobart (71 ha). The one important site not included is Wybalena, of which only part was to be leased to Aborigines (The Mercury, Hobart 19 October 1995). By granting land ownership the State Government avoided the land rights issue.

Aboriginal issues are currently handled by ATSIC's Tasmanian Regional Aboriginal Council (TRAC). Among the Flinders Island community, where one-tenth of the population is Aboriginal, the ownership and management of Wybalena had long been a divisive issue but in November 1996 the municipal council and the Aboriginal community finally signed an agreement on joint ownership and management (ATSIC News, 7, 2, March

1998). In 1997 the TRAC ranked thirteen priorities in the following order: housing; law and justice; health; education; community information, awareness, and assistance; employment and training; women's issues; land, cultural heritage, and environment; youth; children's services; elderly; arts and crafts; and recreation (TRAC, 1997, p. 16).

Conclusion

The provision of Commonwealth funds for TRAC priorities will almost certainly be affected adversely by the substantial number of persons in employment who declared their Aboriginality in the census for the first time in 1996, particularly given Tasmania's strong performance among the ATSIC regions on the NATSIS indicators. Already in the context of national economic reform and smaller government Commonwealth funding for Aboriginals has been scaled down, notably for legal aid, which threatens inter alia the welfare of children in custody battles, and Aboriginal study grants (Abstudy), which will preclude some indigenous people from gaining post-secondary qualifications and thereby improving their chances of employment. The 1994 NATSIS revealed that in the previous twelve months the percentage of Tasmanian Aboriginals who had needed to use legal services was 17% (Australia also 17%), most requiring legal aid, and that of those who had left school and wanted to do further study the proportion unable to do so for financial reasons was one-quarter.

Education and training, arrest rates, and health status are all strongly related with employment outcomes. An analysis of the 1994 survey data by the ABS (1996) and the Australian National University's Centre for Aboriginal Economic Policy Research (CAEPR) found that the acquisition of post-secondary qualifications doubled the chances of being employed for Aboriginal males and increased the chances even more for females. However, Tasmanian indigenous youth continue to have lower enrolment and retention rates, despite steady improvement, than non-indigenous Tasmanians. The RCADC (1991a,b,c) identified high arrest rates as disadvantageous both to education and subsequent employment. The Survey analysis showed further that unemployment increased the likelihood of arrest, an arrest within the previous five years reduced the likelihood of employment by about half, and a reduction in arrests increased employment prospects. Although Tasmanian Aboriginals had a comparatively low arrest rate, the fact that one-eighth of persons aged 13 years and over had been arrested within the previous five years is of major concern. The Survey analysis yielded only a weak relationship between health and employment, probably owing to the data being self-reported.

However, the interrelationships between unemployment and illhealth and mortality are complex. Although Tasmania compared well with other ATSIC regions in 1994 on income and unemployment indicators, it is the relative income and relative deprivation within a society, rather than comparisons with other societies or absolute standards, that bear the closest relationships with ill health and mortality (Bartley, 1994; Wilkinson, 1997). Bartley demonstrated that the relationship between unemployment and ill health depends not only on relative poverty but also on social isolation and loss of self-esteem, health related behaviour, and a person's workforce history, since a spell of unemployment greatly increases the risk of further unemployment. While disadvantage may be less pronounced among Tasmanian Aboriginals than among Australian Aboriginals, the socioeconomic situation of indigenous Tasmanians, particularly having regard to unemployment and health status relative to non-indigenous Tasmanians, evokes the conclusion to an address given by a distinguished Aboriginal Australian to Australian and New Zealand psychiatrists:

Before there can be any real improvement in the state of Aboriginal health, Aborigines must enjoy the same respect as human beings, and the same socioeconomic conditions and quality of life, as other Australians. None of this will be achieved in a political climate, which accords primacy to balance sheets while people are denied. In that climate, Aboriginal needs will always be denied, the people denigrated. The brutality will continue (O'Shane, 1995).

References

Australian Bureau of Statistics (1995), *National Aboriginal and Torres Strait Islander Survey 1994: Detailed Findings*, ABS Cat. No. 4190.0, AGPS, Canberra.

Australian Bureau of Statistics (1996a), *National Aboriginal and Torres Strait Islander Survey 1994: Tasmania*, ABS Cat No. 4190.6, AGPS, Canberra

Australian Bureau of Statistics (1996b), *Hobart: A Social Atlas*, ABS Cat No. 2030.6, AGPS, Canberra.

Australian Bureau of Statistics (1996c), *National Aboriginal and Torres Strait Islander Survey 1994: Employment Outcomes for Indigenous Australians*, ABS Cat No. 4199.0, AGPS, Canberra.

Australian Bureau of Statistics (1996d), *National Aboriginal and Torres Strait Islander Survey 1994: Hobart ATSIC Region*, ABS Cat. No. 4196.0.00.029, AGPS, Canberra.

Australian Bureau of Statistics (1996e), *Census of Population 1996: Selected Social and Housing Characteristics for Statistical Local Areas: Tasmania*, ABS Cat. No. 2015.16, AGPS, Canberra.

Australian Bureau of Statistics (1997a), *1996 Demography: Tasmania*, ABS Cat No. 2015.0, AGPS, Canberra.

Australian Bureau of Statistics (1997b), *Selected Social and Housing Characteristics: Australia*, ABS Cat. No. 2015.0, AGPS, Canberra.

Australian Bureau of Statistics (1997c), *Selected Social and Housing Characteristics: Tasmania*, ABS Cat. No. 2015.6, AGPS, Hobart.

Australian Bureau of Statistics (1997d), *National Aboriginal and Torres Strait Islander Survey 1994: Social Atlas*, ABS Cat. No. 4155.0, AGPS, Canberra.

Australian Bureau of Statistics (1998a), *Experimental Estimates of the Aboriginal and Torres Strait Islander Population 30 June 1991-30 June 1996*, ABS Cat. No. 3230.0, AGPS, Canberra.

Australian Bureau of Statistics (1998b), *1996 Deaths Australia*, ABS Cat. No. 3302.0, AGPS, Canberra.

Australian Bureau of Statistics (1998c), *Census of Population and Housing 1996: Selected Characteristics of Urban Centres and Localities: Tasmania*, ABS Cat. No. 2016.6, AGPS, Canberra.

Bartley, M. (1994), 'Unemployment and Ill Health: Understanding the Relationship', *Journal of Epidemiology and Community Health*, Vol. 48, pp. 333-7.

Borrie, W D. (1975), 'The Aboriginal Populations', *First Report of the National Population Inquiry: Population and Australia: A Demographic Analysis and Projection*, Vol. 2, pp. 455-529; ref. on p. 458.

Cameron, P. (1994), 'A Matriarchal Heritage', in P. Cameron, and V. Matson-Green, 'Pallawah Women: Their Historical Contribution to Our Survival', *Tasmanian Historical Research Association, Papers and Proceedings*, Vol. 41, No. 2, pp. 65-70; ref. on pp. 65-7.

Cave, J.J. (1992), 'Aboriginal Over-Representation in Prisons: What Can Be Learned From Tasmania?', *Australian and New Zealand Journal of Criminology*, Vol. 25, No. 2, pp. 156-168.

Clark, J. (1986), *The Aboriginal People of Tasmania*, 2nd edn, Hobart: Tasmanian Museum and Art Gallery.

Crowley, T. (1993), 'Tasmanian Aboriginal Languages: Old and New Identities', M. Walsh, and C. Yallop, (eds), *Language and Culture in Aboriginal Australia*, Aboriginal Studies Press, Canberra, pp. 51-71.

Fincher, R. and Niewenhuysen, J. (eds.) (1998), *Australian Poverty: Then and Now*, Melbourne University Press, Melbourne.

Friend, R. (1992), *We Who Are Not Here: Aboriginal People of the Huon and Channel Today*, The Huon Municipal Association, Huonville.

Human Rights and Equal Opportunity Commission (1997a), 'Bringing Them Home': *The Report of the National Inquiry Into the Separation of Aboriginal and Torres Strait Islander Children From Their Families*, HREOC, Sydney.

Human Rights and Equal Opportunity Commission (1997b), 'Bringing Them Home': *A Guide to the Findings and Recommendations of the National Inquiry Into the Separation of Aboriginal and Torres Strait Islander Children From Their Families*, HREOC, Sydney.

Jones, P. *et al.* (1983), 'The Australian National University/Tasmanian National Parks and Wildlife Service Archaeological Expedition to the Franklin River 1982: Summary of Results', *Australian Archaeology*, No. 16, pp. 57-60.

Murray-Smith, S. (ed.) (1979), *Mission To the Islands: The Missionary Voyages in Bass Strait of Canon Marcus Brownrigg 1872-1885*, Cat and Fiddle Press, Hobart.

O'Shane, P. (1995), 'The Psychological Impact of White Colonisation on Aboriginal People', *Australian Psychiatry*, Vol. 3, No. 33, pp. 148-53.

Plomley, N.J.B. (ed.) (1987), *Weep in Silence: A History of the Flinders Island Aboriginal Settlement; With the Flinders Island Journal of George Augustus Robinson, 1835-1839*, Blubberhead Press, Hobart.

Plomley, N.J.B. (1989), 'Disease Among the Tasmanian Aborigines', *Medical Journal of Australia*, Vol. 151, Nos 11-12, pp. 665-9.

Plomley, N.J.B. and Henley, K.A. (1990), 'The Sealers of Bass Strait and the Cape Barren Island Community', *Tasmanian Historical Research Association, Papers and Proceedings*, Vol. 37, pp. 37-127.

Reynolds, H. (1995), *Fate of a Free People*, Penguin, Melbourne.

Rowley, C.D. (1972), *Outcasts in White Australia*, ANU Press, Canberra.

Royal Commission into Aboriginal Deaths in Custody (1991a), 'Final Report', AGPS, Canberra.

Royal Commission into Aboriginal Deaths in Custody (1991b), 'National Report: Overview and Recommendations', AGPS, Canberra.

Royal Commission into Aboriginal Deaths in Custody (1991c), 'Regional Report of the Inquiry in NSW, Victoria and Tasmania', AGPS, Canberra.

Royal Commission into Aboriginal Deaths in Custody (1992), 'Overview of the Response by Governments to the Royal Commission', AGPS, Canberra.

Ryan, L. (1996), *The Aboriginal Tasmanians*, 2nd edn, Allen & Unwin, Sydney.

Saunders, P. (1998), 'The Re-Emergence of Poverty as a Research and Policy Issue', *Academy of the Social Sciences in Australia, Wealth, Work and Well-Being*, The Academy, Canberra.

Scott, P. (1965), 'Land Settlement', in J.L. Davies (ed.), *Atlas of Tasmania*, Dept of Lands and Surveys, Hobart, pp. 43-45.

Scott, P. (1994), 'Global Economic Restructuring, National Economic Reform and Regional Marginalization: A Tasmanian Perspective', in C.D. Chang, S. Jou, and Y. Lu (eds), *Marginality and Development Issues in Marginal Regions*, National Taiwan University, Taipei.

Scott, P. (1999), 'Australian Microeconomic Reform and Tasmania: An Economic and Social Appraisal', in H. Jussila, R. Majoral, and C. Mutambirwa (eds), *Marginality in Space – Past, Present and Future*, Ashgate Publishing, Ltd., Aldershot (UK).

Tasmanian Regional Aboriginal Council (1997), *Annual Report*, TRAC, Hobart.

tunapi (1992), *About Aborigines in Tasmania*, ALBE Resources Unit, Devonport.

West, I. (1984), *Pride Against Prejudice*, Australian Institute of Aboriginal Studies, Canberra.

Wilkinson, R.C. (1997), 'Health Inequalities: Relative or Absolute Material Standards?', *British Medical Journal*, Vol. 314, pp. 591-595.

20 Child labour, the reverse of economic globalization in peripheral regions[1]

LUCÍLIA CAETANO

Introduction

The UN estimated that, in 1996, at least 73 million children of both sexes (approximately 41 million boys and 32.5 million girls) aged between 10 and 14 are in work. This represents 13.2% of the population of this age-band, which is a somewhat conservative figure, as their own report admits (given that housework is not counted). Child labour is one of the most worrying manifestations of marginalization, as it is a sensitive issue that remains largely unexplored, often masked by other concerns.

Developing countries, including those of Southern Europe, have the highest rates of child labour. As examples, we may cite the millions of children in Africa, Asia, Latin America and Southern Europe who pick tea, sugarcane, tobacco and coffee; work in mines quarrying iron-ore, salt and diamonds; make toys in China, clothes in the Honduras, leather bags in Italy, charcoal in Brazil; sell newspapers in Moscow, and are hodmen for builders in Portugal. But there are also even more alarming situations, such as the cases of childhood ruined in the brothels of Bangkok and Manila, or of child soldiers enlisted into militias in Africa or Europe (the former Yugoslavia), or used as exchange currency on diverse markets.

It is in Asia that most child labour is found, involving 44.6 million children (approximately 13% of the child population aged 10 to 14). However, in relative terms, it is overtaken by Africa with 26.3% (23.6 million children), followed by Latin America with 9.8% (5.1 million). Increased urbanization in these areas has meant a growth of child labour in the cities. Nevertheless, it is in agriculture or agriculturally related activities that the phenomenon is most common, and in rural zones, 9 out of 10 children work.

However, the rapid economic growth recorded in Southwest Asia, resulting in a substantial improvement in family incomes has led to a drop in child labour in recent years.

Child labour can be classified in two 'main' categories:

1) Socially acceptable cases: There are certain areas in which child labour is not only tolerated by society, but actively encouraged (despite the sometimes traumatic consequences for the child). These include: show business; television (the Brazilian soap-operas frequently hire child 'actors'); advertising; fashion (models are getting younger all over the world, often as young as 14); music; sport (footballers become professional younger than 16); and cinema (the American film industry is one of the greatest employers of child labour).

2) Unacceptable cases: The most repugnant situations are clearly those that involve the sexual exploitation of children and young people, of either sex. Although this scourge does not discriminate between the developed and developing countries, obviously the latter are the most affected. For example, in the Philippines, of 250 million child workers, 60 thousand are involved in prostitution; and in the young African states, child prostitution has increased alarmingly. There has been an associated growth in international tourism, since, with the increase in AIDS and other sexually transmitted diseases, wealthy clients have started to seek virgins.

Child labour

Causes

There is very little rigorous statistical information about child labour. Consequently, it has been necessary to resort to data provided by the mass media, and to reports prepared by world organizations such as UNICEF (the United Nations Children's Fund) and the OIT (International Work Organization), which have attempted to bring the problem to the attention of the world and find solutions (IGT, 1990/1995). UNICEF recognizes that child labour appears whenever there is poverty. However, it is not true that child labour exists only in the poorer countries. Although it is prevalent in developing countries, it occurs everywhere, from the USA to Morocco, Mexico to India.

Neither is it true that child labour may not be eliminated while poverty persists. In fact, the situation perpetuates poverty, since it is from the poorest groups of society that child labour is recruited, and the child inevitably grows up to become one of the many unqualified and underpaid adults.

It is not true that child labour develops only in economic sectors involved in exportation. Although the UNICEF report on the 'Situation of Children in the World in 1997' recognized that child labour is more visible in the export industries (footballs produced by children in Pakistan for Nike or Reebok, for example), no more than 5% of child workers are involved. The vast majority works in the home, hidden from view, sub-contracted by companies, which are disguised, and in areas of difficult access, and which have themselves been sub-contracted by multinationals. This makes control difficult and masks the scale of the problem (OIT, 1992).

It is recognized that the basic conditions for child labour to occur are poverty, lack of access to schooling, poor nourishment, inadequate health care, lack of information and culture, and family pressure. Employers exploit extreme poverty, which is associated with a low educational level of the family and children, and thus the system is perpetuated. The principal factors are:

- *Economic* (meagre financial resources, family poverty, and large families in which children play an active part in procuring the family income). In the global economy, companies with deficient structures or inefficient organization find that children provide the cheapest form of labour, and are useful for the simplest, least differentiated tasks. They therefore make gains on the level of production, which allows them to be competitive.
- *Educational* (the inability of schools to motivate children, linked to the problem of school failure). Learning difficulties generally result from serious psychological problems displayed by children who are subject to verbal and physical abuse, deprived of food and warm clothing, and suffering from social exclusion. In this context, frequently the child itself seeks alternatives to school in the job market. In Portugal, it was only in 1987 that nine years' schooling became compulsory, and this fact has also retarded attempts to combat child labour.
- *Social* (the mentality of the rest of the family, which tends to support work, considering it beneficial and necessary for the professional training of the child).
- *Cultural* (family tradition in certain professions, and rurality).

Consequences for the child

The consequences for the child of an early introduction into the job market are as follows:

- Physical, psychological and emotional under-development (a child's work should be to play).
- Physical problems due to the inability to support certain efforts.
- Increased risk of accidents due to motor immaturity and inability to assess risk (world statistics prove that young people under 25 years are the age group with the greatest incidence of work-related problems, and represent around 11.4% of accidents).
- The lack of opportunity for professional training and qualification (as a rule, when these children reach active legal age, they are dismissed, as they represent a higher financial burden for the employer. Consequently they become unemployed, or without permanent or legal work, and run the risk of delinquency and marginality).
- The perpetuation of poverty.

Child labour in Portugal

This is a complex and poorly defined subject. It is difficult to quantify because it escapes the authorities, and the public is ill informed about the matter. Official statistics available indicate that child labour has greatly decreased in recent decades. Nevertheless, these numbers are unrealistically low. The IGT (Work Inspection Authority) presented only 167 cases as the official data for 1994, while information relating to unemployment recorded 5300 juveniles under 15 working illegally on a regular basis (Barreto, 1996). Later, in 1997, estimations from CNASTI (National Confederation for Action into Child Labour) indicated more than 100,000 children working illegally, but according to the OIT (International Work Organization); the true figure is nearer 50,000 children. Finally, the Government quotes no more than 35,000 (IGT, 1990/1995).

Labour legislation in force in Portugal: Civil minority and minority for employment

At the beginning of the 20th Century, the industrialized countries established the minimum age for admission into the job market as 12. This has been progressively adjusted in accordance with compulsory schooling, and with the intrinsic development of children and adolescents. Thus, since 1919, the minimum age for work in different economic and professional activities has been established through a series of International Conventions.

Civil majority begins at 18, but for any type of activity, legal capacity with respect to employment is presently acquired at 16. This minimum age for entry into the job market has had a long period of evolution. Decree-Law 408 of 24, November 1969 (Article 122) allowed the minimum working age to be 14 years, but compulsory schooling was demanded, which was established as 6 years by Decree-Law 45,810 of 9, June 1964. Later, Decree-Law 396/91 of 16, October 1991 made 16 the minimum age, while compulsory schooling was increased to nine years in 1987. However, this legislation is not restricting, since it permits minors to engage in 'light' work, which is defined as the execution of simple and clearly-defined tasks that require only elementary knowledge. Nevertheless, this easily opens the way for transgression on the part of the employer, and may lead to the exploitation of child labour. In addition, while there is some measure of protection for formal work, there is none at all for non-salaried work or that which is done within the family.

Child labour: Development and incidence in Portugal

During the 1950s, more than 80% of children aged between 12 and 14 were at work (Table 20.1). Although there was a drop in work declared in subsequent decades, this variation reflects the alteration of the minimum age for beginning active work and the progressive increase of school attendance from the 1960s. This does not mean, however, that the situation is no longer worrying (Valente, 1984).

Table 20.1   Active child population

Ages		1950	1960	1970	1981	1991
10-14	N	—	168,383	84,955	—	—
	%	—	20.05	10.45	—	—
12-14	N	398,802	—	—	86,256	34,395
	%	81.03	—	—	19.44	7.07
15-19	N	738,457	386,047	374,235	470,102	346,518
	%	91.05	51.66	51.20	62.07	40.99

Source: National Institute of Statistics (own version).

Attempts on the part of the IGT to supervise work done in companies confirm the drop in the number of detected cases of child labour, a tendency already revealed in the Population Census. However, there was a sharp increase between 1992 and 1993 (Table 20.2), probably explained by increased activity on the part of the authorities to detect and control this phenomenon (Lopes, 1998).

Table 20.2   Child labour incidence rate; (a) Establishments where minors were found, (b) Children under 14 up to 1991 and under 15 from 1992

	1990	1991	1992	1993	1994	1995
Number of visits	4,861	4,876	2,147	3,666	5,514	2,537
Workers (Total)	114,917	111,924	38,824	64,250	97,749	46,713
Establishments (Total) (a)	254	222	212	261	93	62
Children under 15 (b)	330	286	282	341	121	74
Incidence Rate	0.3	0.3	0.7	0.5	0.1	0.1

Source: Work Inspection Authority in Report of Work Group co-ordinated by ICA and CNASTI on 'Child Labour in Portugal', 1996.

In accordance with information gathered by the IGT, child labour affects mainly children above 13 years of age, and unlike the situation prior to 1991, there were no cases detected of children less than 10 at work (Table 20.3). It affects both sexes equally, according to available data (IGT, 1991).

Table 20.3   Distribution per age of child workers

	1990	1991	1992	1993	1994	1995	1996	Total	%
<10	1	3						4	0,3
10/12	15	10	9	4	2	3	2	45	3,0
12/13	54	61	26	22	9	8	4	184	12,0
13/14	230	212	123	94	37	25	34	755	49,5
14/15			124	221	73	38	81	537	35,2
Total	300	282	282	341	121	74	121	1525	100,0

Source: Work Inspection Authority *Report of Work* Group co-ordinated by ICA and CNASTI on 'Child Labour in Portugal', 1996.

The greatest incidence of child labour is recorded in the northern coastal area, and the administrative districts of Oporto and Braga together represent more than 70% of cases detected by the IGT (Table 20.4 and Figure 20.1). This situation has been determined by the economic structure of the area. This consists mainly of small and micro-companies with usually a very rudimentary organizational structure, which survive on the basis of cheap and unqualified informal labour (Barreto *et al.*, 1996).

Table 20.4   National incidence of child labour

	1990	1991	1992	1993	1994	1995	1996	Total	%
Braga	144	152	171	83	74	36	53	713	45,8
Oporto	103	54	28	146	30	24	49	434	27,9
Aveiro	14	30	31	36	3	2	5	121	7,8
Other	69	50	52	76	14	12	14	287	18,5
Portugal (Cont.)	330	286	282	341	121	74	121	1555	100,0

Source: Work Inspection Authority, in *Work Group Report* co-ordinated by ICA and CNASTI on 'Child Labour in Portugal' 1996.

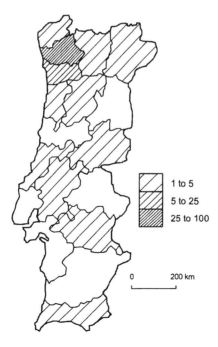

Figure 20.1   Child labour in Portugal (1995)

Economic sectors using child labour

Around 40% of cases of child labour detected in Portugal were in companies involved in the manufacture of clothing and footwear. These are exporting sectors, where competition is very heavy and where a thriving and important parallel economy relies on intensive labour due to low level of technological development (*Diario de Noticias*, 1998). Other sectors involved are construction, and, textile industry, the catering trade connected to seasonal tourism (Table 20.5).

Table 20.5 Child labour per sector of economic activity

	1990	1991	1992	1993	1994	1995	1996	Total	%
Clothing	135	93	69	96	31	16	26	466	30,0
Textiles	29	29	48	19	10	13	7	155	10,0
Footwear	38	68	40	63	35	14	39	297	19,0
Furniture	2	...	5	25	...	...	...	32	2,0
Building	43	24	34	47	19	9	11	187	12,0
Catering	43	24	29	16	4	4	10	130	8,3
Total Industries	330	286	282	341	121	74	121	1555	100,0

Source: Work Inspection Authority, *Report of Work* Group co-ordinated by ICA and CNASTI on 'Child Labour in Portugal', 1996.

Combating child labour

The position of the international community

The Commission of the European Union has tried to regulate child labour through successive directives. Directive 94/33/CEE of the Council of 22, June 1994 deals with the protection of young people at work, and established a plan of action that aimed to protect children and young people against working conditions that could damage their health, safety or development. This Directive prohibits Child Labour amongst Member States, with exemption granted to cases of children under 14 who are covered by systems of alternative training or apprenticeships, provided that the work respects conditions laid down by law concerning hours, and restrictions on certain categories of work. However, the Directive prohibits night work (between 8pm and 6am for children, and between 10pm and 6am for adolescents) (European Commission, 1994).

The debate on child labour held in Geneva by the OIT from the 10 to 20, June 1996 published numbers of a worrying scale. World-wide, one in eight children between 10 and 14 practices a profession. These include forms of slavery (agriculture, manufacture of textiles and carpets, brickmaking, building and sex) observable in certain regions of Asia and Africa. The same conclusions were reached at the Oslo Summit from 27 to 30, October 1997, in which 40 countries participated.

UNICEF (United Nations' Children's Fund) suggests as a possible solution economic boycott and sanctions on countries that consent to the practice. At the Oslo Summit, the German vice-minister for economic co-operation proposed indicating on packaging that products were not made using child labour, or, more drastically, prohibiting the exportation of products that are suspected of involving child labour. However, the application of these measures has been held up by the social and economic characteristics of the countries concerned, and especially, by multinationals interested in easy profits. It is only through sensitization and dissemination of information to the agents involved that this shocking situation will be changed.

It is important to urge politicians to become committed to the subject of child labour, to reinforce the legal framework through the adoption of a new convention, and elaborate a programme of international co-operation to combat this practice. Priority will be given to the prevention of forced work and slavery, exposure to toxic products, physical violence and child prostitution.

More recently, from 2 to 18, June 1998, the OIT (International Work Organization) at its 86th World Conference in Geneva discussed the abolition of extreme forms of child labour. It highlighted the adoption of legislation, which would involve penal sanctions for extreme forms of child labour on the part of countries adhering to the New Convention. It also proposed implementing rehabilitation programme for children particularly minors of 12 and girls.

Given the complexity of the causes, there is a need for a strong political commitment to resolve this social and economic problem. The process is aided, however, by changes in social mentality, advances in technology and the remodelling of legislation.

National action

At the 86th International Conference on Work, the Secretary of State for Social Security and Labour Relations (Diário de Notícias, 18, June 1998, p. 21) recognized that 'situations of child labour still occur in certain areas of Portugal'. However, he offered assurances that a National Plan to eliminate this was under way, supported by rigorous studies launched in collaboration with the OIT.

There is an awareness that children's work is done more and more frequently within their family, in jobs originating from outside. This is particularly the case in the clothing and footwear industries, which subcontract the finishing of their products to intermediaries, who distribute work to the home. In Felgueiras and Amarante near Oporto, children from the age of 10 or 11 begin to sew shoes. This is a legal system, which nevertheless constitutes a new form of child exploitation and is difficult for the Work Inspection Authorities to control. In this context, it is practically impossible to establish the true scale of the problem. In addition, the Work Inspection Authorities have had serious internal problems with regards to material and human resources: there are not enough inspectors, and they have often not had sufficient training.

The Work Inspection Authorities (IGT), conscious of the fact that a more rigorous control of companies has resulted in the transferral of child labour to the home, has asked the Public Ministry to consider the possibility of issuing search warrants to enable them to search houses where there are strong suspicions of child labour, in conjunction with the police. This measure is supported by the National Confederation for Action into Child Labour (CNASTI), and it will be launched in the Vale do Ave, which is suspected of having a high occurrence of transferral of illegal child labour to the home.

It is the multiple sub-contracting of work, frequent in the sectors of footwear, textiles and clothing that are largely responsible for this situation. Producers find child labour economically advantageous in that they pay salaries that are much lower than the national average without the additional burdens of Social Security, holidays, or bonuses. Fines, which are insignificant, do not discourage this practice.

The extension of the Guaranteed Minimal Income to poor families, together with the obligation for children to attend school for the legal minimum period, will help to give children the kind of childhood necessary for their physical, mental and social development, and lay the foundations for future adults and future society.

In order to reinforce the struggle against child labour, the Government has replaced the National Commission for the Fight Against Child Labour with a Plan for the Elimination of the Exploitation of the Child Labour, which has wider-reaching powers and a larger budget. In addition, the traditional methods of combating illegal child labour will be complemented by an educational policy better suited to deal with children at risk, in an attempt to control school desertion and the initiation into the world of work.

In accordance with the recommendations of the OIT Conference held in June 1998, other measures to be adopted include a far-reaching campaign of sensitization and information, legislation involving heavy sanctions for extreme forms of child labour, and rehabilitation programmes for children at risk.

Conclusion

Child labour has a similar character and develops within similar contexts in all areas involved. The situation is generated by degrading social and economic conditions of families who regard their children as a complementary (or unique) source of income, and this is exploited by companies who wish to avoid social costs and fair salaries, and benefit from a flexible labour supply. In this way, they fraudulently make their product competitive. In the rural areas, children have always been regarded as having an important part to play in the family's work, especially in agriculture. The popular proverb 'a child's work is small, but shouldn't be despised' eloquently reflects this reality.

These are areas with high birth rates and large families, where the population is largely young, and poverty is a constant. But alongside the economic causes of child labour, cultural mentality and family traditions also play a part, and parents often hope that their children will enter the world of work early as a way of integrating into society and the professional world. In some cases, it is the children themselves who instigate the situation, seduced by consumerism and the desire to have their own money. Failure at school aggravates this marginality. References available point to a reduction in child labour. However, there are strong indications that much child labour has been transferred to the home and thus escapes the attentions of the authorities, perpetuating marginalization.

278

Note

1   Summary of the Reports on this theme by the students of the subject 'Regional and Local Development' of the academic year 1997/1998.

References

Barreto, A. *et al.* (1996), *A Situação Social em Portugal, 1960-1995*, Instituto de Ciências Sociais, Universidade de Lisboa.

Diário de Notícias (newspaper), 18, June 1998, p. 21.

European Commission (1994), *4th Report of the Commission of the Council at the European Parliament and Economic and Social Committee on the application of the Community Charter on Basic Social Rights of Workers*, Brussels.

Expresso (newspaper) 30, May 1998, 'Tarefas domiciliárias encobrem trabalho infantil', Caderno Economia & Negócios, pp. 1-3.

Lopes, Isabel (1998), 'Inspecção quer fazer buscas domiciliárias', *Expresso* (newspaper), 6, June 1998, Caderno Economia, p. 3

Recenseamentos-Gerais da População, Instituto Nacional de Estatística.

Trabalho Infantil (1991), Report of Activities, Instituto de Desenvolvimento e Inspecção das Condições de Trabalho, Inspecção-Geral do Trabalho, IGT.

Trabalho de Menores - As medidas adoptadas face à resolução nº146 da OIT (1992), Ministério do Emprego e da Segurança Social, Lisbon.

Trabalho de Menores 1990/1995, Reports of Activities, Instituto de Desenvolvimento e Inspecção das Condições de Trabalho, Inspecção-Geral do Trabalho, IGT.

Valente, Domingos Antunes (1984), *A Problemática do Trabalho Infantil em Portugal*, (Lisbon).

21 The plight of women in the margins of rural life in Africa: The case of Zimbabwe

ASSEFA MEHRETU, CHRIS MUTAMBIRWA AND
JANE MUTAMBIRWA

Introduction

Certain traditions and societal attitudes in African culture have contributed significantly to marginalization of women in the rural margins of Africa. But even more limiting to women's progress in Africa was colonial marginalization of rural life in general. Patterns of marginalization of women include:

1) traditional sexism that places women as less important and as a consequence, their functions,
2) the traditional roles associated with married life and the responsibilities of females in the rural household,
3) lack of potable water and source of domestic fuel with easy access,
4) the problems of accessibility to health services,
5) the limited opportunities to formal education,
6) the inequities of direct political participation at the decision-making levels of the state,
7) the limited access to economic opportunities,
8) the biases of post-colonial laws some of which reflect the colonial heritage,
9) the deleterious effects of urbanisation on rural communities in which women are the majority; and
10) the lack of locational choices that women face with marriage.

The purpose of this research is to study the structure and process of female marginality in rural Zimbabwe from the perspectives of both *contingent* and *systemic* causes of marginality, and to explore the reasons why women are especially vulnerable to marginalization. The paper will also address policy implications that would tackle marginality toward improving the quality of women's life in rural Zimbabwe.

Typology of marginality

Marginality is a condition of socioeconomic and spatial distress resulting from either the unintended consequences of traditions and markets, or from cognitive systems of hegemonic inequity in social and economic relations. (Mehretu and Sommers, 1998; see also Friedmann, 1988, p. 114). Social and spatial marginality occurs when there is a convergence of political, cultural, economic, and resource problems in a region. Political and cultural marginality are particularly crucial as they can be used by hegemonic groups to legitimize their privilege and exploitation of others. In addressing women's marginality in Zimbabwe, we will apply the typology of marginality advanced by Sommers and Mehretu who have divided generic marginality into two principal modes which they have termed as *contingent* and *systemic* marginality (Sommers and Mehretu, 1998).

According to Sommers and Mehretu, *contingent marginality* occurs spontaneously as a function of either accepted dominant cultural norms and traditions or free market mechanisms. *Contingent marginality* is assumed to be inherent to the *laissez-faire* system and its appearance in some communities and regions is considered 'accidental' or 'temporary'. It is also considered 'self-correcting.' In other words, *contingent marginality* is an anomalous condition of social and regional inequality within the context of what is a fair and equitable system of enterprise.

Sommers and Mehretu (1998) indicate that *systemic marginality* is a polarized development caused by a system of inequitable social relations in a society where a hegemonic order uses formal and informal institutions to victimize individuals or collectives some of whom may manifest social, political, economic and locational vulnerability. Factors that make communities and their territories vulnerable to *systemic marginality* operate outside the market system often involving political and economic elite that use hegemonic pressures to victimize weak constituencies (see also Palmer, 1977; Mehretu, 1989). *Systemic marginality* is presently most applicable in societies which do not have democratic governments and free markets and in those countries with pseudo radical and totalitarian governments with kleptocratic tendencies (see also Young, 1988; Friedmann, 1988, pp. 108-144).

Marginalization of women in Sub-Saharan Africa

In sub-Saharan Africa (SSA), there are many ways in which women can face both *contingent* and *systemic marginality*. The sources of *contingent marginality* for most women in SSA are found in the culturally determined division of labour within households. Most households in SSA are rural and women are the most constant anchors for these households (Abegaz, 1990; Bryceson, 1993; Buvinic, 1983; Cecelski, 1985; Chiuri, 1992; Leghorn and Parker, 1981; Muchena, 1994; Omosa, 1992). But, the important roles they play as anchors of the rural household, ironically also make them vulnerable to *contingent marginality*. First, women in SSA, especially mothers and wives carry an inordinately high portion of the work burden to support basic requirements for the subsistence and reproduction of their households (Hafkin and Bay, 1976; Buvinic, 1983; Cecelski, 1985; World Bank, 1989; Obbo, 1990; Gallin and Ferguson, 1991; Muchena, 1994). Second, the sources of the work burden are multifaceted as women account for most of the labour input into all three principal sector of the rural economy which are:

1) home-making chores,
2) farm/non-farm production, and
3) rural transportation (Sunny, 1992; Muchena, 1994; Mehretu and Mutambirwa, 1992).

Third, rural work burden from all three sectors listed above has increased over time primarily for three reasons:

1) the carrying capacity of the resource base has declined requiring more energy and time inputs to carry out farm work, livestock grazing, firewood supply and domestic water sourcing (White, 1972; Shiva, 1989; Collins, 1991; Chiuri, 1992,
2) customary social and factor biases against sectors dominated by women have prevented development assistance to improve their condition (Shiva 1991; Gallin and Ferguson, 1991), and
3) males have externalized and/or urbanized their economic links at much higher rates than females who continue to maintain stronger links with their home-base in rural areas (Potts and Mutambirwa, 1990; Gallin and Ferguson, 1991).

The sources of *systemic marginality* of women in SSA reside in the colonial and post colonial methods of territorial administration which often were highly prejudicial to the welfare of women. There are especially four areas which have systematically marginalized women. First, the commodification of high potential land for cash crop production in colonial and postcolonial times, meant that rural women lost access to good soils and water to carry out subsistence food production. They have to manage with inferior land endowments (Kay, 1970; Riddell, 1978; Moyo, 1985; Palmer 1990). Second, the colonial and postcolonial system of production adversely affected the rural household by leaching the male labour out of the rural economy leaving the burden of farm work and food production to women, children and the old folk (Arrighi, 1970; Zinyama, 1986; Potts and Mutambirwa, 1990). Third, land degradation due to overpopulation on lands of deficient potential meant that women had to work harder on impoverished soils to eke out subsistence with occasional ecological collapse which threatened food securities (Mehretu 1994). Fourth, rural enterprises dominated by women have not been able to benefit from infrastructural and innovative technologies which are applied mostly to urban areas or commodity extractive sectors (Muchena, 1994). The rural food sector is deficient in electricity, potable water supply, roads, schools and clinics. Little to no technology goes into food production. The *systemic marginalization* of rural households due to such factors has:

1) prevented women from realizing opportunity benefits that accrue to social and economic engagements in the rural economy that are assumed to have superior benefit-cost outcomes,
2) adversely affected the overall quality of living for women who generally suffer most from rural burdens, and
3) contributed to the exposure of the extended family, especially children, to episodic vulnerabilities caused by natural and human-made crises (Buvinic, 1983; Cecelski, 1985; Sunny, 1992).

Contingent marginality of women in Zimbabwe

By and large, traditional roles of women associated with married life contain the major influences on the lifestyles and livelihoods of females in Zimbabwe. In particular, most factors of contingent marginality of women arise from certain aspects of traditional marriage customs like 'lobola', which involves dowry and often misconceived as making women objects of possession. Furthermore, Zimbabwean children carry the father's totem name which means they belong to the father. By this tradition, mothers have no security as they cannot claim custody of the children or own property. Women with or without modern education in Zimbabwe have never been comfortable with this situation (Mutambirwa, 1984).

The modern economy has introduced further contingent marginality of women. In addition to child bearing and nurturing, mothers are responsible for a variety of tasks in the rural household. Mehretu and Mutambirwa, (1992, 1996) have shown that women in rural Zimbabwe not only are responsible for agricultural production but also spend excessive time and energy carrying out routine domestic chores which adversely affect their nutrition and health (see also Weinrich, 1979). Unfortunately both men and women seem to have accepted this as normal, even though it inflicts a considerable degree of contingent marginality for women (Mutambirwa et al 1998).

Regular responsibilities of women include routine domestic chores of cooking, cleaning, laundry and caring for family members especially children, and farming. Rarely would Zimbabwean men perform cooking tasks or any of the tasks in the domestic sector when women are around and are able to do such works (Mehretu and Mutambirwa, 1992). Women, especially head females, are rarely relieved of such tasks even when they are not in good health. As can be expected, the burden from domestic chores and farm work become even heavier as the head female gets older with more children and older extended family members join the household.

Women in the rural margins of Zimbabwe also perform many trip generating chores. Research by Mehretu and Mutambirwa (1992 and 1996) in the communal areas of Chiduku and Murewa has demonstrated that female members of the household spend about 30 hours per week on trip generating chores and most of this is borne by head females. The drain these chores cause on the daily time and energy budgets of women, adversely affects their nutritional status and health, especially since most of these chores involve head and back loads (Buvinic, 1983; Bryceson, 1993; Leghorn and Parker, 1981). Most of these tasks require being in excellent physical shape which is not easy for rural women as they give their spouses and children priority in nutrition (MacCormack, 1988; Piwoz, 1985).

Systemic marginality of women

One of the most striking phenomena of women's plight in the rural margins of Zimbabwe is the geographic dimension of their systemic marginality. This was based on the deliberate construction of geographic peripheries by the colonial regime to marginalize Zimbabwe's indigenous population. It began with the various acts of land apportionment and influx control

(Mafeje, 1977). The present land ownership system in Zimbabwe is a relic of the colonial system of land apportionment which had divided the country into two major domains, commercial and communal, and introduced a spatially mismatched settlement organization of people and lands with good agricultural potential (GOZ, 1981, 1982, 1983; Mandaza, 1986; Weinrich, 1979; Mehretu, 1995).

The communal lands, to which Africans were relegated, covered about half of the country's rural margins with the worst land potential, but contained close to three-quarters the country's population. On the other hand, half of the country, and the best land endowments, were designated as commercial land and relegated to the colonial minority population (Kay, 1970; Palmer, 1977, 1990). The communal lands are not only deficient in natural endowments (Surveyor General, 1984), they are also located in the most remote parts of the country devoid of towns and infrastructure (Kay, 1970; Mehretu, 1994, 1995). The great majority of the residents of these lands are women (CSO 1990) which means they are the ones that will have to eke out subsistence from such deficient land resources with little to no opportunity for growth and prosperity (Muchena, 1994). Even though the systemic marginalization of people using land apportionment was directed at the Africans as a whole, those that were most vulnerable and suffered from it were women who, unlike rural men, had no options for alternative employment (Brown, 1959).

The systemic spatial marginalization of the Africans in Zimbabwe was partly based on the colonial logic of creating cheap labour pools that could not be sufficiently occupied in the communal lands. They had to seek employment outside these rural margins which usually meant on colonial farms as migrant labourers (Arrighi, 1970; Mafeje, 1977). They would however maintain their families in the rural margins to which they would eventually retire. Communal lands began to experience population pressure, loss of carrying capacity and consequently land degradation (Kay, 1975; Whitlow, 1988). Increased population also meant increased deforestation and overgrazing, making parts of the communal lands extremely marginal and impoverished.

Relics of systemic marginality continue to limit women's opportunities for progress. This is seen, for instance, in sectors dominated by women in rural margins which generally do not attract much attention from development projects. Although women make the principal producers of food products in rural margins, extension services are only slowly responding to this fact (Muchena, 1994). Rural development projects components like loans, high-yielding varieties, fertilizers, agricultural implements and other agricultural inputs are slow to reach women not only because of historical inertia that targets men as the primary beneficiaries of such investments, but also because women lack the requirements of collateral and other pre-conditions for access to such opportunities (Lele, 1975).

Therefore, the overall impact of the spatial organization of access to land assets that the colonial system engineered with a deliberate mismatch between African population density and resource potential, continues to make rural women most vulnerable to systemic marginality and miss out on a variety of life improving developments that they are structurally incapable of engaging.

Policy options for gender sensitive development

Dealing with contingent marginality

Policy options for gender sensitive development programs have to be divided into short-term and long-term strategies. Most factors that make women vulnerable to contingent marginality are perhaps amenable to short term and less radical solutions. As pointed out, contingent marginality continues to be responsible for much of the drudgery and poor quality of life experienced by women in the rural margins of Zimbabwe. One of these realities resides in the attitudes by both men and women to accept the status quo with regards the women's place and their function in rural society. In order to remove culture-based attitudes that are deleterious to women's progress, both men and women have to accept gender equality and enable female children an equitable access to education. Government intervention in providing gender sensitive training toward liberating women from contingent marginality in schools as well as outside schools, would enable women to realize their potential toward the betterment of their life.

Information is crucial in women's progress. Along with literacy programs, women should be provided with means to get access to information which make them much more aware of the nature of their problems and how they might successfully work towards their resolution. Government agencies and non-governmental organizations should facilitate the provision of enabling support systems, such as radios, audio-visual facilities, reading materials and other means of information dissemination. With effective use of such media, lessons on methods of agricultural enterprise, crafts production, food processing, hygiene, child immunization, prevention of communicable diseases and ways to enhance political participation, can be effectively disseminated. National radio and TV media should regularly feature life in rural margins with objectives to sensitize urban and elite audiences to the plight of women in rural margins.

An important preoccupation of women in rural margins is the food security for the household. For this reason, agriculture for subsistence is a critical activity in rural margins, and women carry the major burden in producing food crops (Muchena, 1994). One of the most ironic situations in rural development in countries like Zimbabwe is that women, who are largely responsible for food supply for the household, are not the ones targeted to benefit directly from the extension systems that are designed to improve production of food. A major policy shift to reduce the contingent marginality of women is to feminize the extension service. The strategic use of appropriate technology to increase food security would be a step in the right direction.

The traditional and cultural division of labour that assigns women the tasks of trip-generating time and energy costs of distance are among the most limiting factors of women's contingent marginality. The quality of women's rural life would be greatly improved is they could be relieved of the daily burdens of fetching water and firewood for domestic use. Often, women also have to take the household laundry to water points to wash them by carrying them on their back or head. These are tasks that require the expenditure of time and energy. The simple provision of tap water, which many city people take for granted, would relieve women of tremendous pressure on their health and quality of life. Provision of clean tap water also has many positive spin-offs including improved hygiene and reduction of water-borne diseases.

As indicated earlier, wood is the principal source of domestic fuel. Women spend time and energy to fetch wood. In the communal areas of Zimbabwe, this is creating a double-edged problem. Dependence on wood fuel not only drains women's energy and time to collect it, but also it has become a serious factor in deforestation and land degradation as woodlands are depleted in what is a marginal land to begin with (Whitlow 1979, 1988; Moore and Vaughan, 1994). With increased depletion for forests, distances that women have to travel have increased leading to a vicious spiral in human-environment relations. This is another area for state and non-state cooperation to look into potential substitutes for fuel wood. Provision of reasonably priced fuels including the use of solar power should be looked into. The costs of provisioning such alternative fuels maybe high but such costs should be compared with first, the opportunity benefits foregone by women because of energy and time wasted on fetching wood, and second, the loss of land resources from excessive deforestation and degradation.

Colonial and post-colonial pressures on rural margins have also caused many tasks that belong to males in the household were more and more taken up by female members. The case in point is herding livestock for grazing and watering. The surveys in Chiduku and Murewa indicate that women contribute close to 40% of the effort in caring for livestock (Mehretu and Mutambirwa, 1992, 1996). Policy options in this regard will range from men taking more responsibility for this sector to reducing the number of livestock in rural margins. Intermediate steps may include introducing methods for better livestock management including fencing, controlled grazing, and easy access to livestock watering points.

In the wider sense, the contingent factors of marginality of women in rural areas require enabling social and economic infrastructure in order to improve the quality of life in the rural margins of Zimbabwe. This can reassert the traditional roles of women as mothers and homemakers and not as all-purpose labourers of the household. The convoluted interpretations of traditional marriage customs, which are responsible for the wrong attitudes that have developed in both men and women about the roles of females, will need to be corrected.

Dealing with systemic marginality

In the case of women in the rural margins of Zimbabwe, there are two specific sources of systemic marginality. The first is the expedient distortion of traditional customs and mores about matrimony and women's role in the household by the colonial system, and its imposition of policies had gender biases. The second source of systemic marginality is inherent in the various laws on land apportionment and limits on movement and residence. As indicated earlier, these laws, although they were done to marginalize and weaken the African population, their adverse impact on rural women was by far the most important. Policies to advance the cause of women should address the following two problems.

First, colonial and post-colonial customary laws of marriage need to be amended because they militate against women's progress and maintain their vulnerability to systemic marginality. There are many constraints which beset married women when it comes to property rights, custody of children, freedom of choice with regards place to live or work, conducting major financial deals (which normally require the husband's sanction or endorsement and thereby restricting them from independent access to economic opportunities).

Second, issues of structure that militate against women's progress need to be tackled. The post-colonial government has been slow in changing some of the inherited structures of the dual economy which still exist in the country. The disparities in per capita incomes and resource endowments between the commercial and communal lands are enormous. Likewise the social and economic infrastructure available and taken for granted in the urban and commercial areas, are scarce or absent in the communal lands. As a result people living in the communal lands are greatly disadvantaged and suffer continued systemic marginality whose origins are in colonial policies. The much awaited land redistribution and resettlement has not occurred. Policies to liberate women from systemic marginality have to take into account the current mismatch between population density and land with good potential. The present population pressure on land in rural margins would not only continue to impoverish women but also make communal land resources lose their carrying capacity and render future generations of rural residents even more destitute.

In the colonial period, systemic marginality was achieved not only by the land apportionment system but also by preventing technologies and non-farm activities from reaching the rural margins. The system was set up to deny able-bodied men to find alternative employment in their own rural base, but instead to seek opportunities outside it leaving their women, children and old folks behind. That inertia continues after independence. The lack of technology and modernization has intensified women's vulnerability to systemic marginalization. Although the fundamental structure of women's systemic marginality in rural Zimbabwe is dependent on the land question, strategic and appropriate use of technology can mitigate women's plight in rural margins.

Political representation of women in the communal lands is very weak. Women's participation in politics has improved but it is restricted to the educated and/or urbanized women who have successfully run for offices. But, this has not permeated in the rural margins where women are the majority. What would be desirable is to have direct participation by the rural residents themselves, so that they can speak and stand for their rights. Policy options to increase political participation of women in rural margins may include the creation of incentives by the state for educated women to run from their traditional home districts in communal areas to represent women's issues.

Conclusions

Three sets of conclusions may be drawn from the above. The first is that there are multidimensional aspects to the plight of women in the rural margins of Africa as illustrated by the case study of Zimbabwe. Basic to women's marginality is gender bias. Sexism and the distortion of cultural and traditional customs have contributed to contingent marginality of women. In the hierarchy of favour and privilege inherent in colonialism, aspects of contingent marginality have been converted to systemic marginality. This was aggravated by the colonial structure of separate settlement and land rights that made deliberate uses of systemic marginality to weaken Africans. This was most prejudicial to women's welfare. Post-colonial policies and projects to redress such problems have not been effectively conceived and implemented.

The second set relates to problems of post-colonial rural transformation in the development process. In Zimbabwe, the slow and haphazard implementation of land reform and redistribution (as intended by the war of liberation) continues to marginalize rural inhabitants, the majority of whom are females. Shortfalls in the provision and implementation of adequate social and economic infrastructure in the rural margins, have failed to address marginality in either their contingent or systemic modalities.

The third conclusion is simply an invocation for government to focus more closely on factors responsible for female marginality and to redress them with deliberate intent. The following may be considered:

1) direct involvement of women in defining the problems and causes for their marginality,
2) involving women in designing appropriate solutions to their problems,
3) creating an enabling environment for men to appreciate and comprehend the underlying problems and causes of marginality of females,
4) devise appropriate social, political and economic policies to address directly and effectively the problems of female marginality, and
5) involve local government functionaries to facilitate implementation of plans and projects aimed at eradicating the causes of female marginality.

The majority of women in Africa live in rural areas where they experience many problems which adversely affect their quality of life. It has been argued that much of this is due to the persistent contingent and systemic marginalization of women. Therefore, government policy should purposefully aim at eradicating the underlying factors that contribute to the vulnerability of women to contingent and systemic marginality. If this is not accomplished a priori, rural development projects would not reach their intended target as they would be easily subverted by the underlying factors of gender bias maintained by contingent and systemic marginality.

There are some positive signs for qualified optimism. A major post-colonial policy measure introduced in the early eighties and has considerable promise is the speedy implementation of equal access to education (GOZ, 1981, 1982, 1983). The principle of 'education for all' has provided improved accessibility by constructing more primary schools throughout the rural areas. Although financial constraints were soon to dampen the euphoria on the equity in the educational system, it demonstrated that government policies for social infrastructure, especially for education, can be a strategic intervention in enhancing women's welfare (Mutambirwa et al., 1998). The building of rural clinics and health centres, however limited, has contributed immensely to the improvement in women's life (Mutambirwa, 1989). There has also been a modest success in advancing agricultural technology using the extension system (Muchena, 1994). Government push in these directions with an equitable resolution of the land questions will go a long way to improve life in the rural margins.

More currently, there has been a number of civic organizations devoted to the plight of women. The specific goals of these civic organizations include the creation of enabling environments for the participation of women in political, social and economic activities. They also try to promote awareness among women and men on the significance of contingent and systemic factors responsible for female marginality. They push agendas to empower women by demanding equal opportunity and affirmative action. Examples include Women's Action Group (WAG), the Indigenous Business Women Organization (IBWO), Women in Law, and Banking Co-operatives (Mutambirwa et al., 1998). Women's participation in civil society and local government is a precondition for them to reflect their own needs and desires. Enabling them to participate in the social and political process is to begin tackling their marginality from bottom up.

References

Abegaz, Zewdie and Junge, B. (1990), *Women's Workload and the Time Use in Four Peasant Associations in Ethiopia*, UNICEF, Addis Ababa.

Arrighi, Geovanni (1970), 'Labour Supplies in Historical Perspective: A Study of the Proletarianization of African Peasantry in Rhodesia', *Journal of Development Studies*, vol. 6, pp. 197-234.

Brown, K. (1959), *Land in Rhodesia*, African Bureau, London.

291

Bryceson, Deborah (1993), 'Rural Household Transport in Africa: Reducing the Burden on Women', *World Development*, vol. 21, pp. 1715-1728.

Buvinic, M. (1983), 'Women's Issues in Third World Poverty: A Policy Analysis', in M. Buvinic, M.A. Lycette and W.P. McGreevey (eds), *Women and Poverty in the Third World*, The Johns Hopkins Press, Baltimore, MD.

Cecelski, E. (1985), *The Rural Energy Crisis, Women's Work and Basic Needs: Perspectives and Approaches to Action*, ILO Rural Employment Policy Research Programme, Geneva.

Central Statistical Office (CSO) (1990), *Population Census: Compilations by Province, District Councils and Enumeration Areas*, CSO, Harare, Zimbabwe.

Chiuri, Wanjiku and Nzioki, Akinyi (1992), 'Women: Invisible Managers of Natural Resources', in A. Shanyisa Khasiani (ed.), *Ground Work: African Women as Environmental Managers*, African Center for Technology Studies, Nairobi, pp. 19-25.

Collins, Jane L. (1991), 'Women and Environment: Social Reproduction and Sustainable Development', in Rita S. Gallin and Anne Ferguson (eds.), *The Women and International Development Annual*, Volume 2, Westview, Boulder, pp. 33-58.

Friedmann, John (1988), *Life Space and Economic Space*, Transaction Books, New Brunswick, NJ.

Gallin, Rita S. and Ferguson, Anne (1991), 'Conceptualizing Difference: Gender, Class and Action', in Rita S. Gallin, and Anne Ferguson (eds), *The Women and International Development Annual*, Volume 2, pp. 1-30, Westview, Boulder, CO.

Government of Zimbabwe (GOZ) (1981), *Growth with Equity*, Government Printer, Harare.

Government of Zimbabwe (GOZ) (1982, 1983), *Transitional National Development Plan*, Vol. 1 and 2, Government Printer, Harare.

Hafkin, N. and Bay, E.G. (1976), *Women in Africa: Studies in Socio-Economic Change*, Stanford University Press, Stanford, CA.

Kay, George (1970), *Rhodesia: A Human Geography*, Africana Publishing Corporation, New York.

Kay, George (1975), 'Population Pressures and Development Prospects in Rhodesia', *The Rhodesia Science News*, vol. 9, pp. 7-13.

Leghorn, L. and Parker, K. (1981), *Women's Worth: Sexual Economics and the World of Women*, Routledge and Kegan Paul, Boston.

Lele, Uma (1975), *The Design of Rural Development: Lessons from Africa*, Johns Hopkins University Press, Baltimore.

MacCormack, C. P. (1988), 'Health and the Social Power of Women', *Social Science and Medicine*, vol. 26, pp. 677-683.

Mafeje, Archie (1977), 'Neo-Colonialism, State Capitalism, or Revolution?', in Peter C.W. Gutkind and Peter Waterman (eds), *African Social Studies*, Heinemann, London, pp. 412-422.

Mandaza, Ibo (1986), 'Zimbabwe: The Political Economy of Transition', in Ibo Mandaza (ed.), *The Political Economy of Transition, 1980-1986*, CODESRIA, Dakar, Senegal, pp. 1-20.

Mehretu, Assefa. (1989), *Regional Disparity in Sub-Saharan Africa*, Westview Press, Boulder, CO.

Mehretu, Assefa (1994), 'Social Poverty Profiles in Communal Areas', in Mandivamba Rukuni and Carl K. Eicher (eds), *Zimbabwe's Agricultural Revolution*, University of Zimbabwe Publications, Harare, pp. 56-69.

Mehretu, Assefa. (1995), 'Spatial Mismatch Between Population Density and Land Potential: The Case of Zimbabwe', *Africa Development*, vol. 20, pp. 125-146.

Mehretu, Assefa and Mutambirwa, Chris (1992a), 'Time and Energy Costs of Distance in Rural Life Space of Zimbabwe: Case Study in the Chiduku Communal Area', *Social Science and Medicine*, vol. 34, pp. 17-24.

Mehretu, Assefa and Mutambirwa, Chris (1992b), 'Gender Differences in Time and Energy Costs of Distance for Regular Domestic Chores in Rural Zimbabwe: A Case Study in the Chiduku Communal Area', *World Development*, vol. 20, pp. 1675-1683.

Mehretu, Assefa and Mutambirwa, Chris (1996), 'Transport Burdens on Women in Rural Zimbabwe', Paper presented at the Association of American Geographers 92nd Meeting, 9-13 April, Charlotte, North Carolina.

Mehretu, Assefa and Sommers, Lawrence, M. (1994), 'Patterns of Macrogeographic and Microgeographic Marginality in Michigan', *The Great Lakes Geographer*, vol. 1, pp. 67-80.

Moore, Henrietta, L. and Vaughan, Megan (1994), Cutting Down Trees: Gender, Nutrition, and Agricultural Change in the Northern Province of Zambia, 1890-1990, Heinemann Press, Portsmouth.

Moyo, S. (1995), *The land question in Zimbabwe*, SAPES, Harare.

Muchena, Olivia (1994), 'The Changing Perceptions of Women in Agriculture', in Mandivamba Rukuni and Carl K. Eicher (eds), *Zimbabwe's Agricultural Revolution*, University of Zimbabwe Publications, Harare, pp. 348-360.

Mutambirwa, Chris (1990), 'Changing Patterns of African Rural-Urban Migration and Urbanization in Zimbabwe, Easter and Southern Africa', *Geographical Journal*, vol. 1, pp. 26-39.

Mutambirwa, J. (1984), *Shona Pathology, Religio-medical practices, Obstetrics, Paediatrics and Concepts of Growth and Development in Relation to Scientific Medicine*, Unpublished Thesis, University of Zimbabwe, Harare.

Mutambirwa, J. (1989), 'Health Problems in Rural Communities, Zimbabwe', *Social Science and Medicine*, Vol. 29, pp. 927-932.

Mutambirwa, J., Utete, V., Mutambirwa, C. and Maramba, P. (1998), 'Consequences of Family Planning on Women's Quality of Life in Zimbabwe', in M. Mhloyi, (ed.), *Women and Development in Zimbabwe: The Role of Family Planning*, Weaver Press, Harare.

Obbo, C. (1990), 'East African Women, Work, and the Articulation of Dominance', in I. Tinker (ed.), *Persistent Inequalities*, Oxford University Press, New York, NY.

Omosa, Mary (1992), 'Women and the Management of Domestic Energy', in Shanyisa A. Khasiani, (ed.), *Ground Work: African Women as Environmental Managers*, African Center for Technology Studies, Nairobi, pp. 41-54.

Palmer, R.H. (1977), *Land Racial Discrimination in Rhodesia*, University of California Press, Berkeley, CA.

Palmer, R.H. (1990), 'Land reform in Zimbabwe: 1980-90', *African Affairs*, vol. 89, pp. 163-181.

Piwoz, E.G., Gail, E. and Viteri, F.E. (1985), 'Studying Health and Nutrition Behavior by Examining Household Decision-Making, Intra-Household Resource Distribution and the Role of Women in these Processes', *Food Nutrition Bulletin*, vol. 7, pp. 1-31.

Potts, D. and Mutambirwa, C. (1990), 'Rural-Urban Linkages in Contemporary Harare: Why Migrants Need Their Land', *Journal of Southern African Studies*, vol. 16, pp. 678-698.

Riddell, R. (1978), 'The Land Problem in Rhodesia', *Gwelo Socio-Economic Series*, No. 11, Gwelo, Zimbabwe.

Shiva, Vandana (1989), *Staying Alive: Women, Ecology and Development*, Zed Press, London.

Sommers, Lawrence M. and Mehretu, Assefa (1998), 'International Perspectives on Socio-Spatial Marginality', in Heikki Jussila, Walter Leimgruber, and Roser Majoral (eds), *Perceptions of Marginality*, Ashgate, Aldershot, UK, pp. 135-145.

Sunny, Grace (1992), 'Women's Role in the Supply of Fuelwood', in Shanyisa A. Khasiani, (ed.), *Ground Work: African Women as Environmental Managers*, African Center for Technology Studies, Nairobi, pp. 55-65.

Surveyor General (1984), *Zimbabwe: Natural Regions and Farming Areas Map*, Surveyor General's Office, Harare.

Weinrich, A.K.H. (1979), *Women and Racial Discrimination in Rhodesia*, UNESCO, Paris.

White, Gilbert, F., Bradley, David, J. and White, Anne (1972), *Drawers of Water: Domestic Water Use in East Africa*, Chicago, University of Chicago Press, Chicago, IL.

Whitlow, J.R. (1979), *The Household Use of Woodland Resources in Rural Areas*, Natural Resources Board, Harare, Zimbabwe.

Whitlow, J.R. (1988), *Land Degradation in Zimbabwe*, Natural Resources Board, Harare, Zimbabwe.

World Bank (1989), *Sub-Sahara Africa: From Crisis to Sustainable Growth*, World Bank, Washington, DC.

Young, C. (1988), 'The African Colonial State and its Political Legacy', in D. Rothchild, and N. Chazan (eds), *The Precarious Balance: State and Society in Africa*, Westview Press, Boulder, CO, pp. 25-66.

Zinyama, Lovemore (1990), 'Rural Household Structures, Absenteeism and Agricultural Labor: A Case Study of Two Subsistence Farming Areas in Zimbabwe', *Singapore Journal of Tropical Geography*, vol. 7, pp. 163-173.

Part 4 – Conclusions and summary

22 Conclusions and summary

HEIKKI JUSSILA AND ROSER MAJORAL

This book on the issues of *Globalization and Marginality in Geographical Space*, has looked at this topic from three main points of view:

1. From the *effects* point of view discussing the issue on general global level,
2. The issue has been taken up from *policy and politics* point of view focusing on the questions emerging either international, national or regional level; and
3. This volume has examined the *change* the point of view, i.e., change from economic to social issues.

First article of the *Effects of Globalization* section is by Leimgruber and it combines general theoretical approach with case-studies that all use the same approach to 'measure' how globalization affects an given area. The article examines the globalization from varying points of view and finally it concludes that 'at the end the 20th century, marginality and marginalization continue to be important issues' and that 'despite considerable efforts very little has changed: regional disparities have not disappeared and inequality is still a major problem'.

In the second article of *Effects of Globalization* section by Sommers *et al.* the regions aspect of globalization used by Leimgruber is replaced by a transnational corporation point of view and it uses the 'binoculars of managers of transnational corporation'. The article shows that the aspects of localizing manufacturing efficiently (a single firm or plant) in the whole world within a transnational corporation do not take into account the weaker 'players' of the game. In their conclusions Sommers *et al.* stress the importance of finding policy tools that could counter act this as they call 'deleterious effects of contingent and systemic marginality'.

The third article of *Effects of Globalization* section by Archer and Lonsdale look at one of the most globalized economies within the US, the Great Plains. They, too, show the importance of transnationals in the current process of globalization. However, they demonstrate that besides the transnationals the process of deregulation of various production sectors, including agricultural world markets, has a very direct relevance to the

Great Plains, since it has meant the dismantling of some long established agricultural support programs, and this will probably increase the economic problems of farmers. According to the article the contribution of this region in the world supply of food will continue to be significant but probably unstable due to the effects of globalization.

The fourth article of *Effects of Globalization* section by Cepparo de Grosso analyzes the issue of globalization and the role policies of economic and local development can play in this process in Argentina. The emphasis of her article is to look at the ways the region is targeting its resources in order to cope with the issue of marginalization due to the lack of competence within the region. The article stresses the importance of creating new forms of organization and in this way to search for more open and perhaps also more prosperous future. The risks in deregulation policies are evident and one does need to find a balance, since the current trend seems to reinforce the already existing regional inequalities within the region.

The last article of *Effects of Globalization* section by Goverde examines globalization trends from 'macro' policy point of view. The issue is both global and regional, how to tackle integration and avoid marginalization of areas within the region, Europe. The article approaches the question globalization from the 'European' point of view. The issues discussed include the 'agro-political cultures' within Europe as to show the basic mentalities of how to 'govern' rural and/or agricultural questions. This is then taken up on a global level when confronting it with the globalization of agribusiness and its effects on European production systems.

The second part of the book addresses the issues of *Policies and Politics of Change*. In these chapters policies refer to the actions or the development paths governments have chosen to pursue to confront global economic or deregulation needs. This part contains case-study articles, which analyze cases from Finland, Italy, Norway, Portugal, Spain and the USA. The common tone for all these articles is the stress that policies and politics of change that are designed to operate on national or intra-national level do not enough take into account the diversity that exists at regional level.

The *Policies and Politics* section starts with an article discussing Finnish policy initiatives regarding the European Union (see the article of Muilu). This article speaks about the possibilities the North can give to the European Union as a whole. The central argument of the article is that there is the need to reinforce the image of the North within the Union much in the same way as the Mediterranean has been given a special focus. In this sense the concept of 'Northern dimension', presented in the article, is a tool for the EU to define the 'interests' of the Union on the region. However, while there is an official 'euphoria' toward the concept, there are also critical comments. The most profound is that so far the idea is based on 'political speeches' rather than real action. The article, however, clearly points out that the proposed concept is the first step to look at the North differently not as a periphery, but as a region of resources for the EU in a globalizing world.

The second article of the section on *Policies and Politics* by Häkkilä examines the case of rural northern Finland. The question that is taken up is the role of EU norms and legislation for rural policy, especially for agriculture, that in some instances are not at all suitable for the region. However, the article shows that especially the programmes for rural diversification have gained from the membership, since the national policies for the rural development prior the EU-membership were being cut and the financial resources available were diminishing. According this article when a rural region is prepared to a change it will be able to adapt its actions accordingly and in this sense globalization does not necessarily need to be a threat.

The third article of *Policies and Politics* sections by Andreoli *et al.* examines an Italian case. The article analyses a case of the introduction of new policy tools and what these tools require from those who implementing them and from those who aiming to use services provided for regional development by these new tools. According to the article there is a need to test usability of 'new' tools of rural development before wider diffusion and that one needs to patient when starting something new. The article shows that new policy tools make it possible to cope better with the issues that arrive from the globalizing markets. The proposed development tools and methods stress the importance of local action and local co-operation. Building an 'atmosphere' of co-operation is one of the main targets of the Italian case, since through co-operation it is easier to overcome the problems and threats arriving from the currently globalizing world.

The fourth article of *Policies and Politics* section the Portuguese case by Moreno analyses the issue of policies at local micro-regional level. The region analyzed is Algarve with divided regional structure. Firstly there is the coastal tourist region and secondly the mountainous periphery that has been suffering since the beginning of tourist boom. The EC integration process was decisive for Algarve's rural regions, since this process enabled the generation of the first real rural development programmes. These programmes had one important aim: think globally but act locally. Currently the region is starting to face the different aspects of globalization. The examples range from golf course development by some tourists to ideas of a 'complete nature reserve' by some (deep) ecologists. The conflict of local development that manifests in this area is indeed global and also those that 'create' the conflicts are in a way outsiders, that do not always listen to those who live in the area.

The fifth article of *Policies and Politics* section, the Norwegian case by Berg, looks at the policy changes from the point of view of corporatization of service and public utilities as a response to globalization. These changes usually aim at cost savings and they look for more efficiency. These changes do not always take into account that service provision in a remote area might suffer from these changes, since globalization and market pressures create dilemmas for the new corporations producing services and public utilities. On markets the public corporations operate as any company and they play according to the same rules as the private corporations. This means that usually those that have the possibility to make difference have the edge in the market, while the weaker or marginalized players pay a higher price of the same service. However, the Norwegian examples do not clearly show if the corporatization has really been a negative move from the viewpoint of rural, peripheral or marginal areas or customers.

The sixth case in *Policies and Politics* section, presented by Kale, is from the USA and it looks at the policy issues from the regulation and deregulation perspectives and addresses the consequences of governmental regulation on the economies of the US Pacific Northwest. According to the article 'numerous observers believe environmental regulations of varying types adversely affect remote areas more than more urbanized areas', but the article does not clearly show that governmental regulations have affected negatively on rural areas. The second approach of the article is deregulation that in the US deal mostly transportation and energy. According to the article the US policies of transport and energy deregulation seem on surface to be successful, but they have lead to a poorer service for smaller cities and areas were population densities are low. In the Pacific Northwest the consequence has been a development of a variety of strategies to help to cope with economic change. They include traditional tools like tourism development and less traditional as nature tourism and even accepting chemical waste sites have been used. In US one potential emerging trend is the movement of 'lone eagles' to remote areas. Lone eagles are businesspersons living in location where information technologies allow them to conduct business from their homes or small offices. At the moment this number is small but it is growing and can in future help some small communities.

The last article of the *Policies and Politics* section, the Spanish case by Lopez-Palomeque, analyses tourism planning and how it affects regional development. In southern Europe areas that are traditionally least developed are affected by new sectoral and spatial manifestations of the productive system, and many traditionally rural and peripheral areas have either through tourism or second homes gained importance that has radically changed the vision of the rural areas. They are not at today's world necessarily 'doomed' of being marginal, but they can become economically important and start to attract investments and one starts to see enclaves or pockets of development in an otherwise 'lagging' area. The policy changes that have followed are those that stress more strategic planning and the structural and physical planning has today less importance. This in turn leads to the above mentioned enclaves or pockets of development.

Part three of this volume contains eight articles that analyse different aspects of marginality in the light of change *From Economic to Social Issues*. The emphasis of the articles is on the question of process. The economic aspect of marginality is important, but at the same time the role of social issues of marginality is increasing. It is this increase in the social aspect of spatial dimension of marginality that creates new questions of how, why, and where we are seeing marginalization in space and in time.

The first article of the *From Economic to Social Issues* section by Andreoli *et al.* explains why traditionally marginal areas of a region do not necessarily today belong to socially marginal areas. The analysis of marginality is been confronted with the aspect of rural – urban continuum in order to see if there is a connection between economic continuum and social continuum of marginality. The most apparent finding of the article is that the social marginality is more concentrated on the urbanized areas than on rural areas. This suggests that the social values are more stable in the rural areas than in urban areas, although not all variables used in the analysis support this finding. However, spatially the economic and rural marginal areas were remarkably different almost being opposite images of the study area, Region of Tuscany.

The second article of the *From Economic to Social Issues* section by Marques and Delgado analyses Portuguese society and its ability to adapt to the process of globalization, mass communication and European integration. They, e.g., conclude that as country 'Portugal is still inferior in many aspects in comparison with western countries as whole'. They point out that the globalization process, that brings in centralization processes does not help in bringing the country 'in par' with those that have had an 'head start' in globalization and internationalization process, within the country itself there is a tendency to leave marginal areas out of integration including only the most central, i.e., coastal regions. Despite the macro trends at regional level it is possible to find differences that create a heterogeneous image of the country. An image that at 'global' level is usually hidden, but that requires regions to search their main potentials.

The third article of the *From Economic to Social Issues* section by Stanley discusses issues of globalization and marginalization at local mill town level. The article shows how the history of mill towns came to being in the southern states of US. In mill towns there was a 'total' dependence from the mill for all activities. The mill towns were places that lived and breath through the mill. The mills initially provided also housing for their workers, housing that later led to house privatization, since the funds of the mill invested in them were needed elsewhere. According to Stanley this was the first sign of the changes that were to come. The article shows the US textile industry was not altogether prepared to the globalization processes that arrived. Consequently, the globalization process has hit hard the mill town in US and according to the article 'it seems that the policies that are based on subsidies do not provide a solution for those that were left suffering based on a miscalculation of global markets and market forces'.

The fourth article of the *From Economic to Social Issues* section by Sanchez-Aguilera and Majoral analyses the Spanish case from the viewpoint of population and demography. The analysis on population concentrates on the issues of imbalances in Spanish economy and the consequences these imbalances have had on population development in Spain on municipality level. The high degree of concentration of economic activity has led to uneven population distribution, which is reflected as an imbalance in economic and social development. They conclude that 'there is a sharp contrast between the northern and southern halves of the country, the south presenting on the whole lower mean ages of the overall population, which in turn correlate with lower overall mean ages of the farming population, thus enhancing the possibility that younger farming generations will replace the older ones'. In European level the population on rural areas, especially in 'very remote' rural areas is ageing rapidly and at the moment it seems that one has not been able to find solutions to alleviate this problem and at the same time centres seem to attract more people. A problem that we face at the coming millennium.

The fifth article of the *From Economic to Social Issues* section by Rusanen *et al.* discusses these same issues when analyzing the 'social neighbourhoods' in Finland and Sweden. The article looks at population from a slightly different point of view, but the main 'message' is clear, the peripheral and remote areas are getting more 'uninhabited' and the area were you will find most of the population is getting smaller and smaller in spatial and to some extent also in temporal terms. The use of 'hermit' analysis of grid-square material shows well how the geographically large countries like Finland and Sweden are getting in economic terms, measures as the 'density and concentration of population' smaller. In this respect they resemble the situations of Spain where a few large centres make up a very large proportion of the population.

The sixth article of the *From Economic to Social Issues* section by Peter Scott discusses the 'cultural' aspects of marginalization in the form of Aboriginals in Tasmania. In his opening statement he quotes the Melbourne Journal the Age, that says; 'Aboriginality in the island state (Tasmania) is not an issue of colour; it is an issue of culture...'. In global sense the issue of Tasmanian Aboriginals has not changed, although their 'relative' well-being has risen. The problems of marginalization through your birth or cultural origin seem to continue, since the enrolment of indigenous youth to higher education tends to be lower than the average in Tasmania. It is this respect that the article advocates that 'Aborigines must enjoy the same respect as human beings, and same socioeconomic conditions' before it is possible to have any real improvement. In this respect the question is that the evil circle of culture and marginalization at global level needs to be broken before it is possible to have real change. Policies and politics that do not go into the roots are not enough.

The seventh article of the *From Economic to Social Issues* section by Caetano looks at the question of economic globalization and its consequences from the point of view of child labour, the 'reverse' sides of employment. The article discusses the issue of child labour in Portugal and it refers to the old traditions in agriculture where children were supposed to help and work on the farm. This tradition has moved to cities and in Portugal the amount of children working is still much higher than on the average in within the European Union, although it is been diminishing during the last years. In her conclusions Caetano finds that child labour has a global character. It develops within similar contexts in all areas involved. Earlier children were largely working in agriculture and this tradition is still continuing, although it is not so intense anymore. The question of cultural mentality, as in Portugal, should not be forgotten, since in many places parents hope that children enter into professional life early in order to integrate into the society. This cultural phenomenon has, however, been used by the transnationals that seek for new production sites and consequently economic marginalization is almost always present as well as globalized production that favours low-cost-countries, where the use of child labour is allowed.

The last article of this *From Economic to Social Issues* section and the whole book by Mehretu *et al.* discusses the issue of women in rural African society by using the case of Zimbabwe as an example. The article demonstrates that traditions and societal attitudes in African culture have contributed significantly to marginalization of women in rural Africa. However, the colonial marginalization has been even more limiting factor for the women's progress in Africa. The article then analyses these issues in the contexts of contingent and systemic marginality and aims to theorize of the current situation. The article also proposes some policy instruments to alleviate the problems of women in Zimbabwe. One of the most important aspects from alleviating problems is education, but also the division of labour needs to be re-examined. Alleviating systemic marginality of women is a long term process, since it includes changes in the political representation of women, and according to the article it would be important that also women from the rural areas should take part and not only the educated urban women. In conclusions the article points out that 'government policy should purposefully aim at eradicating the underlying factors that contribute to the vulnerability of women to contingent and systemic marginality.' The article further points out that rural development projects will not reach their goals unless the gender bias is not changed.

The discussion of the articles in this volume of *Globalization and Marginality in Geographical Space* has throughout the whole volume emphasized the importance of a holistic approach towards the problem arising from the policies of globalization. The general conclusion that can be drawn from all the articles is that of an assurance that rural, peripheral and/or marginal regions of the world have taken the challenge of globalization very seriously. In these areas researchers and local politicians and entrepreneurs alike are looking for ways that alleviate the possible conflicts and problems arising from the increasingly globalized economic development. No region is alone at the moment. The tone of the articles, although sometimes showing some dark images is, nevertheless positive. The articles do show ways to cope with the 'impossible' and the potential solutions do create 'pockets of development' that are the sources of new economic development that most certainly will continue to the new millennium.